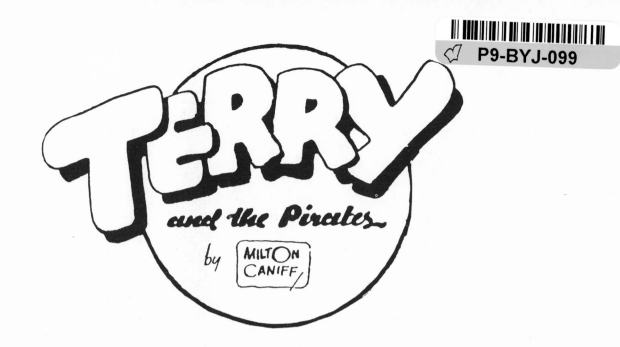

# TERRY
## and the Pirates
by MILTON CANIFF

# RAVEN...

FLYING BUTTRESS classics library

## Our Story So Far...

Terry & Pat escape imprisonment with the help of the German officer Wolff, only to become prisoners of the guerillas. They prove themselves trustworthy after helping save the guerillas' children from a Jap air raid. But now the Japanese commander has devised a new trick: Spread rumors to create panic!

ISBN 0-918348-77-3
LC 87-090446

© NBM 1989
cover designed and painted by Ray Fehrenbach.

THE FLYING BUTTRESS CLASSICS LIBRARY
is an imprint of:

NANTIER · BEALL · MINOUSTCHINE
Publishing co.
new york

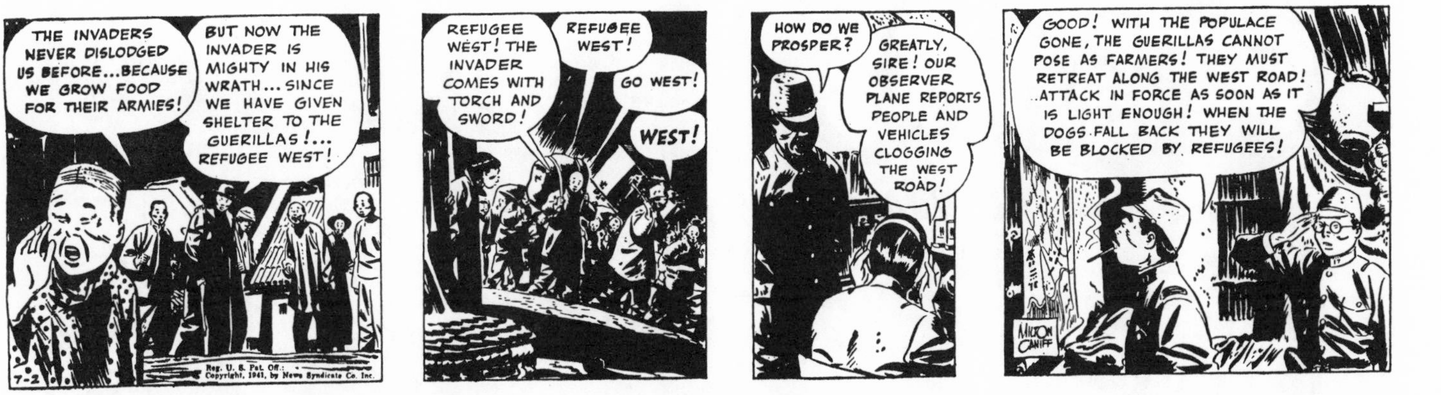
THE INVADERS NEVER DISLODGED US BEFORE...BECAUSE WE GROW FOOD FOR THEIR ARMIES!
BUT NOW THE INVADER IS MIGHTY IN HIS WRATH... SINCE WE HAVE GIVEN SHELTER TO THE GUERILLAS!... REFUGEE WEST!
7-2
Reg. U. S. Pat. Off.: Copyright, 1941, by News Syndicate Co. Inc.
REFUGEE WEST! THE INVADER COMES WITH TORCH AND SWORD!
REFUGEE WEST!
GO WEST!
WEST!
HOW DO WE PROSPER?
GREATLY, SIRE! OUR OBSERVER PLANE REPORTS PEOPLE AND VEHICLES CLOGGING THE WEST ROAD!
GOOD! WITH THE POPULACE GONE, THE GUERILLAS CANNOT POSE AS FARMERS! THEY MUST RETREAT ALONG THE WEST ROAD! ..ATTACK IN FORCE AS SOON AS IT IS LIGHT ENOUGH! WHEN THE DOGS FALL BACK THEY WILL BE BLOCKED BY REFUGEES!
MILTON CANIFF

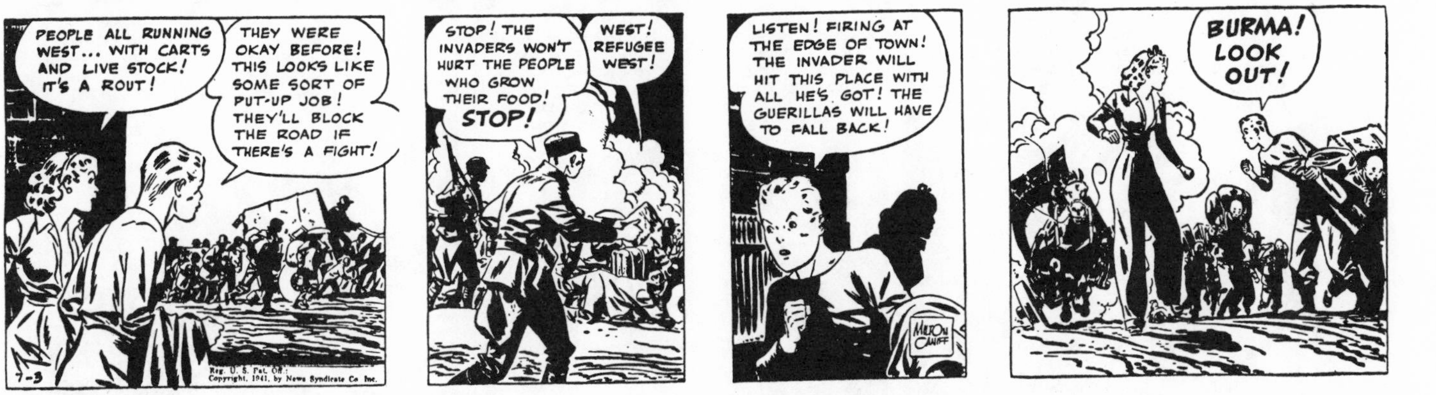
PEOPLE ALL RUNNING WEST... WITH CARTS AND LIVE STOCK! IT'S A ROUT!
THEY WERE OKAY BEFORE! THIS LOOKS LIKE SOME SORT OF PUT-UP JOB! THEY'LL BLOCK THE ROAD IF THERE'S A FIGHT!
7-3
Reg. U. S. Pat. Off.: Copyright, 1941, by News Syndicate Co. Inc.
STOP! THE INVADERS WON'T HURT THE PEOPLE WHO GROW THEIR FOOD! STOP!
WEST! REFUGEE WEST!
LISTEN! FIRING AT THE EDGE OF TOWN! THE INVADER WILL HIT THIS PLACE WITH ALL HE'S GOT! THE GUERILLAS WILL HAVE TO FALL BACK!
MILTON CANIFF
BURMA! LOOK OUT!

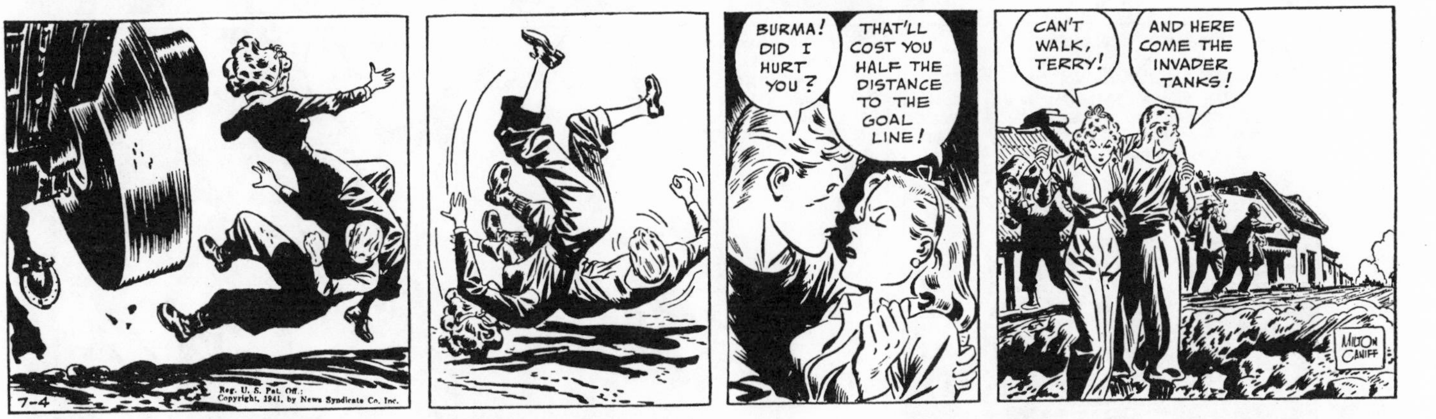
7-4
Reg. U. S. Pat. Off.: Copyright, 1941, by News Syndicate Co. Inc.
BURMA! DID I HURT YOU?
THAT'LL COST YOU HALF THE DISTANCE TO THE GOAL LINE!
CAN'T WALK, TERRY!
AND HERE COME THE INVADER TANKS!
MILTON CANIFF

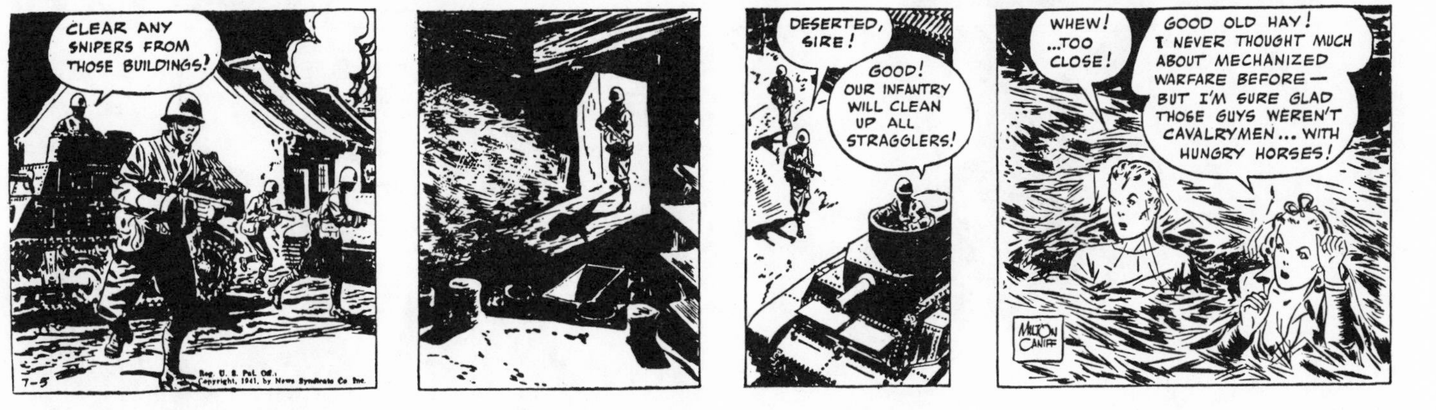
CLEAR ANY SNIPERS FROM THOSE BUILDINGS!
7-5
Reg. U. S. Pat. Off.: Copyright, 1941, by News Syndicate Co. Inc.
DESERTED, SIRE!
GOOD! OUR INFANTRY WILL CLEAN UP ALL STRAGGLERS!
WHEW! ...TOO CLOSE!
GOOD OLD HAY! I NEVER THOUGHT MUCH ABOUT MECHANIZED WARFARE BEFORE — BUT I'M SURE GLAD THOSE GUYS WEREN'T CAVALRYMEN... WITH HUNGRY HORSES!
MILTON CANIFF

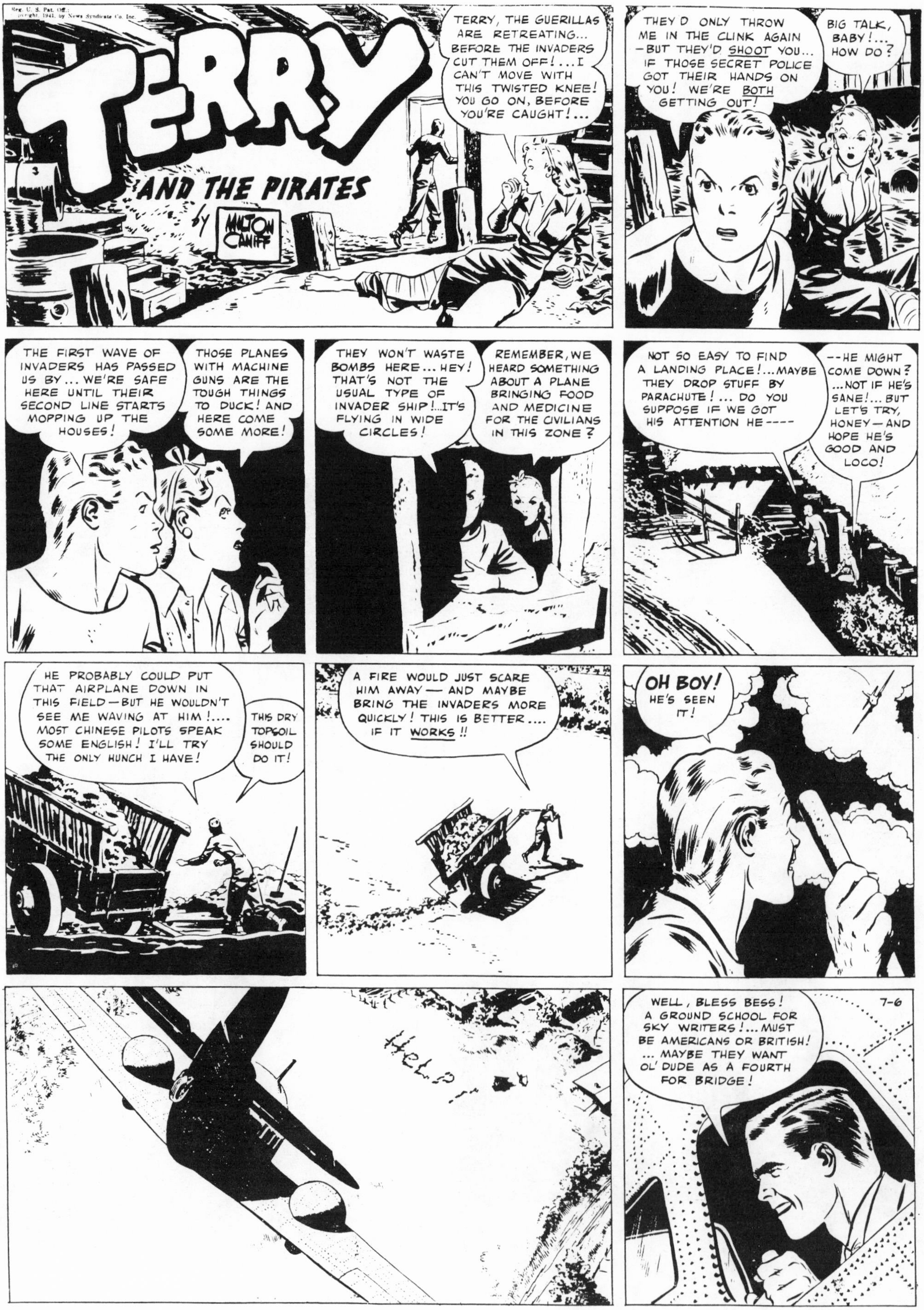
Reg. U. S. Pat. Off.;
pyright, 1941, by News Syndicate Co. Inc.
TERRY AND THE PIRATES
by MILTON CANIFF
TERRY, THE GUERILLAS ARE RETREATING... BEFORE THE INVADERS CUT THEM OFF!... I CAN'T MOVE WITH THIS TWISTED KNEE! YOU GO ON, BEFORE YOU'RE CAUGHT!...
THEY'D ONLY THROW ME IN THE CLINK AGAIN — BUT THEY'D SHOOT YOU... IF THOSE SECRET POLICE GOT THEIR HANDS ON YOU! WE'RE BOTH GETTING OUT!
BIG TALK, BABY!... HOW DO?
THE FIRST WAVE OF INVADERS HAS PASSED US BY... WE'RE SAFE HERE UNTIL THEIR SECOND LINE STARTS MOPPING UP THE HOUSES!
THOSE PLANES WITH MACHINE GUNS ARE THE TOUGH THINGS TO DUCK! AND HERE COME SOME MORE!
THEY WON'T WASTE BOMBS HERE... HEY! THAT'S NOT THE USUAL TYPE OF INVADER SHIP!... IT'S FLYING IN WIDE CIRCLES!
REMEMBER, WE HEARD SOMETHING ABOUT A PLANE BRINGING FOOD AND MEDICINE FOR THE CIVILIANS IN THIS ZONE?
NOT SO EASY TO FIND A LANDING PLACE!... MAYBE THEY DROP STUFF BY PARACHUTE!... DO YOU SUPPOSE IF WE GOT HIS ATTENTION HE----
--HE MIGHT COME DOWN? ...NOT IF HE'S SANE!... BUT LET'S TRY, HONEY — AND HOPE HE'S GOOD AND LOCO!
HE PROBABLY COULD PUT THAT AIRPLANE DOWN IN THIS FIELD — BUT HE WOULDN'T SEE ME WAVING AT HIM!.... MOST CHINESE PILOTS SPEAK SOME ENGLISH! I'LL TRY THE ONLY HUNCH I HAVE!
THIS DRY TOPSOIL SHOULD DO IT!
A FIRE WOULD JUST SCARE HIM AWAY — AND MAYBE BRING THE INVADERS MORE QUICKLY! THIS IS BETTER.... IF IT WORKS!!
OH BOY! HE'S SEEN IT!
HELP!
7-6
WELL, BLESS BESS! A GROUND SCHOOL FOR SKY WRITERS!... MUST BE AMERICANS OR BRITISH! ... MAYBE THEY WANT OL' DUDE AS A FOURTH FOR BRIDGE!

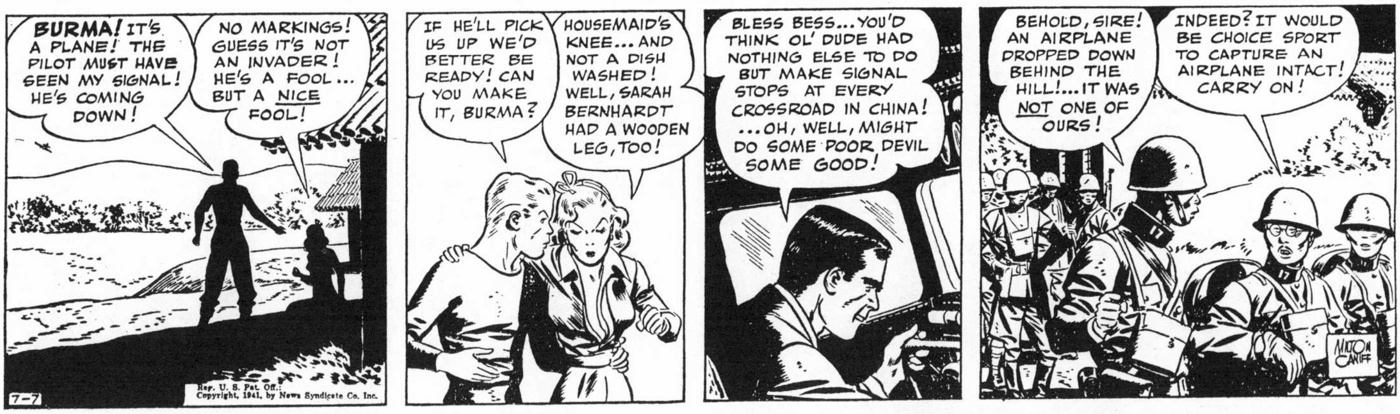
BURMA! IT'S A PLANE! THE PILOT MUST HAVE SEEN MY SIGNAL! HE'S COMING DOWN!
NO MARKINGS! GUESS IT'S NOT AN INVADER! HE'S A FOOL... BUT A NICE FOOL!
7-7
Reg. U. S. Pat. Off.: Copyright, 1941, by News Syndicate Co. Inc.
IF HE'LL PICK US UP WE'D BETTER BE READY! CAN YOU MAKE IT, BURMA?
HOUSEMAID'S KNEE... AND NOT A DISH WASHED! WELL, SARAH BERNHARDT HAD A WOODEN LEG, TOO!
BLESS BESS... YOU'D THINK OL' DUDE HAD NOTHING ELSE TO DO BUT MAKE SIGNAL STOPS AT EVERY CROSSROAD IN CHINA! ...OH, WELL, MIGHT DO SOME POOR DEVIL SOME GOOD!
BEHOLD, SIRE! AN AIRPLANE DROPPED DOWN BEHIND THE HILL!... IT WAS NOT ONE OF OURS!
INDEED? IT WOULD BE CHOICE SPORT TO CAPTURE AN AIRPLANE INTACT! CARRY ON!
MILTON CANIFF

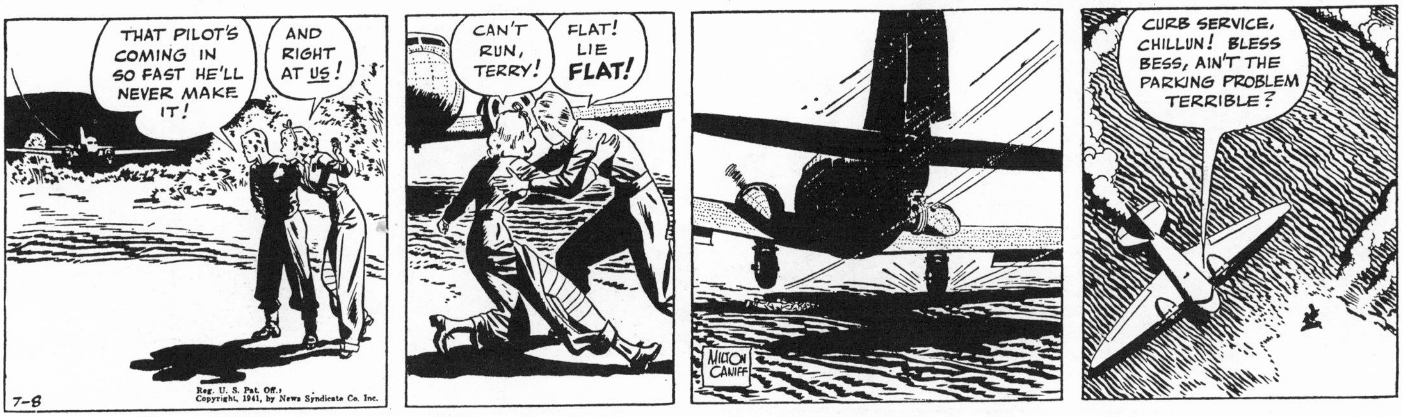
THAT PILOT'S COMING IN SO FAST HE'LL NEVER MAKE IT!
AND RIGHT AT US!
7-8
Reg. U. S. Pat. Off.: Copyright, 1941, by News Syndicate Co. Inc.
CAN'T RUN, TERRY!
FLAT! LIE FLAT!
MILTON CANIFF
CURB SERVICE, CHILLUN! BLESS BESS, AIN'T THE PARKING PROBLEM TERRIBLE?

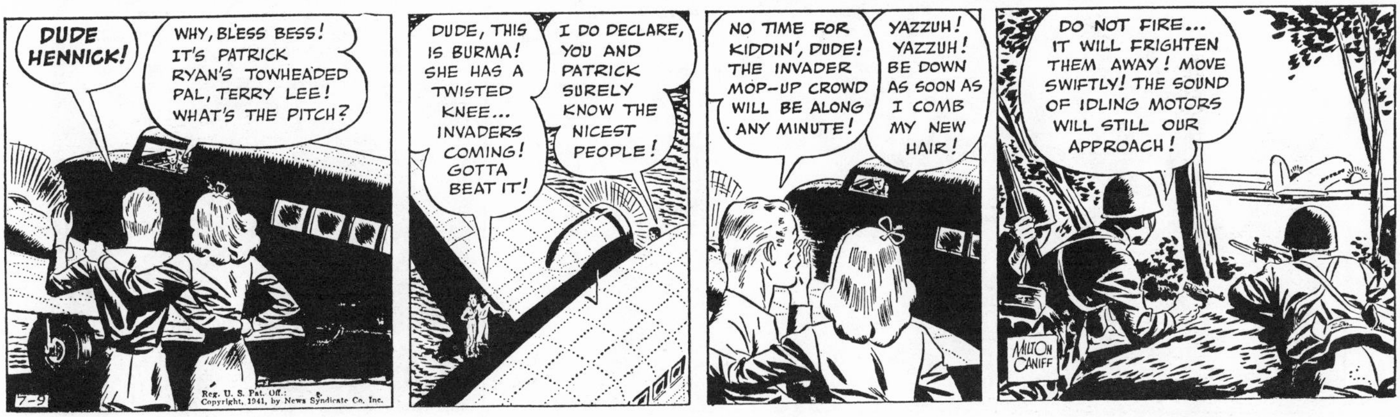
DUDE HENNICK!
WHY, BLESS BESS! IT'S PATRICK RYAN'S TOWHEADED PAL, TERRY LEE! WHAT'S THE PITCH?
7-9
Reg. U. S. Pat. Off.: Copyright, 1941, by News Syndicate Co. Inc.
DUDE, THIS IS BURMA! SHE HAS A TWISTED KNEE... INVADERS COMING! GOTTA BEAT IT!
I DO DECLARE, YOU AND PATRICK SURELY KNOW THE NICEST PEOPLE!
NO TIME FOR KIDDIN', DUDE! THE INVADER MOP-UP CROWD WILL BE ALONG ANY MINUTE!
YAZZUH! YAZZUH! BE DOWN AS SOON AS I COMB MY NEW HAIR!
MILTON CANIFF
DO NOT FIRE... IT WILL FRIGHTEN THEM AWAY! MOVE SWIFTLY! THE SOUND OF IDLING MOTORS WILL STILL OUR APPROACH!

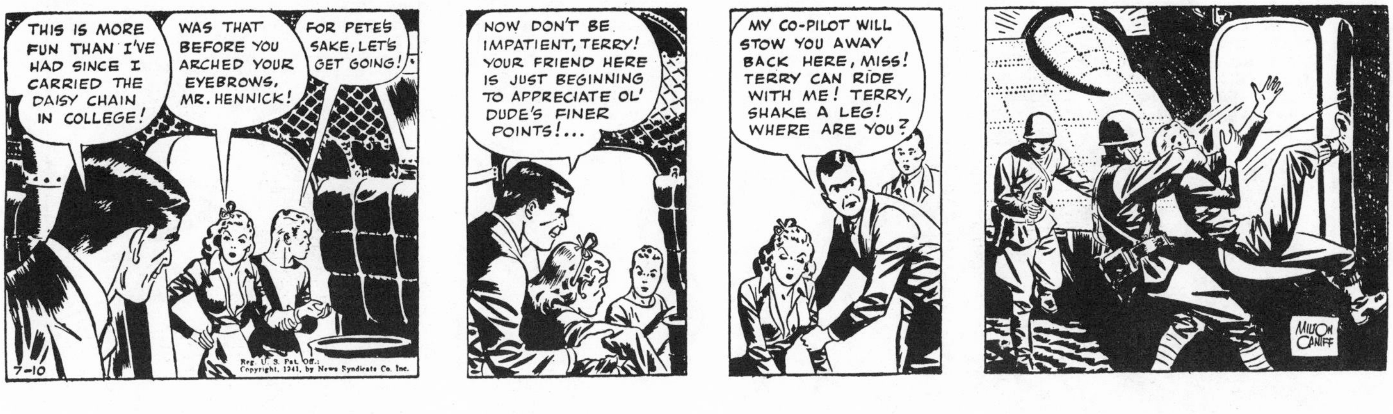
THIS IS MORE FUN THAN I'VE HAD SINCE I CARRIED THE DAISY CHAIN IN COLLEGE!
WAS THAT BEFORE YOU ARCHED YOUR EYEBROWS, MR. HENNICK!
FOR PETE'S SAKE, LET'S GET GOING!
7-10
Reg. U. S. Pat. Off.: Copyright, 1941, by News Syndicate Co. Inc.
NOW DON'T BE IMPATIENT, TERRY! YOUR FRIEND HERE IS JUST BEGINNING TO APPRECIATE OL' DUDE'S FINER POINTS!...
MY CO-PILOT WILL STOW YOU AWAY BACK HERE, MISS! TERRY CAN RIDE WITH ME! TERRY, SHAKE A LEG! WHERE ARE YOU?
MILTON CANIFF

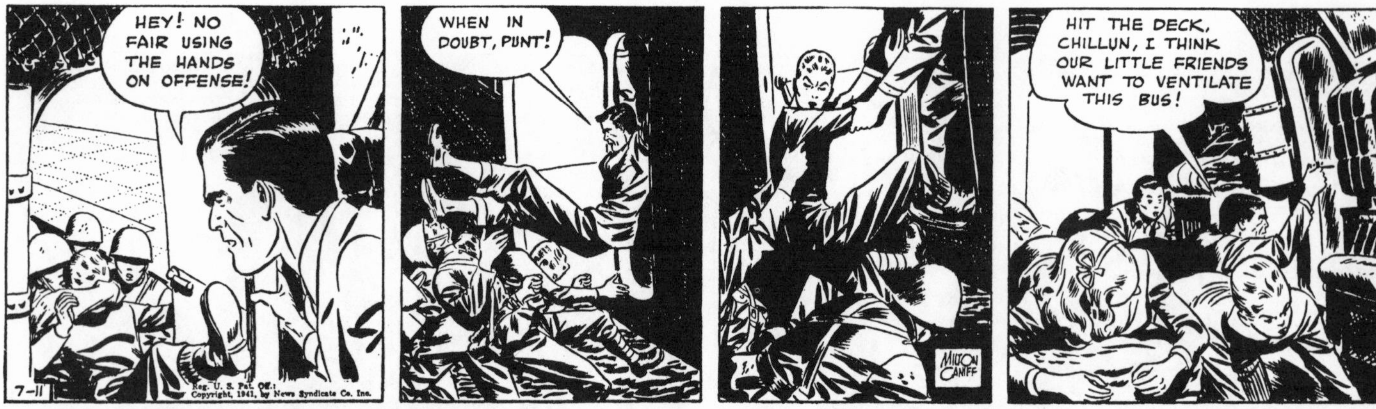
HEY! NO FAIR USING THE HANDS ON OFFENSE!
7-11
Reg. U. S. Pat. Off.: Copyright, 1941, by News Syndicate Co. Inc.
WHEN IN DOUBT, PUNT!
MILTON CANIFF
HIT THE DECK, CHILLUN, I THINK OUR LITTLE FRIENDS WANT TO VENTILATE THIS BUS!

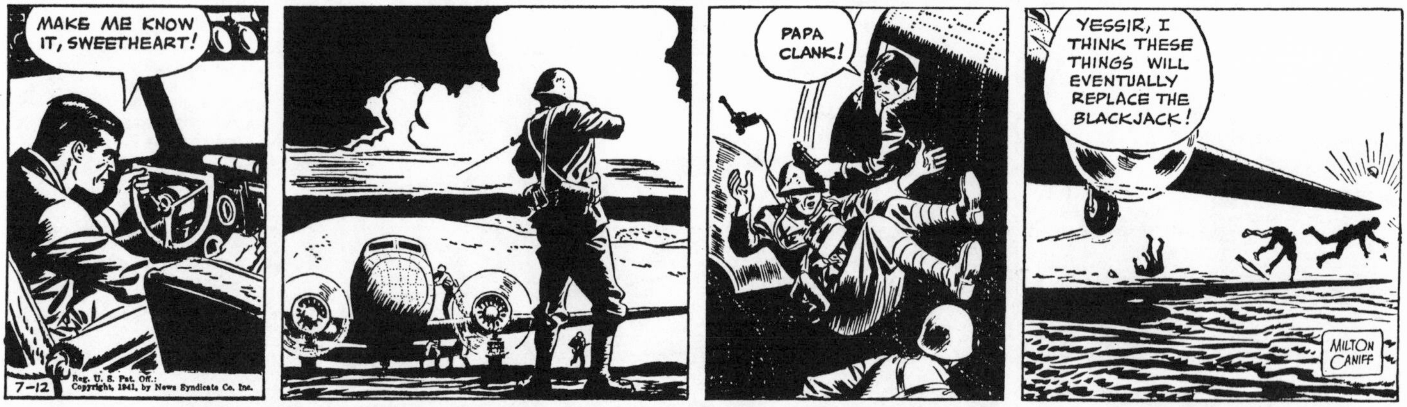
MAKE ME KNOW IT, SWEETHEART!
7-12
Reg. U. S. Pat. Off.: Copyright, 1941, by News Syndicate Co. Inc.
PAPA CLANK!
YESSIR, I THINK THESE THINGS WILL EVENTUALLY REPLACE THE BLACKJACK!
MILTON CANIFF

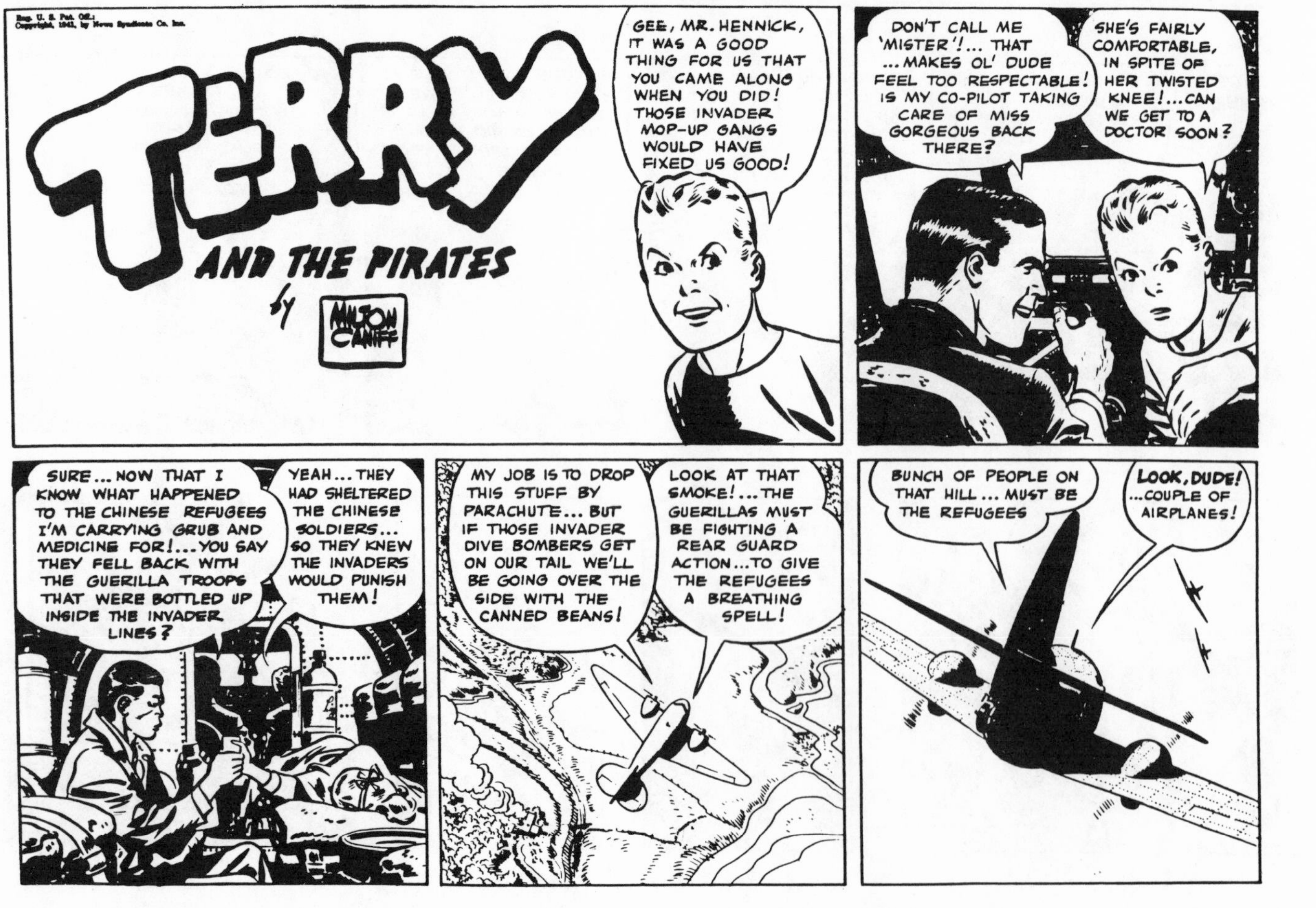
TERRY AND THE PIRATES by MILTON CANIFF
GEE, MR. HENNICK, IT WAS A GOOD THING FOR US THAT YOU CAME ALONG WHEN YOU DID! THOSE INVADER MOP-UP GANGS WOULD HAVE FIXED US GOOD!
DON'T CALL ME 'MISTER'!... THAT ...MAKES OL' DUDE FEEL TOO RESPECTABLE! IS MY CO-PILOT TAKING CARE OF MISS GORGEOUS BACK THERE?
SHE'S FAIRLY COMFORTABLE, IN SPITE OF HER TWISTED KNEE!...CAN WE GET TO A DOCTOR SOON?
SURE... NOW THAT I KNOW WHAT HAPPENED TO THE CHINESE REFUGEES I'M CARRYING GRUB AND MEDICINE FOR!... YOU SAY THEY FELL BACK WITH THE GUERILLA TROOPS THAT WERE BOTTLED UP INSIDE THE INVADER LINES?
YEAH... THEY HAD SHELTERED THE CHINESE SOLDIERS... SO THEY KNEW THE INVADERS WOULD PUNISH THEM!
MY JOB IS TO DROP THIS STUFF BY PARACHUTE... BUT IF THOSE INVADER DIVE BOMBERS GET ON OUR TAIL WE'LL BE GOING OVER THE SIDE WITH THE CANNED BEANS!
LOOK AT THAT SMOKE!... THE GUERILLAS MUST BE FIGHTING A REAR GUARD ACTION... TO GIVE THE REFUGEES A BREATHING SPELL!
BUNCH OF PEOPLE ON THAT HILL... MUST BE THE REFUGEES
LOOK, DUDE! ...COUPLE OF AIRPLANES!

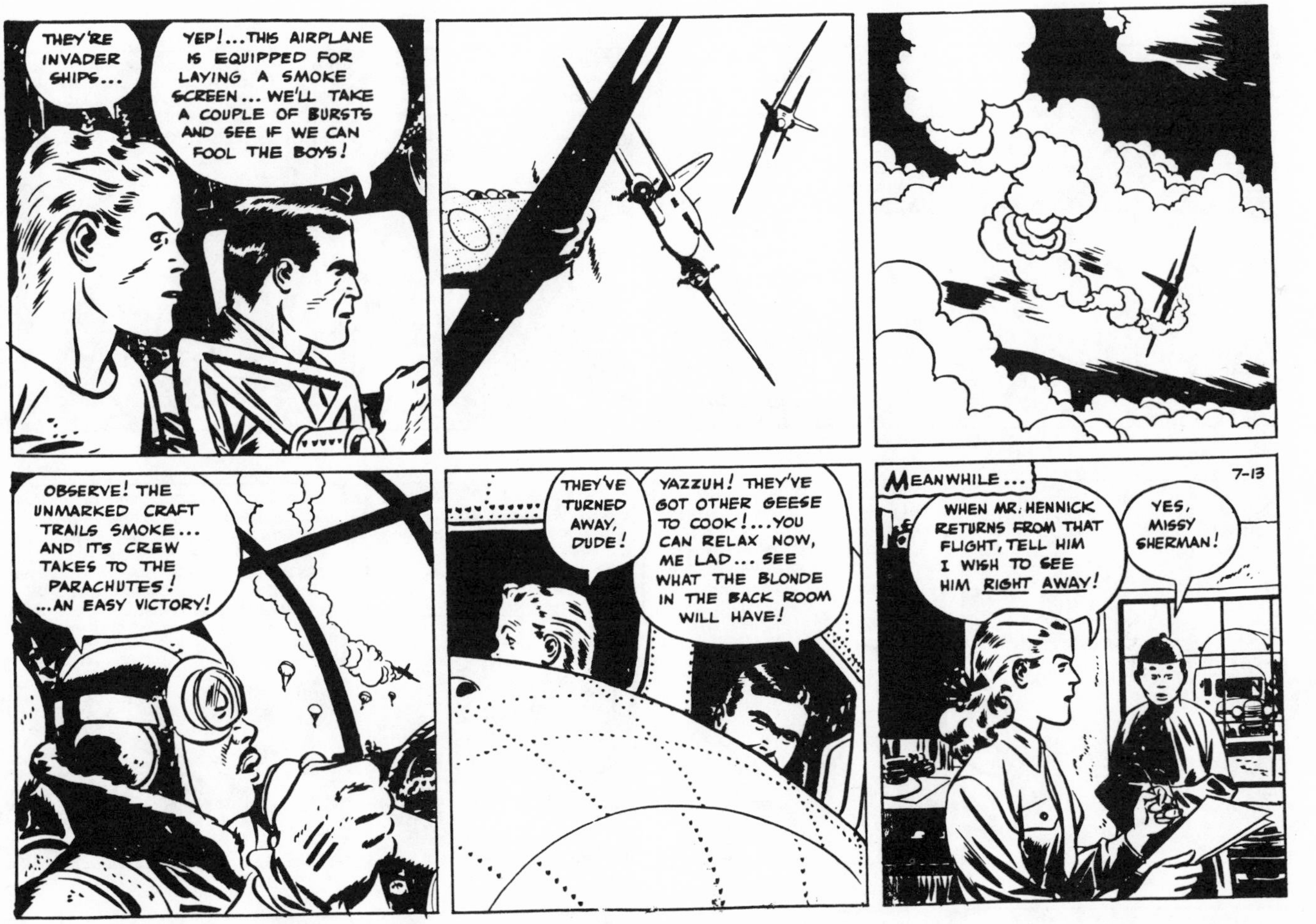
THEY'RE INVADER SHIPS...
YEP!... THIS AIRPLANE IS EQUIPPED FOR LAYING A SMOKE SCREEN... WE'LL TAKE A COUPLE OF BURSTS AND SEE IF WE CAN FOOL THE BOYS!
OBSERVE! THE UNMARKED CRAFT TRAILS SMOKE... AND ITS CREW TAKES TO THE PARACHUTES! ...AN EASY VICTORY!
THEY'VE TURNED AWAY, DUDE!
YAZZUH! THEY'VE GOT OTHER GEESE TO COOK!... YOU CAN RELAX NOW, ME LAD... SEE WHAT THE BLONDE IN THE BACK ROOM WILL HAVE!
MEANWHILE...
7-13
WHEN MR. HENNICK RETURNS FROM THAT FLIGHT, TELL HIM I WISH TO SEE HIM RIGHT AWAY!
YES, MISSY SHERMAN!

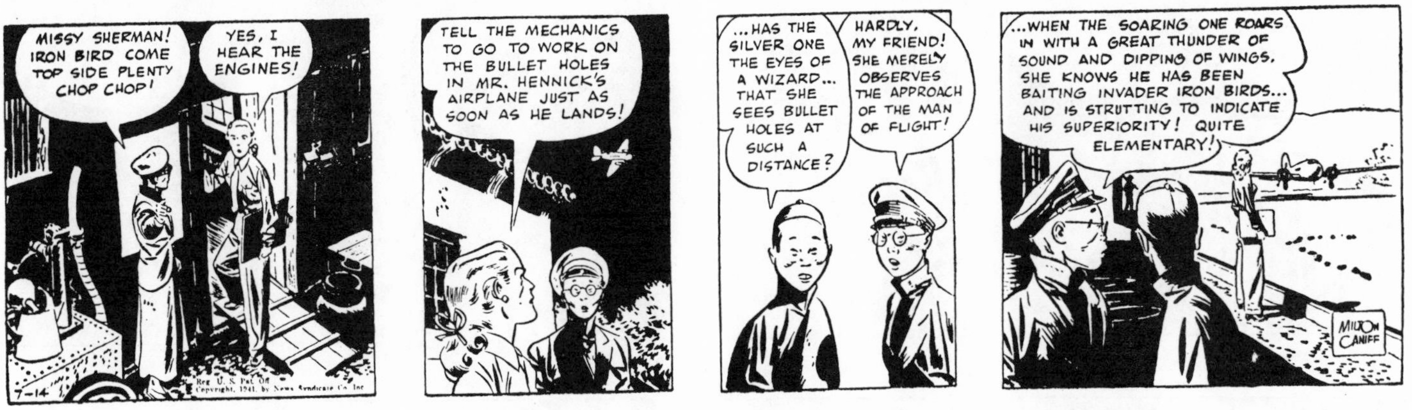
MISSY SHERMAN! IRON BIRD COME TOP SIDE PLENTY CHOP CHOP!
YES, I HEAR THE ENGINES!
7-14
Reg. U. S. Pat. Off. Copyright, 1941, by News Syndicate Co. Inc.
TELL THE MECHANICS TO GO TO WORK ON THE BULLET HOLES IN MR. HENNICK'S AIRPLANE JUST AS SOON AS HE LANDS!
...HAS THE SILVER ONE THE EYES OF A WIZARD... THAT SHE SEES BULLET HOLES AT SUCH A DISTANCE?
HARDLY, MY FRIEND! SHE MERELY OBSERVES THE APPROACH OF THE MAN OF FLIGHT!
...WHEN THE SOARING ONE ROARS IN WITH A GREAT THUNDER OF SOUND AND DIPPING OF WINGS, SHE KNOWS HE HAS BEEN BAITING INVADER IRON BIRDS... AND IS STRUTTING TO INDICATE HIS SUPERIORITY! QUITE ELEMENTARY!
MILTON CANIFF

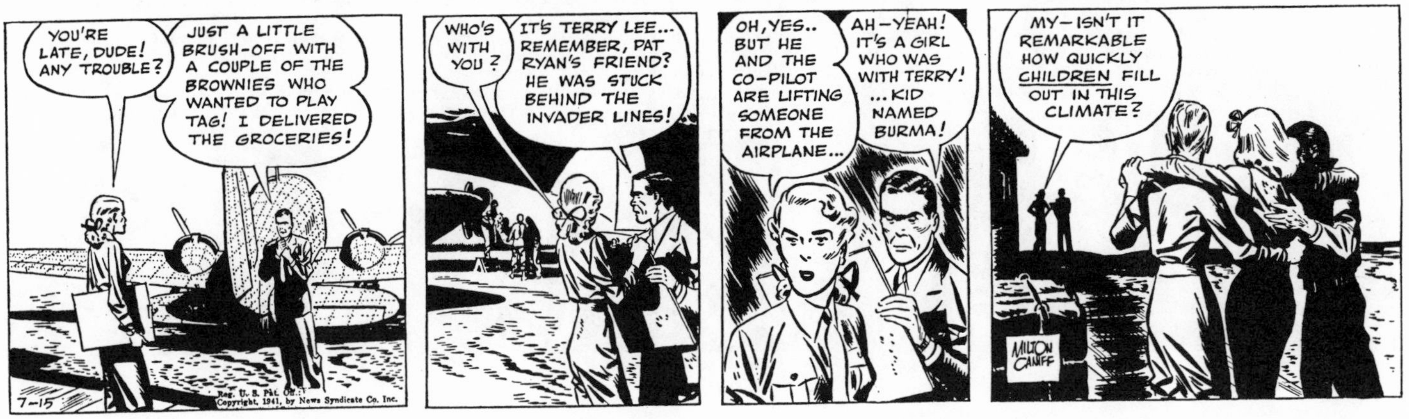
YOU'RE LATE, DUDE! ANY TROUBLE?
JUST A LITTLE BRUSH-OFF WITH A COUPLE OF THE BROWNIES WHO WANTED TO PLAY TAG! I DELIVERED THE GROCERIES!
7-15
Reg. U. S. Pat. Off. Copyright, 1941, by News Syndicate Co. Inc.
WHO'S WITH YOU?
IT'S TERRY LEE... REMEMBER, PAT RYAN'S FRIEND? HE WAS STUCK BEHIND THE INVADER LINES!
OH, YES.. BUT HE AND THE CO-PILOT ARE LIFTING SOMEONE FROM THE AIRPLANE...
AH-YEAH! IT'S A GIRL WHO WAS WITH TERRY! ...KID NAMED BURMA!
MILTON CANIFF
MY-ISN'T IT REMARKABLE HOW QUICKLY CHILDREN FILL OUT IN THIS CLIMATE?

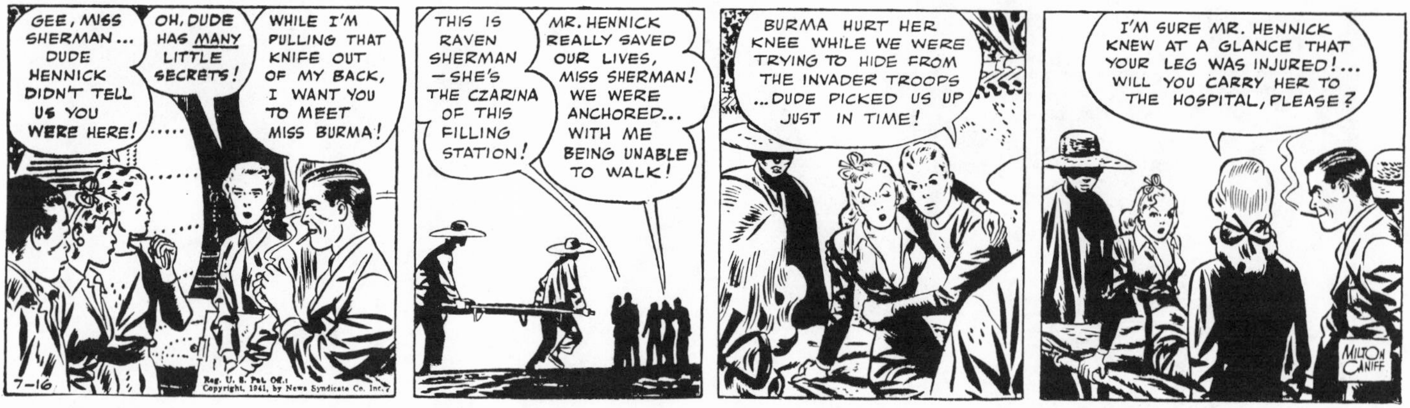
GEE, MISS SHERMAN... DUDE HENNICK DIDN'T TELL US YOU WERE HERE!
OH, DUDE HAS MANY LITTLE SECRETS!
WHILE I'M PULLING THAT KNIFE OUT OF MY BACK, I WANT YOU TO MEET MISS BURMA!
7-16
Reg. U. S. Pat. Off.: Copyright, 1941, by News Syndicate Co. Inc.
THIS IS RAVEN SHERMAN — SHE'S THE CZARINA OF THIS FILLING STATION!
MR. HENNICK REALLY SAVED OUR LIVES, MISS SHERMAN! WE WERE ANCHORED... WITH ME BEING UNABLE TO WALK!
BURMA HURT HER KNEE WHILE WE WERE TRYING TO HIDE FROM THE INVADER TROOPS ...DUDE PICKED US UP JUST IN TIME!
I'M SURE MR. HENNICK KNEW AT A GLANCE THAT YOUR LEG WAS INJURED!... WILL YOU CARRY HER TO THE HOSPITAL, PLEASE?
MILTON CANIFF

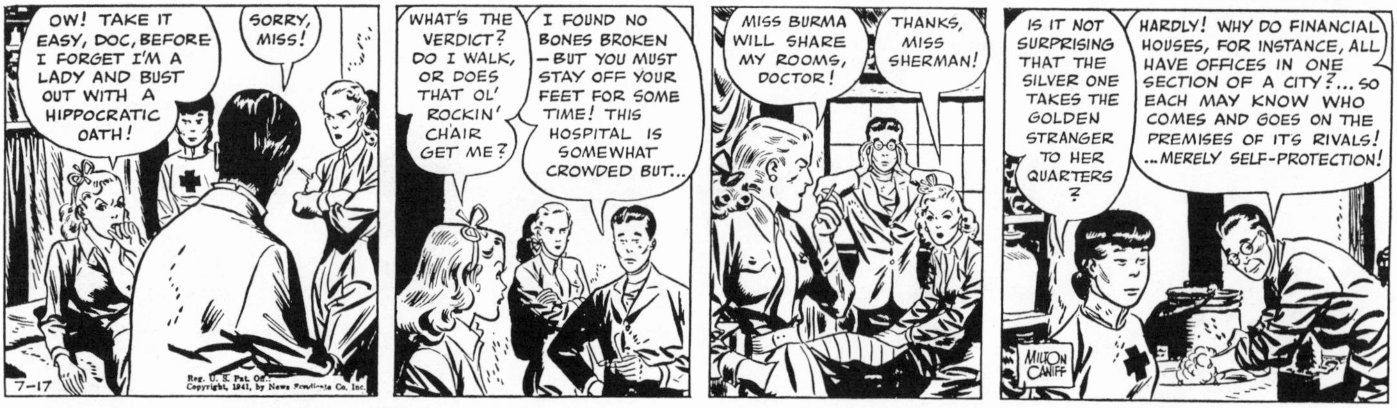
OW! TAKE IT EASY, DOC, BEFORE I FORGET I'M A LADY AND BUST OUT WITH A HIPPOCRATIC OATH!
SORRY, MISS!
7-17
Reg. U. S. Pat. Off.: Copyright, 1941, by News Syndicate Co. Inc.
WHAT'S THE VERDICT? DO I WALK, OR DOES THAT OL' ROCKIN' CHAIR GET ME?
I FOUND NO BONES BROKEN — BUT YOU MUST STAY OFF YOUR FEET FOR SOME TIME! THIS HOSPITAL IS SOMEWHAT CROWDED BUT...
MISS BURMA WILL SHARE MY ROOMS, DOCTOR!
THANKS, MISS SHERMAN!
IS IT NOT SURPRISING THAT THE SILVER ONE TAKES THE GOLDEN STRANGER TO HER QUARTERS?
HARDLY! WHY DO FINANCIAL HOUSES, FOR INSTANCE, ALL HAVE OFFICES IN ONE SECTION OF A CITY?... SO EACH MAY KNOW WHO COMES AND GOES ON THE PREMISES OF ITS RIVALS! ...MERELY SELF-PROTECTION!
MILTON CANIFF

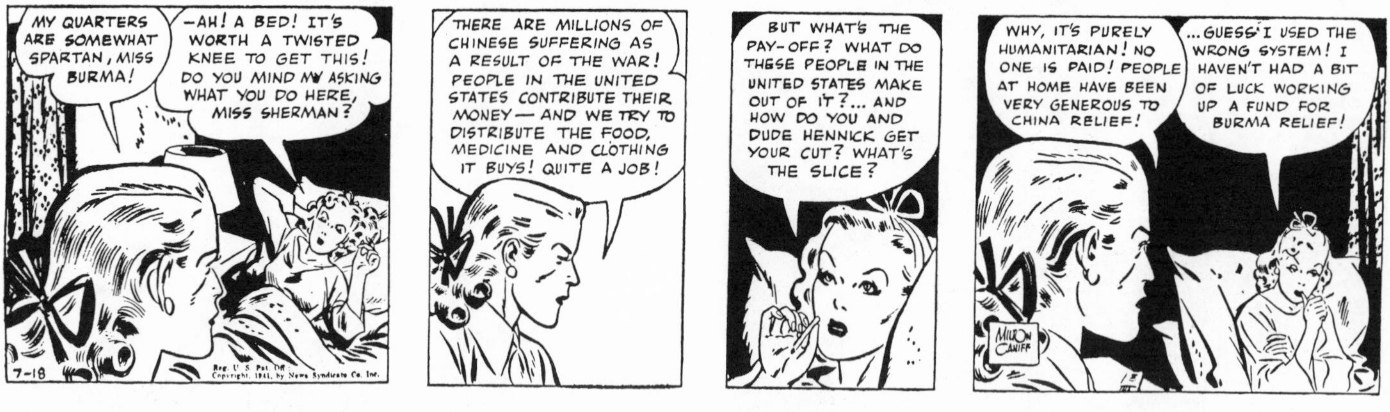
MY QUARTERS ARE SOMEWHAT SPARTAN, MISS BURMA!
—AH! A BED! IT'S WORTH A TWISTED KNEE TO GET THIS! DO YOU MIND MY ASKING WHAT YOU DO HERE, MISS SHERMAN?
7-18
Reg. U. S. Pat. Off.: Copyright, 1941, by News Syndicate Co. Inc.
THERE ARE MILLIONS OF CHINESE SUFFERING AS A RESULT OF THE WAR! PEOPLE IN THE UNITED STATES CONTRIBUTE THEIR MONEY — AND WE TRY TO DISTRIBUTE THE FOOD, MEDICINE AND CLOTHING IT BUYS! QUITE A JOB!
BUT WHAT'S THE PAY-OFF? WHAT DO THESE PEOPLE IN THE UNITED STATES MAKE OUT OF IT?... AND HOW DO YOU AND DUDE HENNICK GET YOUR CUT? WHAT'S THE SLICE?
WHY, IT'S PURELY HUMANITARIAN! NO ONE IS PAID! PEOPLE AT HOME HAVE BEEN VERY GENEROUS TO CHINA RELIEF!
...GUESS I USED THE WRONG SYSTEM! I HAVEN'T HAD A BIT OF LUCK WORKING UP A FUND FOR BURMA RELIEF!
MILTON CANIFF

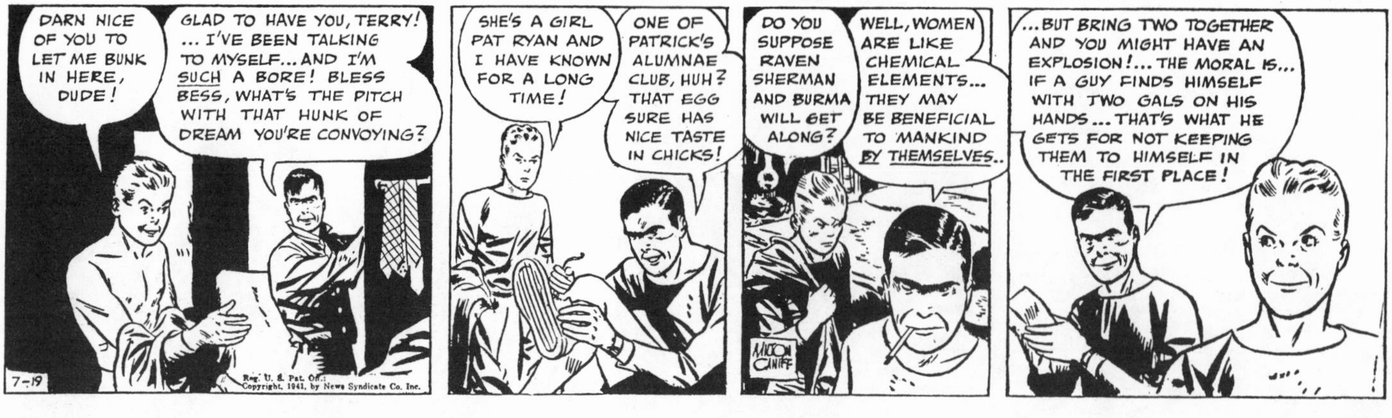
DARN NICE OF YOU TO LET ME BUNK IN HERE, DUDE!
GLAD TO HAVE YOU, TERRY! ... I'VE BEEN TALKING TO MYSELF... AND I'M SUCH A BORE! BLESS BESS, WHAT'S THE PITCH WITH THAT HUNK OF DREAM YOU'RE CONVOYING?
7-19
Reg. U. S. Pat. Off.: Copyright, 1941, by News Syndicate Co. Inc.
SHE'S A GIRL PAT RYAN AND I HAVE KNOWN FOR A LONG TIME!
ONE OF PATRICK'S ALUMNAE CLUB, HUH? THAT EGG SURE HAS NICE TASTE IN CHICKS!
DO YOU SUPPOSE RAVEN SHERMAN AND BURMA WILL GET ALONG?
WELL, WOMEN ARE LIKE CHEMICAL ELEMENTS... THEY MAY BE BENEFICIAL TO MANKIND BY THEMSELVES..
...BUT BRING TWO TOGETHER AND YOU MIGHT HAVE AN EXPLOSION!... THE MORAL IS... IF A GUY FINDS HIMSELF WITH TWO GALS ON HIS HANDS... THAT'S WHAT HE GETS FOR NOT KEEPING THEM TO HIMSELF IN THE FIRST PLACE!
MILTON CANIFF

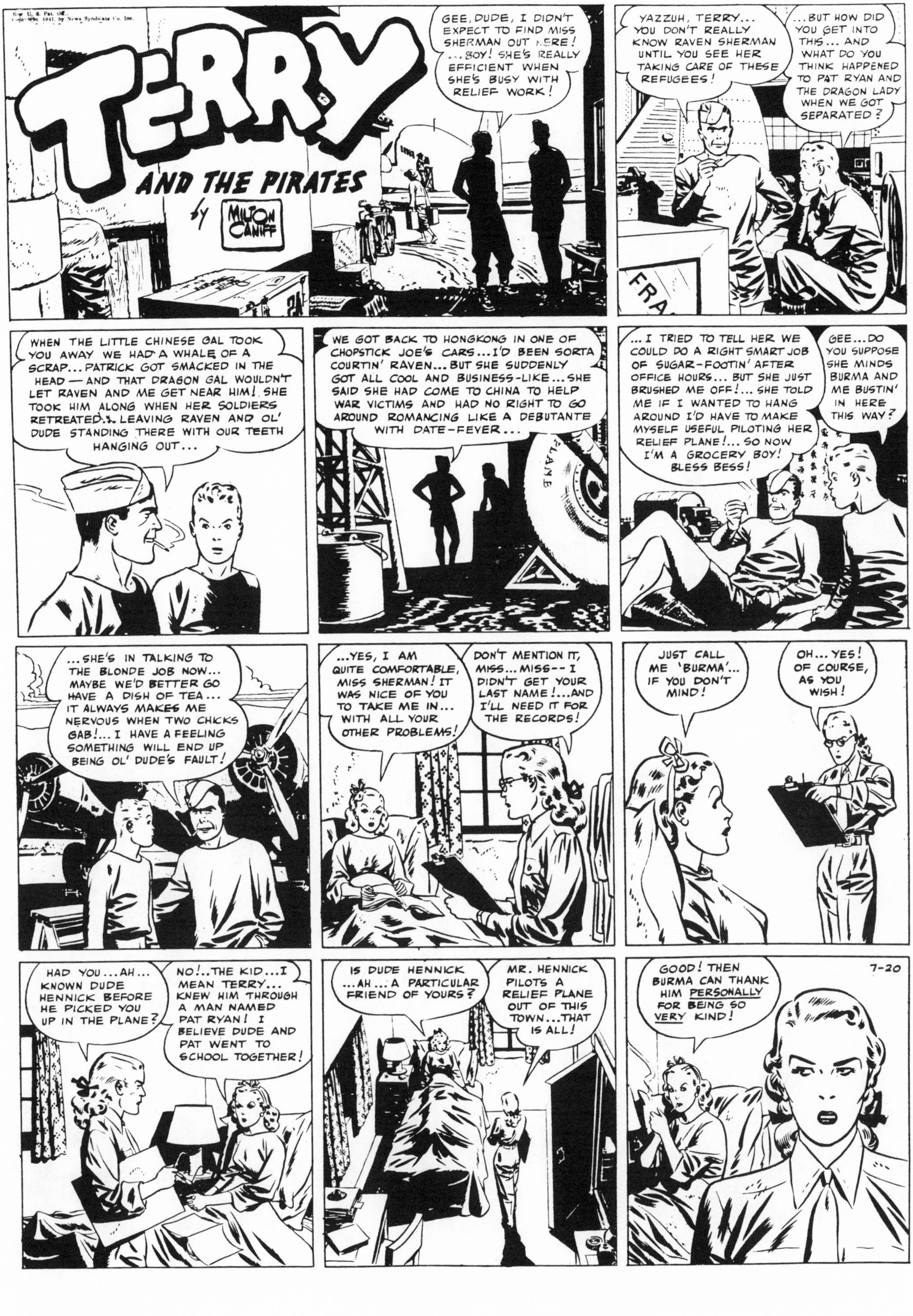
Reg. U. S. Pat. Off.:
Copyright, 1941, by News Syndicate Co. Inc.
TERRY AND THE PIRATES
by MILTON CANIFF
GEE, DUDE, I DIDN'T EXPECT TO FIND MISS SHERMAN OUT HERE! ... BOY! SHE'S REALLY EFFICIENT WHEN SHE'S BUSY WITH RELIEF WORK!
YAZZUH, TERRY... YOU DON'T REALLY KNOW RAVEN SHERMAN UNTIL YOU SEE HER TAKING CARE OF THESE REFUGEES!
...BUT HOW DID YOU GET INTO THIS... AND WHAT DO YOU THINK HAPPENED TO PAT RYAN AND THE DRAGON LADY WHEN WE GOT SEPARATED?
FRA
WHEN THE LITTLE CHINESE GAL TOOK YOU AWAY WE HAD A WHALE OF A SCRAP... PATRICK GOT SMACKED IN THE HEAD — AND THAT DRAGON GAL WOULDN'T LET RAVEN AND ME GET NEAR HIM! SHE TOOK HIM ALONG WHEN HER SOLDIERS RETREATED... LEAVING RAVEN AND OL' DUDE STANDING THERE WITH OUR TEETH HANGING OUT...
WE GOT BACK TO HONGKONG IN ONE OF CHOPSTICK JOE'S CARS... I'D BEEN SORTA COURTIN' RAVEN... BUT SHE SUDDENLY GOT ALL COOL AND BUSINESS-LIKE... SHE SAID SHE HAD COME TO CHINA TO HELP WAR VICTIMS AND HAD NO RIGHT TO GO AROUND ROMANCING LIKE A DEBUTANTE WITH DATE-FEVER...
PLANE
...I TRIED TO TELL HER WE COULD DO A RIGHT SMART JOB OF SUGAR-FOOTIN' AFTER OFFICE HOURS... BUT SHE JUST BRUSHED ME OFF!... SHE TOLD ME IF I WANTED TO HANG AROUND I'D HAVE TO MAKE MYSELF USEFUL PILOTING HER RELIEF PLANE!... SO NOW I'M A GROCERY BOY! BLESS BESS!
GEE... DO YOU SUPPOSE SHE MINDS BURMA AND ME BUSTIN' IN HERE THIS WAY?
...SHE'S IN TALKING TO THE BLONDE JOB NOW... MAYBE WE'D BETTER GO HAVE A DISH OF TEA... IT ALWAYS MAKES ME NERVOUS WHEN TWO CHICKS GAB!... I HAVE A FEELING SOMETHING WILL END UP BEING OL' DUDE'S FAULT!
...YES, I AM QUITE COMFORTABLE, MISS SHERMAN! IT WAS NICE OF YOU TO TAKE ME IN... WITH ALL YOUR OTHER PROBLEMS!
DON'T MENTION IT, MISS... MISS-- I DIDN'T GET YOUR LAST NAME!... AND I'LL NEED IT FOR THE RECORDS!
JUST CALL ME 'BURMA'... IF YOU DON'T MIND!
OH... YES! OF COURSE, AS YOU WISH!
HAD YOU... AH... KNOWN DUDE HENNICK BEFORE HE PICKED YOU UP IN THE PLANE?
NO!.. THE KID... I MEAN TERRY... KNEW HIM THROUGH A MAN NAMED PAT RYAN! I BELIEVE DUDE AND PAT WENT TO SCHOOL TOGETHER!
IS DUDE HENNICK ...AH... A PARTICULAR FRIEND OF YOURS?
MR. HENNICK PILOTS A RELIEF PLANE OUT OF THIS TOWN... THAT IS ALL!
7-20
GOOD! THEN BURMA CAN THANK HIM PERSONALLY FOR BEING SO VERY KIND!

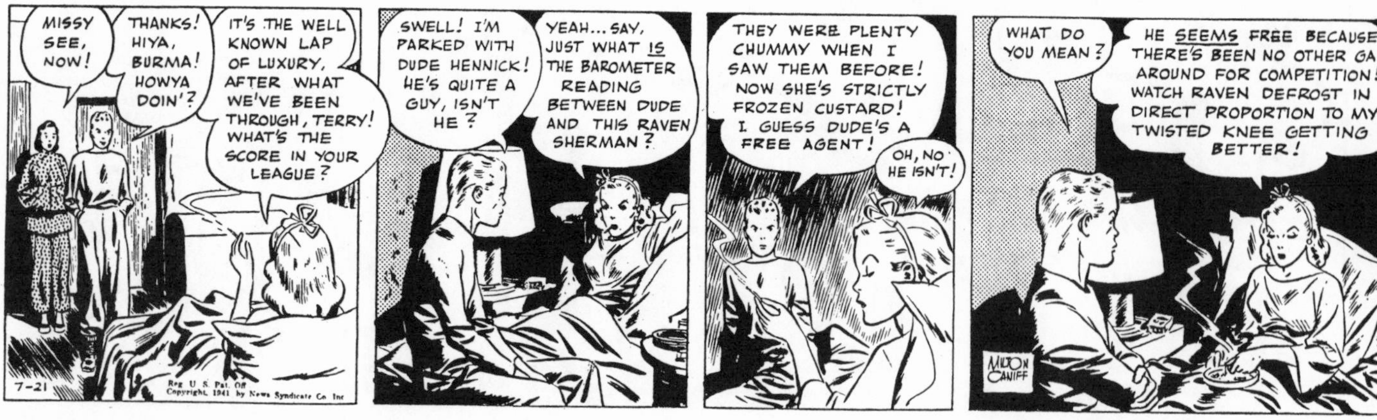
MISSY SEE, NOW!
THANKS! HIYA, BURMA! HOWYA DOIN'?
IT'S THE WELL KNOWN LAP OF LUXURY, AFTER WHAT WE'VE BEEN THROUGH, TERRY! WHAT'S THE SCORE IN YOUR LEAGUE?
7-21
Reg. U. S. Pat. Off. Copyright, 1941, by News Syndicate Co. Inc
SWELL! I'M PARKED WITH DUDE HENNICK! HE'S QUITE A GUY, ISN'T HE?
YEAH... SAY, JUST WHAT IS THE BAROMETER READING BETWEEN DUDE AND THIS RAVEN SHERMAN?
THEY WERE PLENTY CHUMMY WHEN I SAW THEM BEFORE! NOW SHE'S STRICTLY FROZEN CUSTARD! I GUESS DUDE'S A FREE AGENT!
OH, NO HE ISN'T!
WHAT DO YOU MEAN?
HE SEEMS FREE BECAUSE THERE'S BEEN NO OTHER GAL AROUND FOR COMPETITION! WATCH RAVEN DEFROST IN DIRECT PROPORTION TO MY TWISTED KNEE GETTING BETTER!
MILTON CANIFF

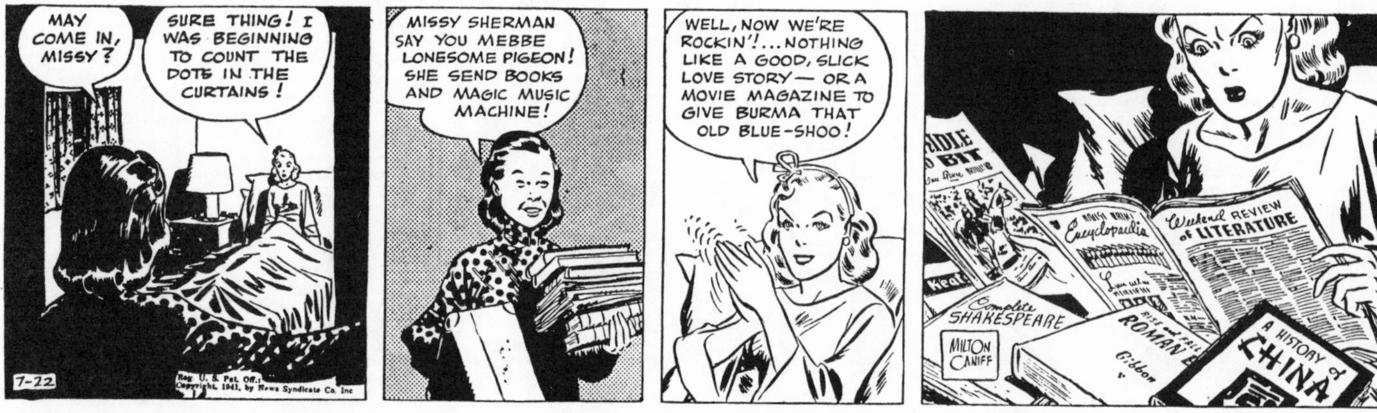
MAY COME IN, MISSY?
SURE THING! I WAS BEGINNING TO COUNT THE DOTS IN THE CURTAINS!
7-22
Reg. U. S. Pat. Off. Copyright, 1941, by News Syndicate Co. Inc
MISSY SHERMAN SAY YOU MEBBE LONESOME PIGEON! SHE SEND BOOKS AND MAGIC MUSIC MACHINE!
WELL, NOW WE'RE ROCKIN'!... NOTHING LIKE A GOOD, SLICK LOVE STORY — OR A MOVIE MAGAZINE TO GIVE BURMA THAT OLD BLUE-SHOO!
Weekend REVIEW of LITERATURE
Encyclopaedia
Complete SHAKESPEARE
ROMAN
Gibbon
A HISTORY of CHINA
MILTON CANIFF

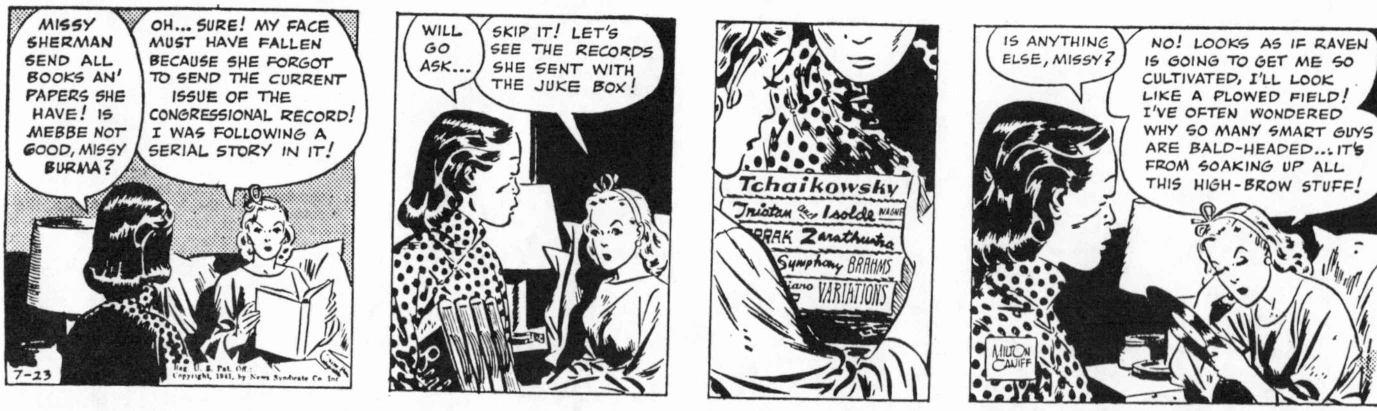
MISSY SHERMAN SEND ALL BOOKS AN' PAPERS SHE HAVE! IS MEBBE NOT GOOD, MISSY BURMA?
OH... SURE! MY FACE MUST HAVE FALLEN BECAUSE SHE FORGOT TO SEND THE CURRENT ISSUE OF THE CONGRESSIONAL RECORD! I WAS FOLLOWING A SERIAL STORY IN IT!
7-23
Reg. U. S. Pat. Off. Copyright, 1941, by News Syndicate Co. Inc
WILL GO ASK...
SKIP IT! LET'S SEE THE RECORDS SHE SENT WITH THE JUKE BOX!
Tchaikowsky
Tristan und Isolde
Zarathustra
Symphony BRAHMS
VARIATIONS
IS ANYTHING ELSE, MISSY?
NO! LOOKS AS IF RAVEN IS GOING TO GET ME SO CULTIVATED, I'LL LOOK LIKE A PLOWED FIELD! I'VE OFTEN WONDERED WHY SO MANY SMART GUYS ARE BALD-HEADED... IT'S FROM SOAKING UP ALL THIS HIGH-BROW STUFF!
MILTON CANIFF

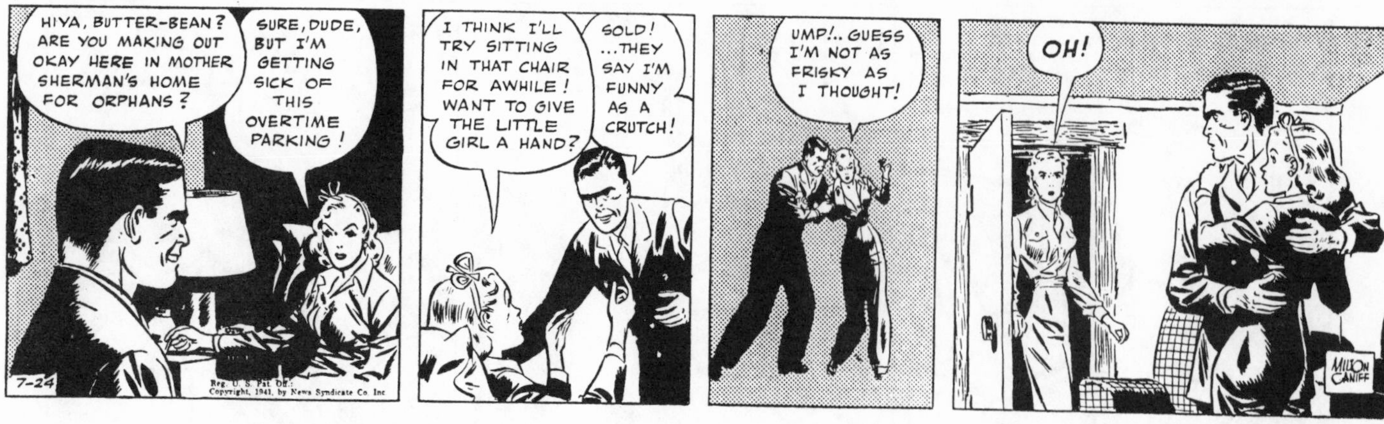
HIYA, BUTTER-BEAN? ARE YOU MAKING OUT OKAY HERE IN MOTHER SHERMAN'S HOME FOR ORPHANS?
SURE, DUDE, BUT I'M GETTING SICK OF THIS OVERTIME PARKING!
7-24
Reg. U. S. Pat. Off. Copyright, 1941, by News Syndicate Co. Inc
I THINK I'LL TRY SITTING IN THAT CHAIR FOR AWHILE! WANT TO GIVE THE LITTLE GIRL A HAND?
SOLD! ...THEY SAY I'M FUNNY AS A CRUTCH!
UMP!.. GUESS I'M NOT AS FRISKY AS I THOUGHT!
OH!
MILTON CANIFF

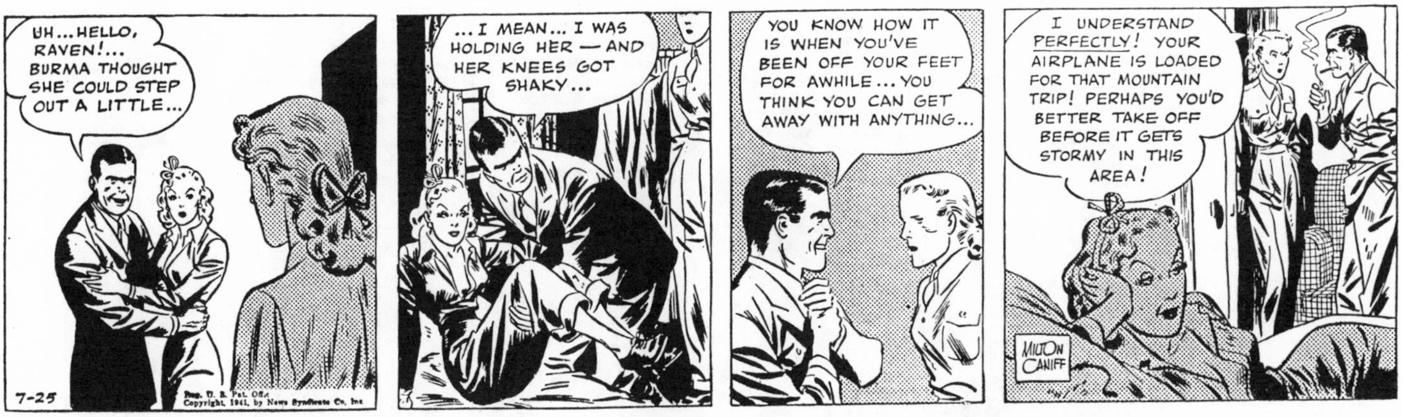

UH... HELLO, RAVEN!... BURMA THOUGHT SHE COULD STEP OUT A LITTLE...
7-25
Reg. U. S. Pat. Off. Copyright, 1941, by News Syndicate Co. Inc.
... I MEAN... I WAS HOLDING HER — AND HER KNEES GOT SHAKY...
YOU KNOW HOW IT IS WHEN YOU'VE BEEN OFF YOUR FEET FOR AWHILE... YOU THINK YOU CAN GET AWAY WITH ANYTHING...
I UNDERSTAND PERFECTLY! YOUR AIRPLANE IS LOADED FOR THAT MOUNTAIN TRIP! PERHAPS YOU'D BETTER TAKE OFF BEFORE IT GETS STORMY IN THIS AREA!
MILTON CANIFF


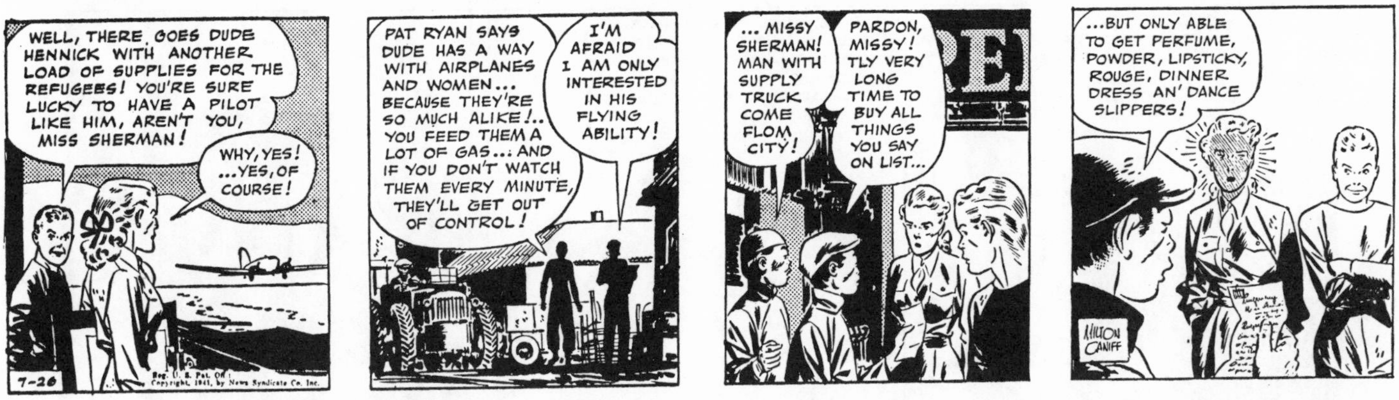

WELL, THERE GOES DUDE HENNICK WITH ANOTHER LOAD OF SUPPLIES FOR THE REFUGEES! YOU'RE SURE LUCKY TO HAVE A PILOT LIKE HIM, AREN'T YOU, MISS SHERMAN!
WHY, YES! ...YES, OF COURSE!
7-26
Reg. U. S. Pat. Off. Copyright, 1941, by News Syndicate Co. Inc.
PAT RYAN SAYS DUDE HAS A WAY WITH AIRPLANES AND WOMEN... BECAUSE THEY'RE SO MUCH ALIKE!.. YOU FEED THEM A LOT OF GAS...AND IF YOU DON'T WATCH THEM EVERY MINUTE, THEY'LL GET OUT OF CONTROL!
I'M AFRAID I AM ONLY INTERESTED IN HIS FLYING ABILITY!
... MISSY SHERMAN! MAN WITH SUPPLY TRUCK COME FLOM CITY!
PARDON, MISSY! TLY VERY LONG TIME TO BUY ALL THINGS YOU SAY ON LIST...
...BUT ONLY ABLE TO GET PERFUME, POWDER, LIPSTICKY, ROUGE, DINNER DRESS AN' DANCE SLIPPERS!
MILTON CANIFF


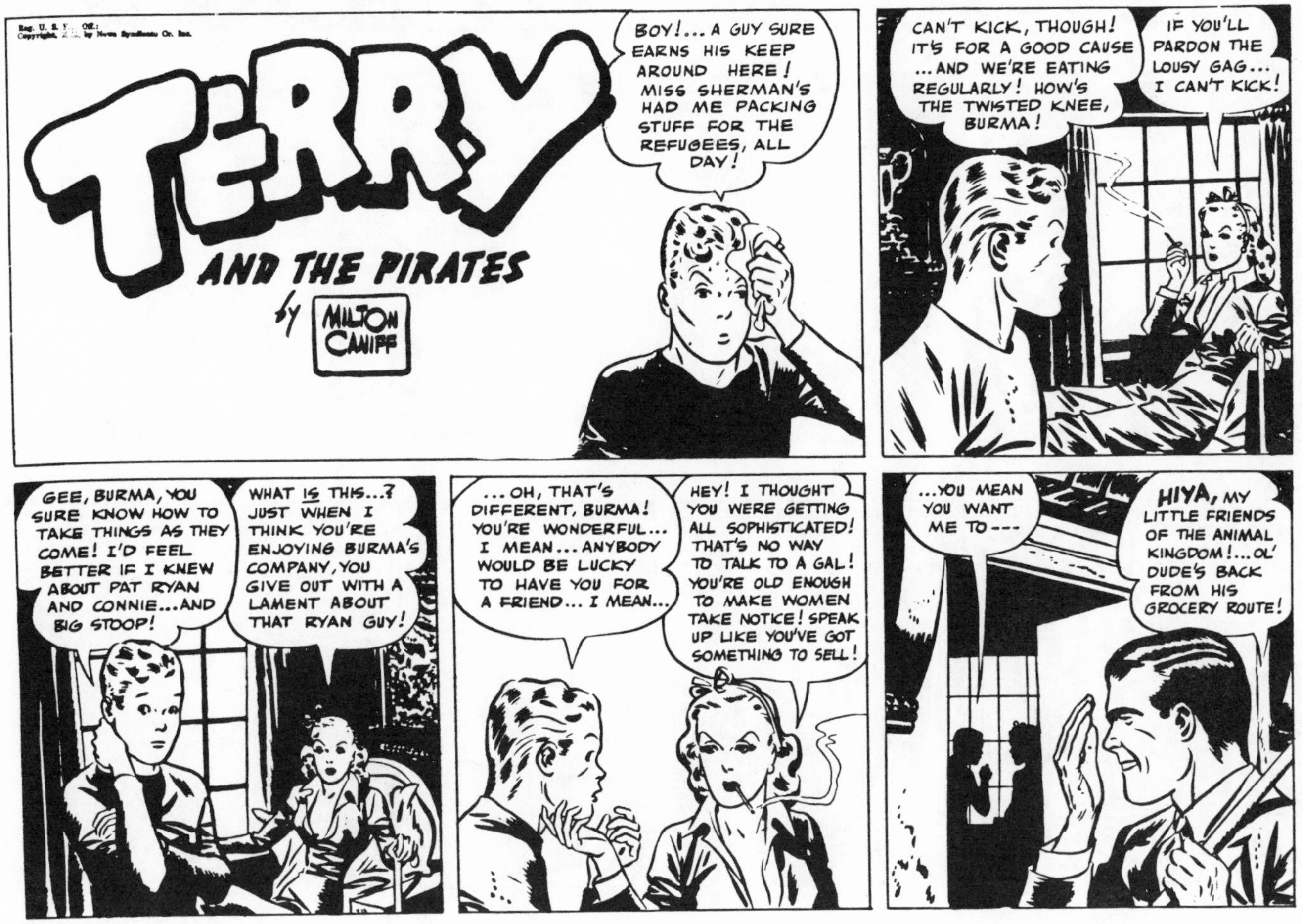

TERRY AND THE PIRATES
by MILTON CANIFF
BOY!... A GUY SURE EARNS HIS KEEP AROUND HERE! MISS SHERMAN'S HAD ME PACKING STUFF FOR THE REFUGEES, ALL DAY!
CAN'T KICK, THOUGH! IT'S FOR A GOOD CAUSE ...AND WE'RE EATING REGULARLY! HOW'S THE TWISTED KNEE, BURMA!
IF YOU'LL PARDON THE LOUSY GAG... I CAN'T KICK!
GEE, BURMA, YOU SURE KNOW HOW TO TAKE THINGS AS THEY COME! I'D FEEL BETTER IF I KNEW ABOUT PAT RYAN AND CONNIE...AND BIG STOOP!
WHAT IS THIS...? JUST WHEN I THINK YOU'RE ENJOYING BURMA'S COMPANY, YOU GIVE OUT WITH A LAMENT ABOUT THAT RYAN GUY!
...OH, THAT'S DIFFERENT, BURMA! YOU'RE WONDERFUL... I MEAN... ANYBODY WOULD BE LUCKY TO HAVE YOU FOR A FRIEND... I MEAN...
HEY! I THOUGHT YOU WERE GETTING ALL SOPHISTICATED! THAT'S NO WAY TO TALK TO A GAL! YOU'RE OLD ENOUGH TO MAKE WOMEN TAKE NOTICE! SPEAK UP LIKE YOU'VE GOT SOMETHING TO SELL!
...YOU MEAN YOU WANT ME TO---
HIYA, MY LITTLE FRIENDS OF THE ANIMAL KINGDOM!...OL' DUDE'S BACK FROM HIS GROCERY ROUTE!

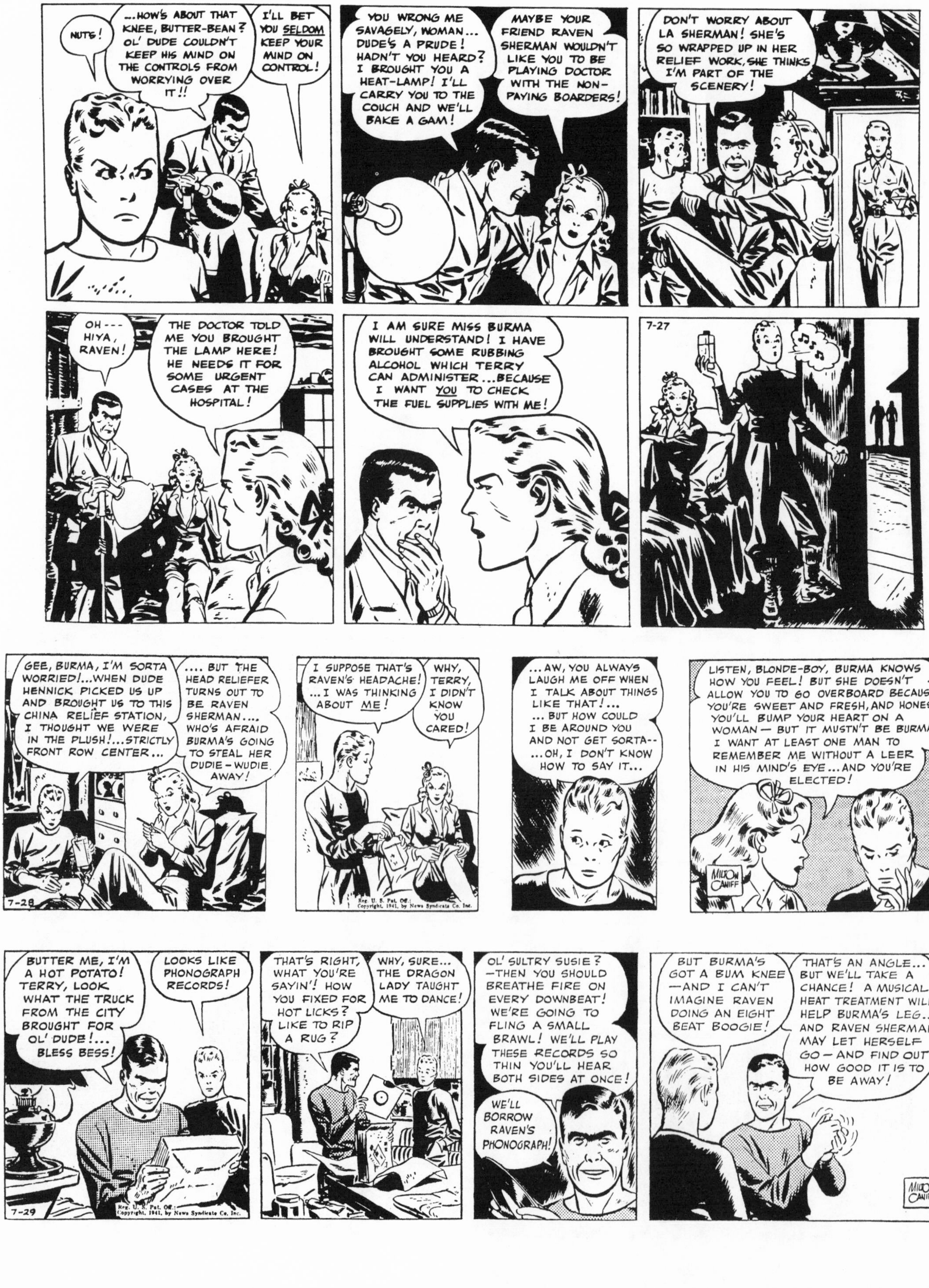

NUTS!
...HOW'S ABOUT THAT KNEE, BUTTER-BEAN? OL' DUDE COULDN'T KEEP HIS MIND ON THE CONTROLS FROM WORRYING OVER IT!!
I'LL BET YOU SELDOM KEEP YOUR MIND ON CONTROL!
YOU WRONG ME SAVAGELY, WOMAN... DUDE'S A PRUDE! HADN'T YOU HEARD? I BROUGHT YOU A HEAT-LAMP! I'LL CARRY YOU TO THE COUCH AND WE'LL BAKE A GAM!
MAYBE YOUR FRIEND RAVEN SHERMAN WOULDN'T LIKE YOU TO BE PLAYING DOCTOR WITH THE NON-PAYING BOARDERS!
DON'T WORRY ABOUT LA SHERMAN! SHE'S SO WRAPPED UP IN HER RELIEF WORK, SHE THINKS I'M PART OF THE SCENERY!
OH--- HIYA, RAVEN!
THE DOCTOR TOLD ME YOU BROUGHT THE LAMP HERE! HE NEEDS IT FOR SOME URGENT CASES AT THE HOSPITAL!
I AM SURE MISS BURMA WILL UNDERSTAND! I HAVE BROUGHT SOME RUBBING ALCOHOL WHICH TERRY CAN ADMINISTER... BECAUSE I WANT YOU TO CHECK THE FUEL SUPPLIES WITH ME!
7-27
GEE, BURMA, I'M SORTA WORRIED!...WHEN DUDE HENNICK PICKED US UP AND BROUGHT US TO THIS CHINA RELIEF STATION, I THOUGHT WE WERE IN THE PLUSH!...STRICTLY FRONT ROW CENTER...
.... BUT THE HEAD RELIEFER TURNS OUT TO BE RAVEN SHERMAN.... WHO'S AFRAID BURMA'S GOING TO STEAL HER DUDIE-WUDIE AWAY!
7-28
I SUPPOSE THAT'S RAVEN'S HEADACHE! ...I WAS THINKING ABOUT ME!
WHY, TERRY, I DIDN'T KNOW YOU CARED!
Reg. U. S. Pat. Off.: Copyright, 1941, by News Syndicate Co. Inc.
...AW, YOU ALWAYS LAUGH ME OFF WHEN I TALK ABOUT THINGS LIKE THAT!... ...BUT HOW COULD I BE AROUND YOU AND NOT GET SORTA-- ...OH, I DON'T KNOW HOW TO SAY IT...
LISTEN, BLONDE-BOY, BURMA KNOWS HOW YOU FEEL! BUT SHE DOESN'T ALLOW YOU TO GO OVERBOARD BECAUSE YOU'RE SWEET AND FRESH, AND HONEST! YOU'LL BUMP YOUR HEART ON A WOMAN — BUT IT MUSTN'T BE BURMA! I WANT AT LEAST ONE MAN TO REMEMBER ME WITHOUT A LEER IN HIS MIND'S EYE... AND YOU'RE ELECTED!
MILTON CANIFF
BUTTER ME, I'M A HOT POTATO! TERRY, LOOK WHAT THE TRUCK FROM THE CITY BROUGHT FOR OL' DUDE!... BLESS BESS!
LOOKS LIKE PHONOGRAPH RECORDS!
7-29
Reg. U. S. Pat. Off.: Copyright, 1941, by News Syndicate Co. Inc.
THAT'S RIGHT, WHAT YOU'RE SAYIN'! HOW YOU FIXED FOR HOT LICKS? LIKE TO RIP A RUG?
WHY, SURE... THE DRAGON LADY TAUGHT ME TO DANCE!
OL' SULTRY SUSIE? —THEN YOU SHOULD BREATHE FIRE ON EVERY DOWNBEAT! WE'RE GOING TO FLING A SMALL BRAWL! WE'LL PLAY THESE RECORDS SO THIN YOU'LL HEAR BOTH SIDES AT ONCE!
WE'LL BORROW RAVEN'S PHONOGRAPH!
BUT BURMA'S GOT A BUM KNEE —AND I CAN'T IMAGINE RAVEN DOING AN EIGHT BEAT BOOGIE!
THAT'S AN ANGLE... BUT WE'LL TAKE A CHANCE! A MUSICAL HEAT TREATMENT WILL HELP BURMA'S LEG... AND RAVEN SHERMAN MAY LET HERSELF GO — AND FIND OUT HOW GOOD IT IS TO BE AWAY!
MILTON CANIFF

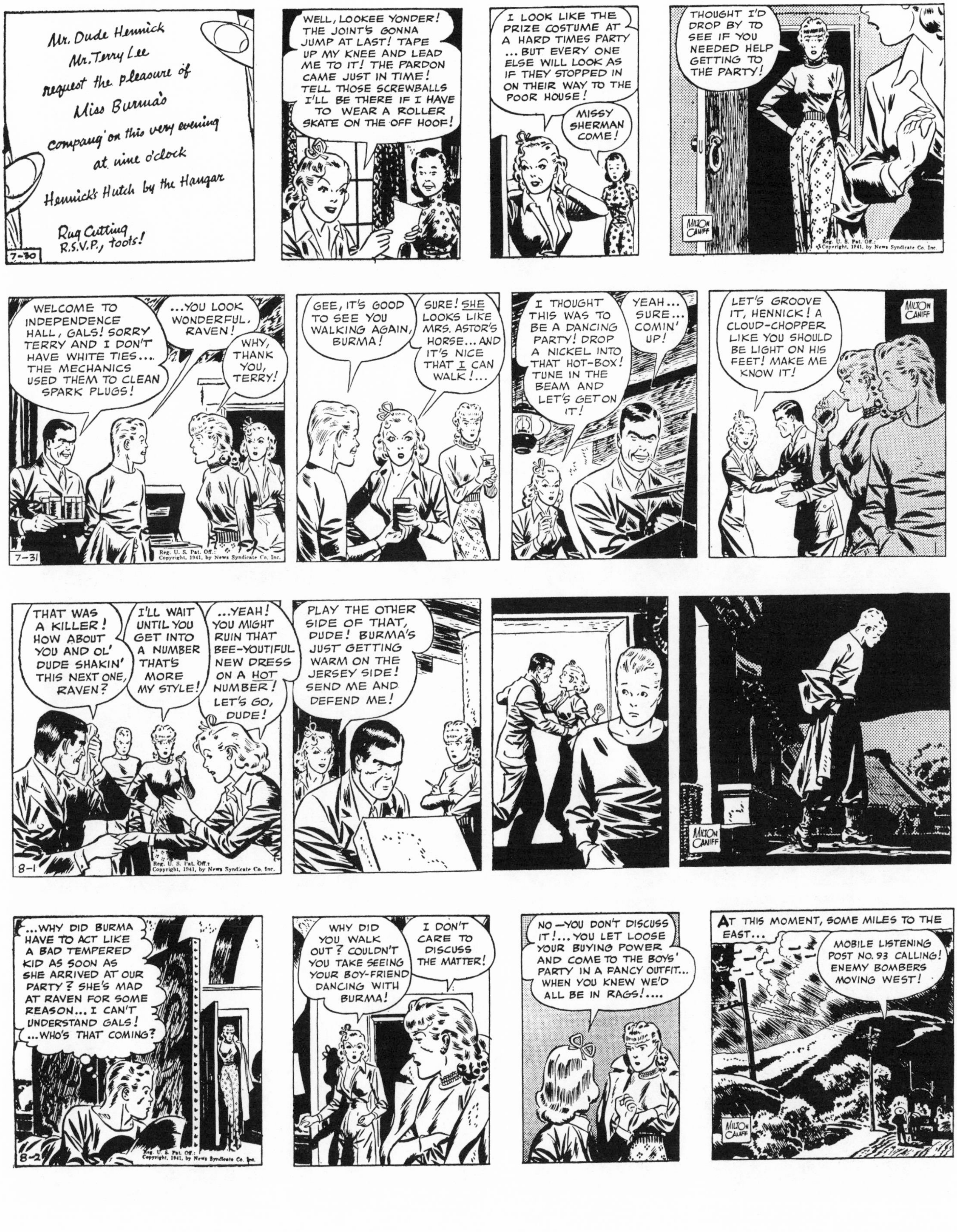
Mr. Dude Hennick
Mr. Terry Lee
request the pleasure of
Miss Burma's
company on this very evening
at nine o'clock
Hennick's Hutch by the Hangar
Rug Cutting
R.S.V.P., toots!
7-30
WELL, LOOKEE YONDER! THE JOINT'S GONNA JUMP AT LAST! TAPE UP MY KNEE AND LEAD ME TO IT! THE PARDON CAME JUST IN TIME! TELL THOSE SCREWBALLS I'LL BE THERE IF I HAVE TO WEAR A ROLLER SKATE ON THE OFF HOOF!
I LOOK LIKE THE PRIZE COSTUME AT A HARD TIMES PARTY ... BUT EVERY ONE ELSE WILL LOOK AS IF THEY STOPPED IN ON THEIR WAY TO THE POOR HOUSE!
MISSY SHERMAN COME!
THOUGHT I'D DROP BY TO SEE IF YOU NEEDED HELP GETTING TO THE PARTY!
MILTON CANIFF
Reg. U. S. Pat. Off.: Copyright, 1941, by News Syndicate Co. Inc.
WELCOME TO INDEPENDENCE HALL, GALS! SORRY TERRY AND I DON'T HAVE WHITE TIES.... THE MECHANICS USED THEM TO CLEAN SPARK PLUGS!
...YOU LOOK WONDERFUL, RAVEN!
WHY, THANK YOU, TERRY!
7-31
Reg. U. S. Pat. Off.: Copyright, 1941, by News Syndicate Co. Inc.
GEE, IT'S GOOD TO SEE YOU WALKING AGAIN, BURMA!
SURE! SHE LOOKS LIKE MRS. ASTOR'S HORSE... AND IT'S NICE THAT I CAN WALK!...
I THOUGHT THIS WAS TO BE A DANCING PARTY! DROP A NICKEL INTO THAT HOT-BOX! TUNE IN THE BEAM AND LET'S GET ON IT!
YEAH... SURE... COMIN' UP!
LET'S GROOVE IT, HENNICK! A CLOUD-CHOPPER LIKE YOU SHOULD BE LIGHT ON HIS FEET! MAKE ME KNOW IT!
MILTON CANIFF
THAT WAS A KILLER! HOW ABOUT YOU AND OL' DUDE SHAKIN' THIS NEXT ONE, RAVEN?
I'LL WAIT UNTIL YOU GET INTO A NUMBER THAT'S MORE MY STYLE!
...YEAH! YOU MIGHT RUIN THAT BEE-YOUTIFUL NEW DRESS ON A HOT NUMBER! LET'S GO, DUDE!
8-1
Reg. U. S. Pat. Off.: Copyright, 1941, by News Syndicate Co. Inc.
PLAY THE OTHER SIDE OF THAT, DUDE! BURMA'S JUST GETTING WARM ON THE JERSEY SIDE! SEND ME AND DEFEND ME!
MILTON CANIFF
...WHY DID BURMA HAVE TO ACT LIKE A BAD TEMPERED KID AS SOON AS SHE ARRIVED AT OUR PARTY? SHE'S MAD AT RAVEN FOR SOME REASON... I CAN'T UNDERSTAND GALS! ...WHO'S THAT COMING?
8-2
Reg. U. S. Pat. Off.: Copyright, 1941, by News Syndicate Co. Inc.
WHY DID YOU WALK OUT? COULDN'T YOU TAKE SEEING YOUR BOY-FRIEND DANCING WITH BURMA!
I DON'T CARE TO DISCUSS THE MATTER!
NO—YOU DON'T DISCUSS IT!... YOU LET LOOSE YOUR BUYING POWER AND COME TO THE BOYS' PARTY IN A FANCY OUTFIT... WHEN YOU KNEW WE'D ALL BE IN RAGS!....
AT THIS MOMENT, SOME MILES TO THE EAST...
MOBILE LISTENING POST NO. 93 CALLING! ENEMY BOMBERS MOVING WEST!
MILTON CANIFF

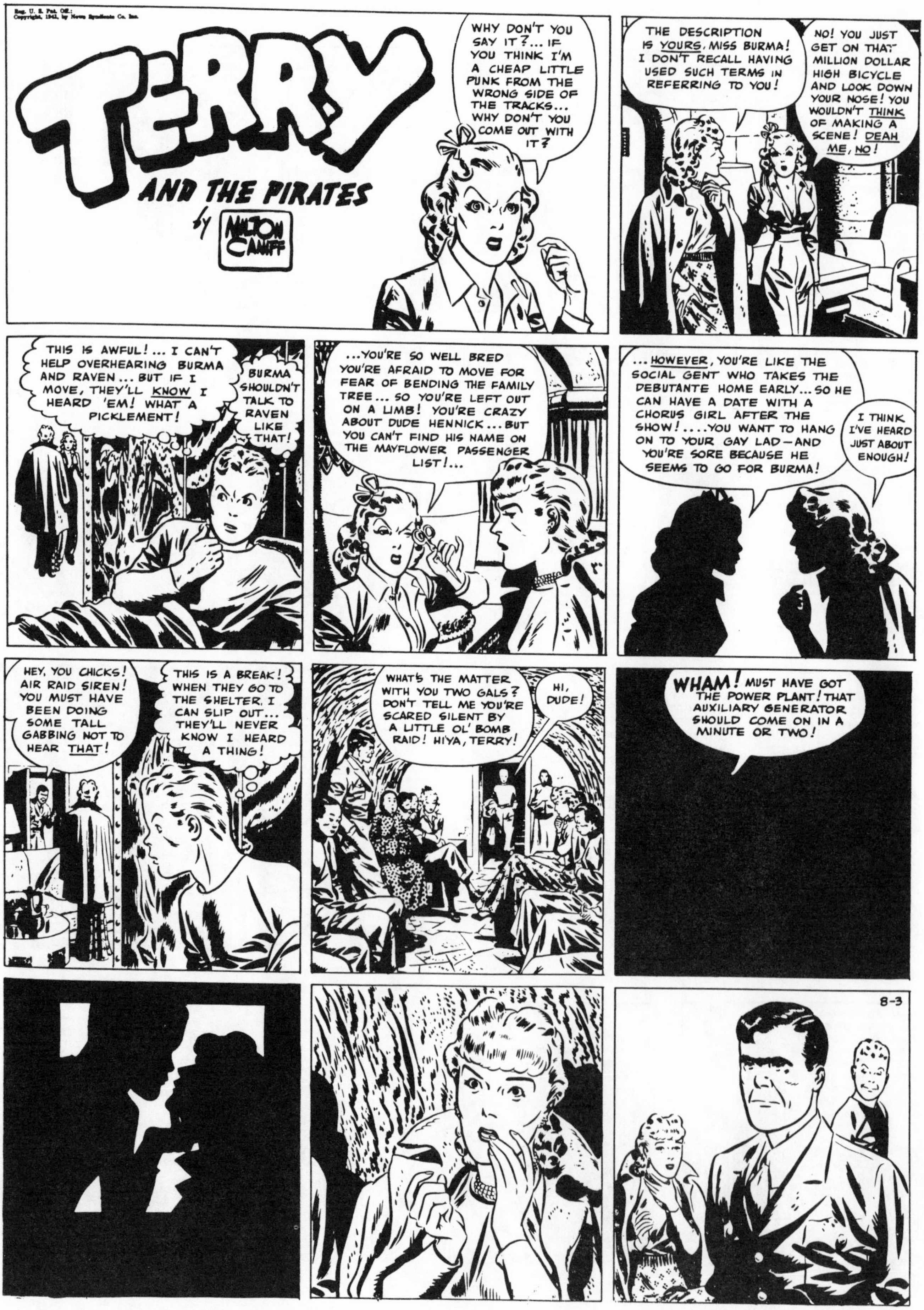
Reg. U. S. Pat. Off.:
Copyright, 1941, by News Syndicate Co. Inc.
TERRY AND THE PIRATES
by MILTON CANIFF
WHY DON'T YOU SAY IT?... IF YOU THINK I'M A CHEAP LITTLE PUNK FROM THE WRONG SIDE OF THE TRACKS... WHY DON'T YOU COME OUT WITH IT?
THE DESCRIPTION IS YOURS, MISS BURMA! I DON'T RECALL HAVING USED SUCH TERMS IN REFERRING TO YOU!
NO! YOU JUST GET ON THAT MILLION DOLLAR HIGH BICYCLE AND LOOK DOWN YOUR NOSE! YOU WOULDN'T THINK OF MAKING A SCENE! DEAH ME, NO!
THIS IS AWFUL! ... I CAN'T HELP OVERHEARING BURMA AND RAVEN ... BUT IF I MOVE, THEY'LL KNOW I HEARD 'EM! WHAT A PICKLEMENT!
BURMA SHOULDN'T TALK TO RAVEN LIKE THAT!
...YOU'RE SO WELL BRED YOU'RE AFRAID TO MOVE FOR FEAR OF BENDING THE FAMILY TREE... SO YOU'RE LEFT OUT ON A LIMB! YOU'RE CRAZY ABOUT DUDE HENNICK... BUT YOU CAN'T FIND HIS NAME ON THE MAYFLOWER PASSENGER LIST!...
... HOWEVER, YOU'RE LIKE THE SOCIAL GENT WHO TAKES THE DEBUTANTE HOME EARLY... SO HE CAN HAVE A DATE WITH A CHORUS GIRL AFTER THE SHOW! ....YOU WANT TO HANG ON TO YOUR GAY LAD—AND YOU'RE SORE BECAUSE HE SEEMS TO GO FOR BURMA!
I THINK I'VE HEARD JUST ABOUT ENOUGH!
HEY, YOU CHICKS! AIR RAID SIREN! YOU MUST HAVE BEEN DOING SOME TALL GABBING NOT TO HEAR THAT!
THIS IS A BREAK! WHEN THEY GO TO THE SHELTER, I CAN SLIP OUT... THEY'LL NEVER KNOW I HEARD A THING!
WHAT'S THE MATTER WITH YOU TWO GALS? DON'T TELL ME YOU'RE SCARED SILENT BY A LITTLE OL' BOMB RAID! HIYA, TERRY!
HI, DUDE!
WHAM! MUST HAVE GOT THE POWER PLANT! THAT AUXILIARY GENERATOR SHOULD COME ON IN A MINUTE OR TWO!
8-3

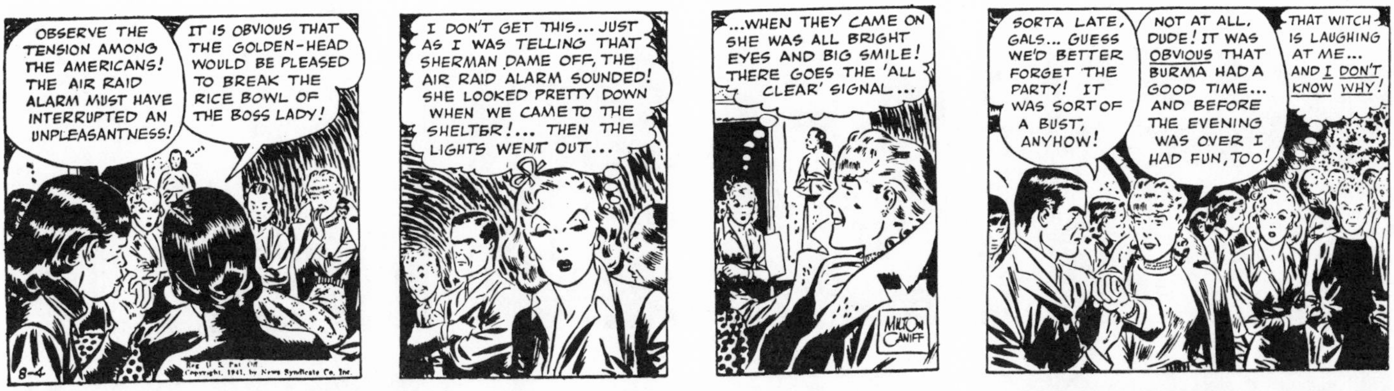
OBSERVE THE TENSION AMONG THE AMERICANS! THE AIR RAID ALARM MUST HAVE INTERRUPTED AN UNPLEASANTNESS!
IT IS OBVIOUS THAT THE GOLDEN-HEAD WOULD BE PLEASED TO BREAK THE RICE BOWL OF THE BOSS LADY!
I DON'T GET THIS... JUST AS I WAS TELLING THAT SHERMAN DAME OFF, THE AIR RAID ALARM SOUNDED! SHE LOOKED PRETTY DOWN WHEN WE CAME TO THE SHELTER!... THEN THE LIGHTS WENT OUT...
...WHEN THEY CAME ON SHE WAS ALL BRIGHT EYES AND BIG SMILE! THERE GOES THE 'ALL CLEAR' SIGNAL...
SORTA LATE, GALS... GUESS WE'D BETTER FORGET THE PARTY! IT WAS SORT OF A BUST, ANYHOW!
NOT AT ALL, DUDE! IT WAS OBVIOUS THAT BURMA HAD A GOOD TIME... AND BEFORE THE EVENING WAS OVER I HAD FUN, TOO!
THAT WITCH IS LAUGHING AT ME... AND I DON'T KNOW WHY!
MILTON CANIFF
8-4
Reg. U.S. Pat. Off.: Copyright, 1941, by News Syndicate Co. Inc.

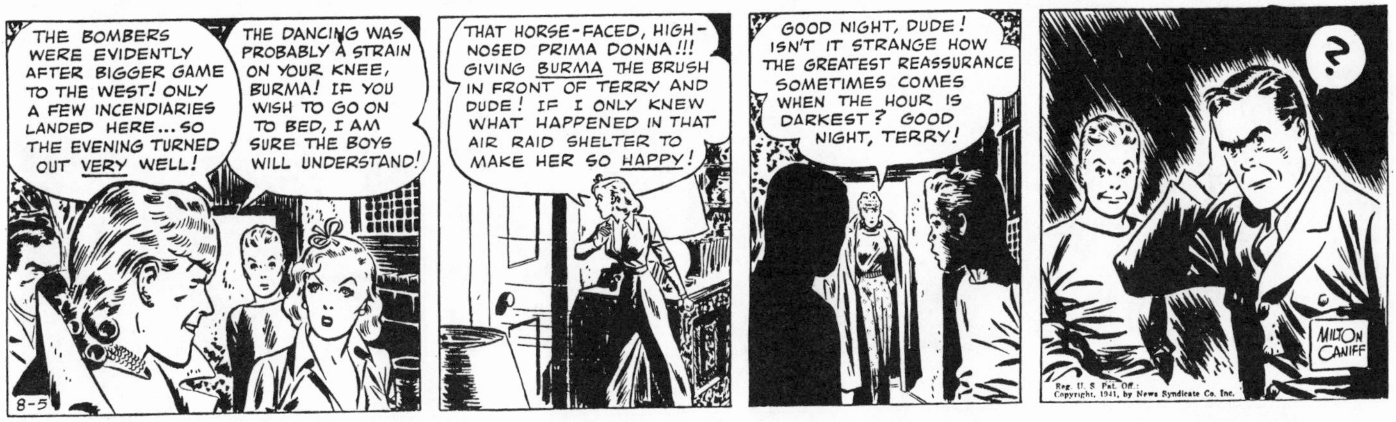
THE BOMBERS WERE EVIDENTLY AFTER BIGGER GAME TO THE WEST! ONLY A FEW INCENDIARIES LANDED HERE... SO THE EVENING TURNED OUT VERY WELL!
THE DANCING WAS PROBABLY A STRAIN ON YOUR KNEE, BURMA! IF YOU WISH TO GO ON TO BED, I AM SURE THE BOYS WILL UNDERSTAND!
THAT HORSE-FACED, HIGH-NOSED PRIMA DONNA!!! GIVING BURMA THE BRUSH IN FRONT OF TERRY AND DUDE! IF I ONLY KNEW WHAT HAPPENED IN THAT AIR RAID SHELTER TO MAKE HER SO HAPPY!
GOOD NIGHT, DUDE! ISN'T IT STRANGE HOW THE GREATEST REASSURANCE SOMETIMES COMES WHEN THE HOUR IS DARKEST? GOOD NIGHT, TERRY!
?
MILTON CANIFF
8-5
Reg. U.S. Pat. Off.: Copyright, 1941, by News Syndicate Co. Inc.

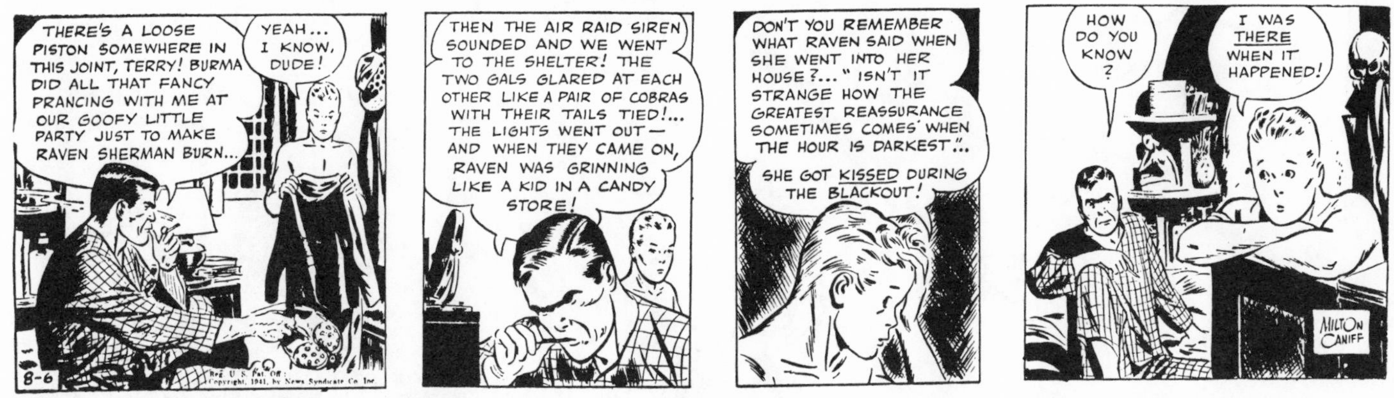
THERE'S A LOOSE PISTON SOMEWHERE IN THIS JOINT, TERRY! BURMA DID ALL THAT FANCY PRANCING WITH ME AT OUR GOOFY LITTLE PARTY JUST TO MAKE RAVEN SHERMAN BURN...
YEAH... I KNOW, DUDE!
THEN THE AIR RAID SIREN SOUNDED AND WE WENT TO THE SHELTER! THE TWO GALS GLARED AT EACH OTHER LIKE A PAIR OF COBRAS WITH THEIR TAILS TIED!... THE LIGHTS WENT OUT— AND WHEN THEY CAME ON, RAVEN WAS GRINNING LIKE A KID IN A CANDY STORE!
DON'T YOU REMEMBER WHAT RAVEN SAID WHEN SHE WENT INTO HER HOUSE?..." ISN'T IT STRANGE HOW THE GREATEST REASSURANCE SOMETIMES COMES WHEN THE HOUR IS DARKEST"...
SHE GOT KISSED DURING THE BLACKOUT!
HOW DO YOU KNOW?
I WAS THERE WHEN IT HAPPENED!
MILTON CANIFF
8-6
Reg. U.S. Pat. Off.: Copyright, 1941, by News Syndicate Co. Inc.

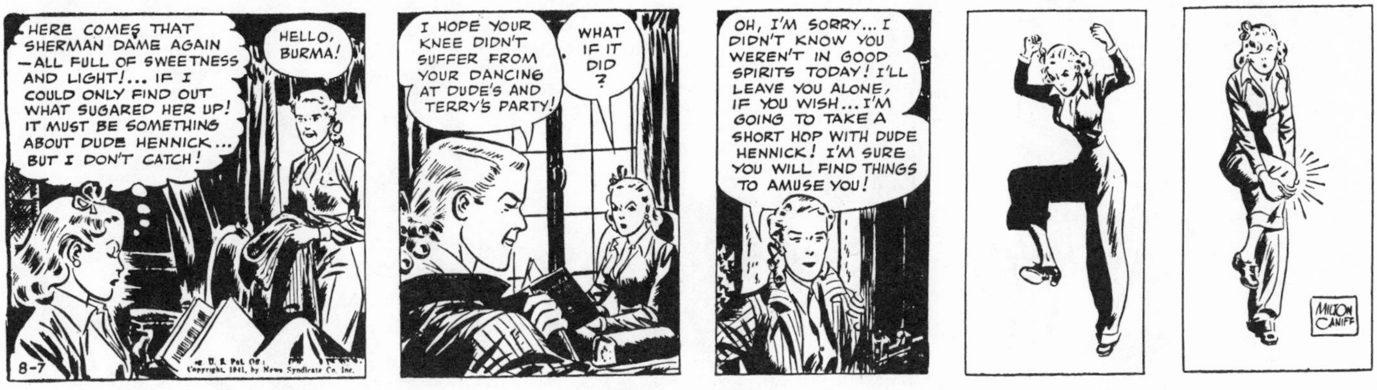
HERE COMES THAT SHERMAN DAME AGAIN —ALL FULL OF SWEETNESS AND LIGHT!... IF I COULD ONLY FIND OUT WHAT SUGARED HER UP! IT MUST BE SOMETHING ABOUT DUDE HENNICK... BUT I DON'T CATCH!
HELLO, BURMA!
I HOPE YOUR KNEE DIDN'T SUFFER FROM YOUR DANCING AT DUDE'S AND TERRY'S PARTY!
WHAT IF IT DID?
OH, I'M SORRY... I DIDN'T KNOW YOU WEREN'T IN GOOD SPIRITS TODAY! I'LL LEAVE YOU ALONE, IF YOU WISH... I'M GOING TO TAKE A SHORT HOP WITH DUDE HENNICK! I'M SURE YOU WILL FIND THINGS TO AMUSE YOU!
MILTON CANIFF
8-7
Reg. U.S. Pat. Off.: Copyright, 1941, by News Syndicate Co. Inc.

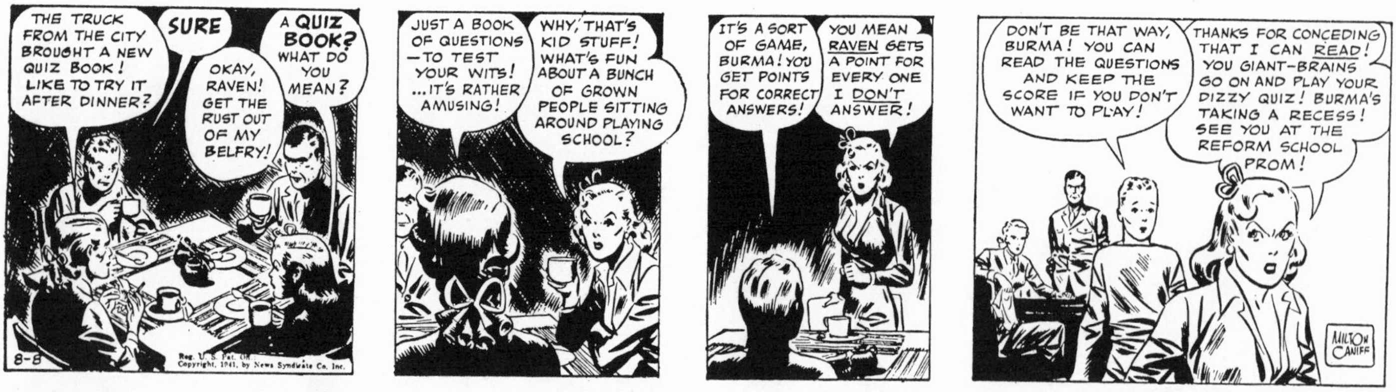
THE TRUCK FROM THE CITY BROUGHT A NEW QUIZ BOOK! LIKE TO TRY IT AFTER DINNER?
SURE
OKAY, RAVEN! GET THE RUST OUT OF MY BELFRY!
A QUIZ BOOK? WHAT DO YOU MEAN?
8-8
Reg. U. S. Pat. Off. Copyright, 1941, by News Syndicate Co. Inc.
JUST A BOOK OF QUESTIONS —TO TEST YOUR WITS! ...IT'S RATHER AMUSING!
WHY, THAT'S KID STUFF! WHAT'S FUN ABOUT A BUNCH OF GROWN PEOPLE SITTING AROUND PLAYING SCHOOL?
IT'S A SORT OF GAME, BURMA! YOU GET POINTS FOR CORRECT ANSWERS!
YOU MEAN RAVEN GETS A POINT FOR EVERY ONE I DON'T ANSWER!
DON'T BE THAT WAY, BURMA! YOU CAN READ THE QUESTIONS AND KEEP THE SCORE IF YOU DON'T WANT TO PLAY!
THANKS FOR CONCEDING THAT I CAN READ! YOU GIANT-BRAINS GO ON AND PLAY YOUR DIZZY QUIZ! BURMA'S TAKING A RECESS! SEE YOU AT THE REFORM SCHOOL PROM!
MILTON CANIFF

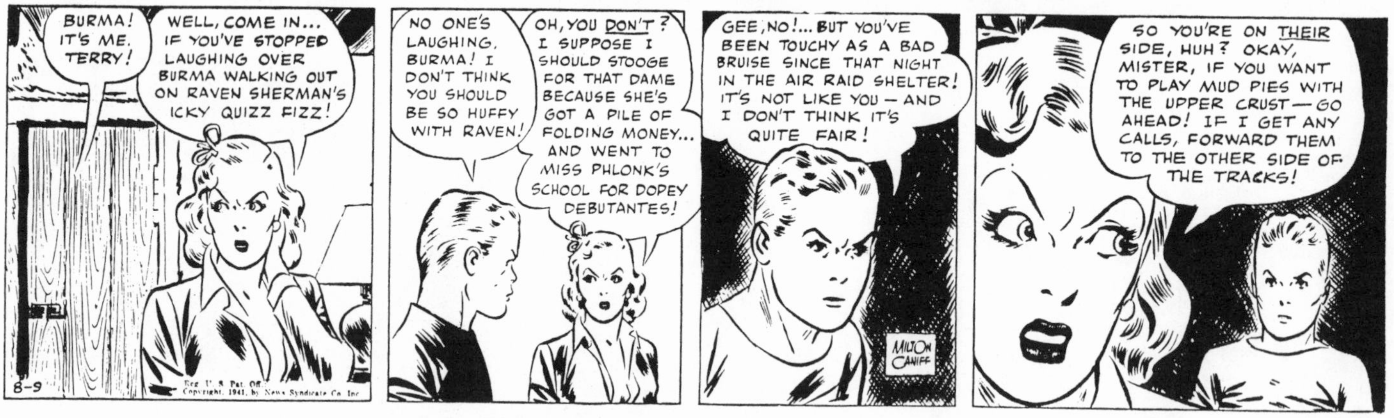
BURMA! IT'S ME. TERRY!
WELL, COME IN... IF YOU'VE STOPPED LAUGHING OVER BURMA WALKING OUT ON RAVEN SHERMAN'S ICKY QUIZZ FIZZ!
8-9
Reg. U. S. Pat. Off. Copyright, 1941, by News Syndicate Co. Inc.
NO ONE'S LAUGHING, BURMA! I DON'T THINK YOU SHOULD BE SO HUFFY WITH RAVEN!
OH, YOU DON'T? I SUPPOSE I SHOULD STOOGE FOR THAT DAME BECAUSE SHE'S GOT A PILE OF FOLDING MONEY... AND WENT TO MISS PHLONK'S SCHOOL FOR DOPEY DEBUTANTES!
GEE, NO!... BUT YOU'VE BEEN TOUCHY AS A BAD BRUISE SINCE THAT NIGHT IN THE AIR RAID SHELTER! IT'S NOT LIKE YOU — AND I DON'T THINK IT'S QUITE FAIR!
MILTON CANIFF
SO YOU'RE ON THEIR SIDE, HUH? OKAY, MISTER, IF YOU WANT TO PLAY MUD PIES WITH THE UPPER CRUST — GO AHEAD! IF I GET ANY CALLS, FORWARD THEM TO THE OTHER SIDE OF THE TRACKS!

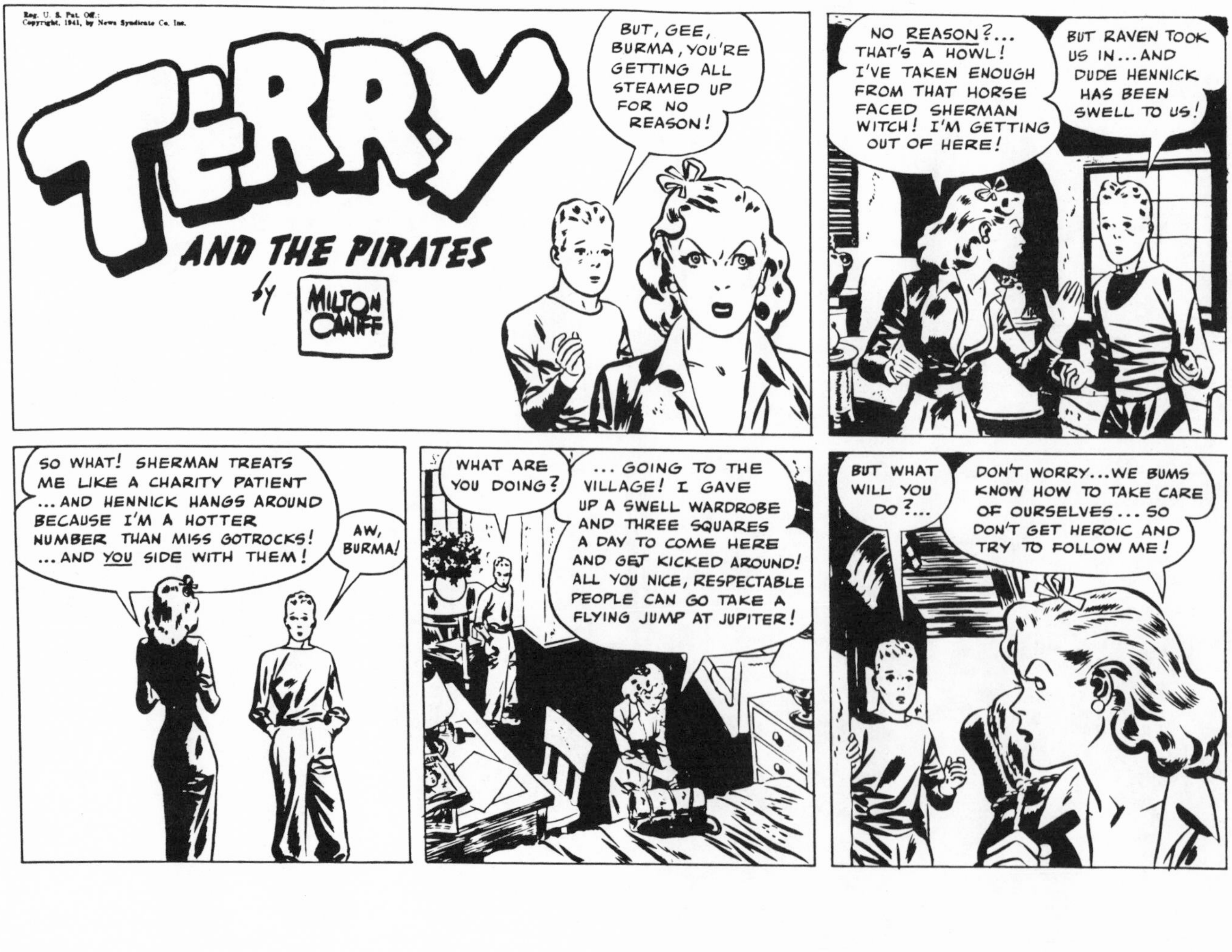
Reg. U. S. Pat. Off. Copyright, 1941, by News Syndicate Co. Inc.
TERRY AND THE PIRATES
by MILTON CANIFF
BUT, GEE, BURMA, YOU'RE GETTING ALL STEAMED UP FOR NO REASON!
NO REASON?... THAT'S A HOWL! I'VE TAKEN ENOUGH FROM THAT HORSE FACED SHERMAN WITCH! I'M GETTING OUT OF HERE!
BUT RAVEN TOOK US IN... AND DUDE HENNICK HAS BEEN SWELL TO US!
SO WHAT! SHERMAN TREATS ME LIKE A CHARITY PATIENT ...AND HENNICK HANGS AROUND BECAUSE I'M A HOTTER NUMBER THAN MISS GOTROCKS! ...AND YOU SIDE WITH THEM!
AW, BURMA!
WHAT ARE YOU DOING?
... GOING TO THE VILLAGE! I GAVE UP A SWELL WARDROBE AND THREE SQUARES A DAY TO COME HERE AND GET KICKED AROUND! ALL YOU NICE, RESPECTABLE PEOPLE CAN GO TAKE A FLYING JUMP AT JUPITER!
BUT WHAT WILL YOU DO?...
DON'T WORRY... WE BUMS KNOW HOW TO TAKE CARE OF OURSELVES... SO DON'T GET HEROIC AND TRY TO FOLLOW ME!

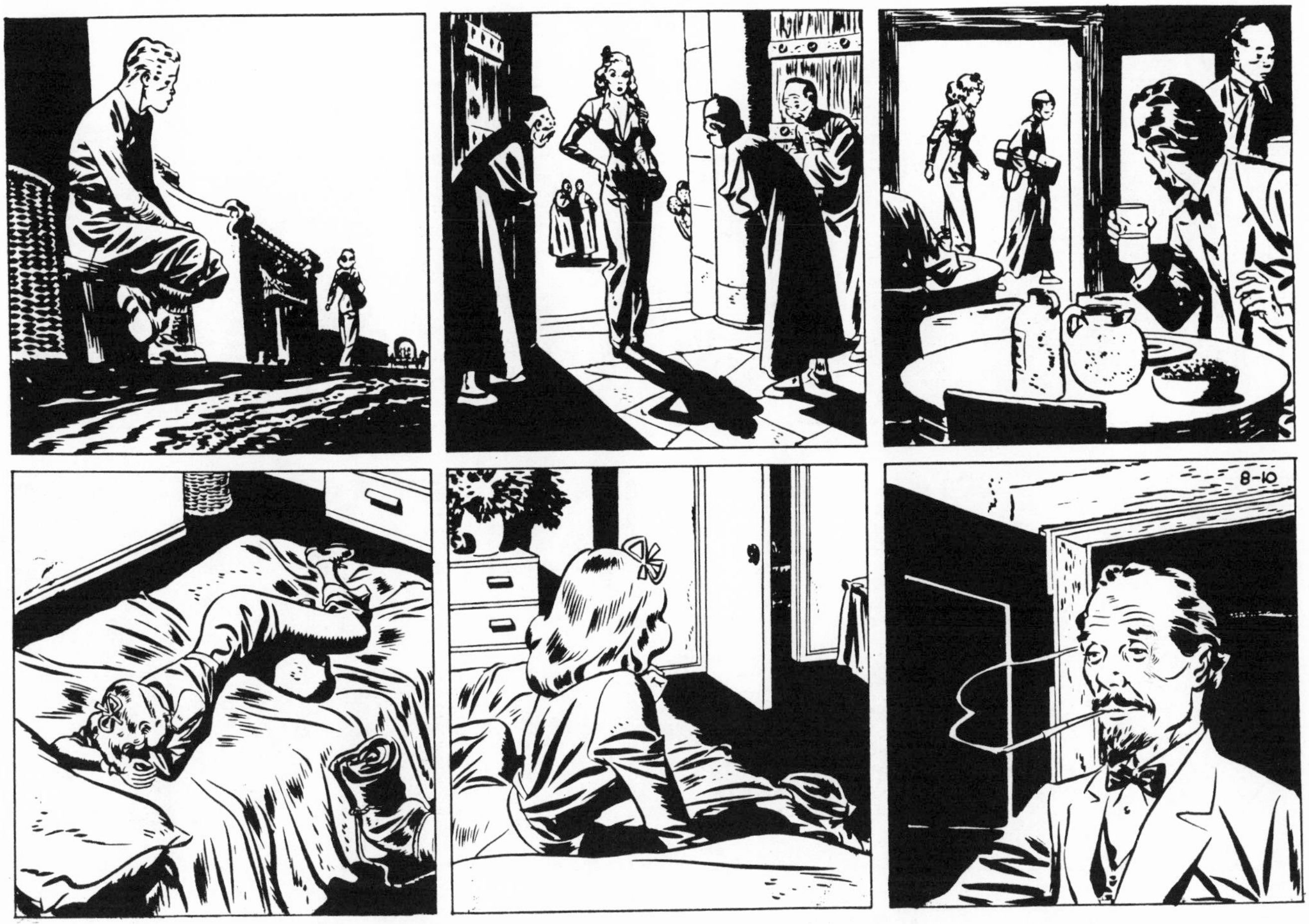
8-10

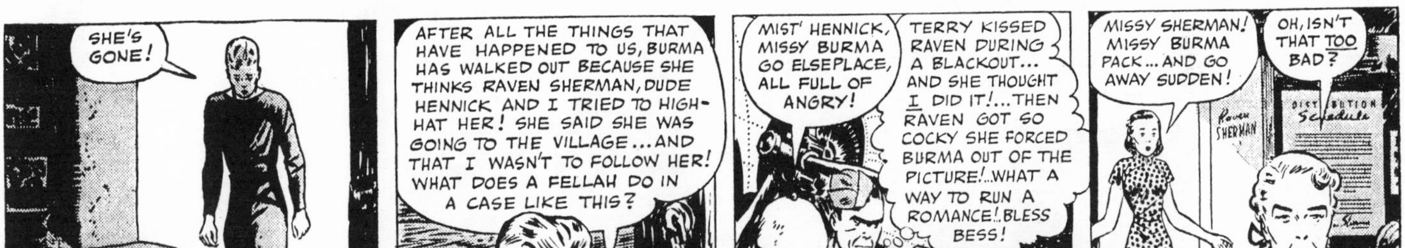
SHE'S GONE!
8-11
Reg. U. S. Pat. Off. Copyright, 1941, by News Syndicate Co. Inc.
AFTER ALL THE THINGS THAT HAVE HAPPENED TO US, BURMA HAS WALKED OUT BECAUSE SHE THINKS RAVEN SHERMAN, DUDE HENNICK AND I TRIED TO HIGH-HAT HER! SHE SAID SHE WAS GOING TO THE VILLAGE... AND THAT I WASN'T TO FOLLOW HER! WHAT DOES A FELLAH DO IN A CASE LIKE THIS?
MIST' HENNICK, MISSY BURMA GO ELSEPLACE, ALL FULL OF ANGRY!
TERRY KISSED RAVEN DURING A BLACKOUT... AND SHE THOUGHT I DID IT!... THEN RAVEN GOT SO COCKY SHE FORCED BURMA OUT OF THE PICTURE!..WHAT A WAY TO RUN A ROMANCE!..BLESS BESS!
MISSY SHERMAN! MISSY BURMA PACK... AND GO AWAY SUDDEN!
OH, ISN'T THAT TOO BAD?
MILTON CANIFF

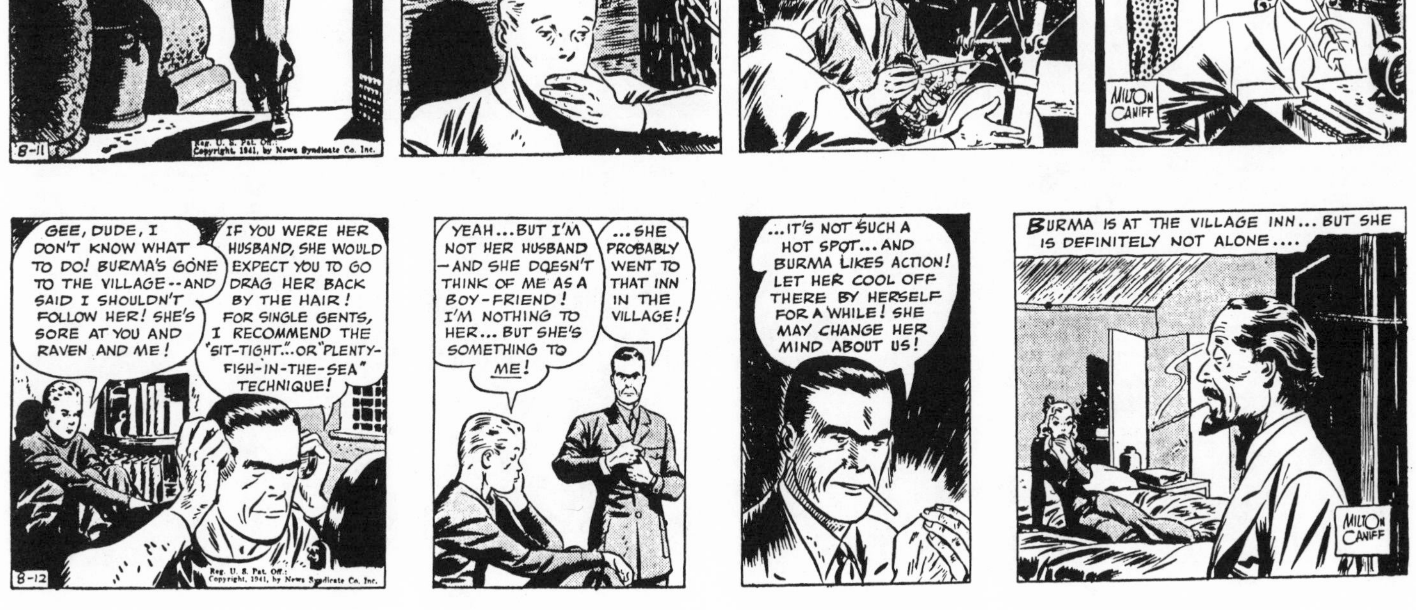
GEE, DUDE, I DON'T KNOW WHAT TO DO! BURMA'S GONE TO THE VILLAGE--AND SAID I SHOULDN'T FOLLOW HER! SHE'S SORE AT YOU AND RAVEN AND ME!
IF YOU WERE HER HUSBAND, SHE WOULD EXPECT YOU TO GO DRAG HER BACK BY THE HAIR! FOR SINGLE GENTS, I RECOMMEND THE "SIT-TIGHT"...OR "PLENTY-FISH-IN-THE-SEA" TECHNIQUE!
8-12
Reg. U. S. Pat. Off. Copyright, 1941, by News Syndicate Co. Inc.
YEAH... BUT I'M NOT HER HUSBAND -AND SHE DOESN'T THINK OF ME AS A BOY-FRIEND! I'M NOTHING TO HER... BUT SHE'S SOMETHING TO ME!
...SHE PROBABLY WENT TO THAT INN IN THE VILLAGE!
...IT'S NOT SUCH A HOT SPOT... AND BURMA LIKES ACTION! LET HER COOL OFF THERE BY HERSELF FOR A WHILE! SHE MAY CHANGE HER MIND ABOUT US!
BURMA IS AT THE VILLAGE INN... BUT SHE IS DEFINITELY NOT ALONE....
MILTON CANIFF

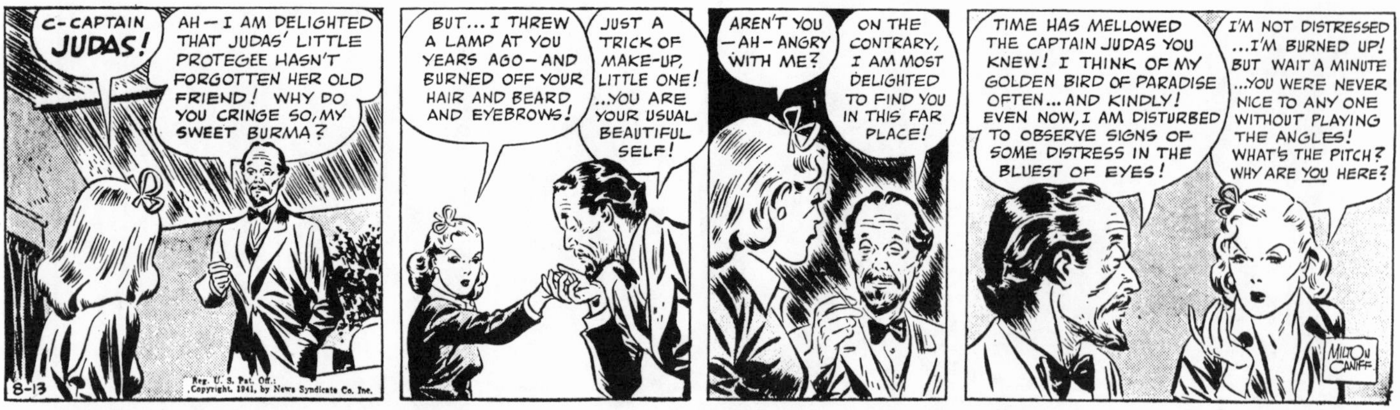
C-CAPTAIN JUDAS!
AH—I AM DELIGHTED THAT JUDAS' LITTLE PROTEGEE HASN'T FORGOTTEN HER OLD FRIEND! WHY DO YOU CRINGE SO, MY SWEET BURMA?
BUT... I THREW A LAMP AT YOU YEARS AGO—AND BURNED OFF YOUR HAIR AND BEARD AND EYEBROWS!
JUST A TRICK OF MAKE-UP, LITTLE ONE! ...YOU ARE YOUR USUAL BEAUTIFUL SELF!
AREN'T YOU —AH— ANGRY WITH ME?
ON THE CONTRARY, I AM MOST DELIGHTED TO FIND YOU IN THIS FAR PLACE!
TIME HAS MELLOWED THE CAPTAIN JUDAS YOU KNEW! I THINK OF MY GOLDEN BIRD OF PARADISE OFTEN... AND KINDLY! EVEN NOW, I AM DISTURBED TO OBSERVE SIGNS OF SOME DISTRESS IN THE BLUEST OF EYES!
I'M NOT DISTRESSED ...I'M BURNED UP! BUT WAIT A MINUTE ...YOU WERE NEVER NICE TO ANY ONE WITHOUT PLAYING THE ANGLES! WHAT'S THE PITCH? WHY ARE YOU HERE?
8-13
Reg. U. S. Pat. Off.: Copyright, 1941, by News Syndicate Co. Inc.
MILTON CANIFF

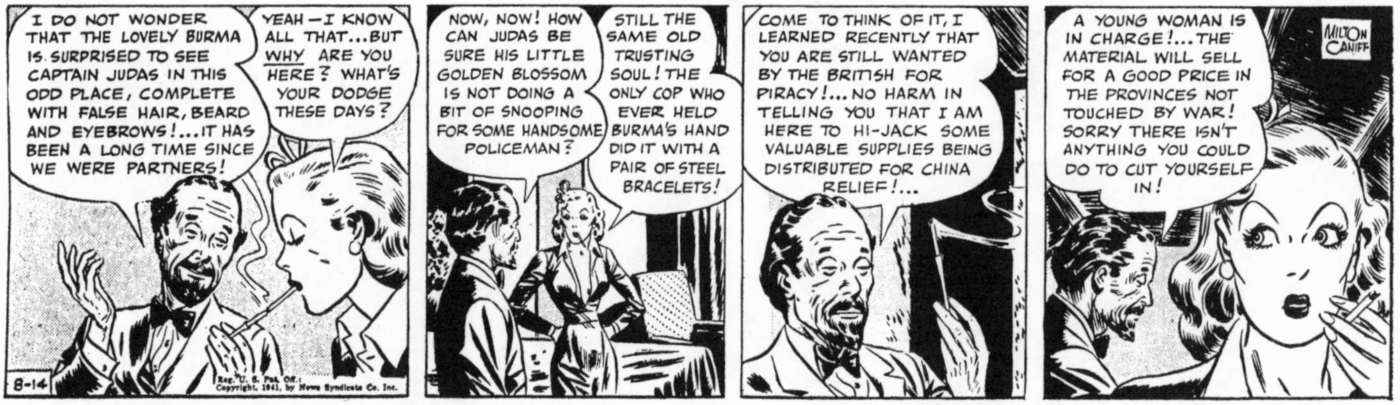
I DO NOT WONDER THAT THE LOVELY BURMA IS SURPRISED TO SEE CAPTAIN JUDAS IN THIS ODD PLACE, COMPLETE WITH FALSE HAIR, BEARD AND EYEBROWS!... IT HAS BEEN A LONG TIME SINCE WE WERE PARTNERS!
YEAH—I KNOW ALL THAT... BUT WHY ARE YOU HERE? WHAT'S YOUR DODGE THESE DAYS?
NOW, NOW! HOW CAN JUDAS BE SURE HIS LITTLE GOLDEN BLOSSOM IS NOT DOING A BIT OF SNOOPING FOR SOME HANDSOME POLICEMAN?
STILL THE SAME OLD TRUSTING SOUL! THE ONLY COP WHO EVER HELD BURMA'S HAND DID IT WITH A PAIR OF STEEL BRACELETS!
COME TO THINK OF IT, I LEARNED RECENTLY THAT YOU ARE STILL WANTED BY THE BRITISH FOR PIRACY!... NO HARM IN TELLING YOU THAT I AM HERE TO HI-JACK SOME VALUABLE SUPPLIES BEING DISTRIBUTED FOR CHINA RELIEF!...
A YOUNG WOMAN IS IN CHARGE!... THE MATERIAL WILL SELL FOR A GOOD PRICE IN THE PROVINCES NOT TOUCHED BY WAR! SORRY THERE ISN'T ANYTHING YOU COULD DO TO CUT YOURSELF IN!
8-14
Reg. U. S. Pat. Off.: Copyright, 1941, by News Syndicate Co. Inc.
MILTON CANIFF

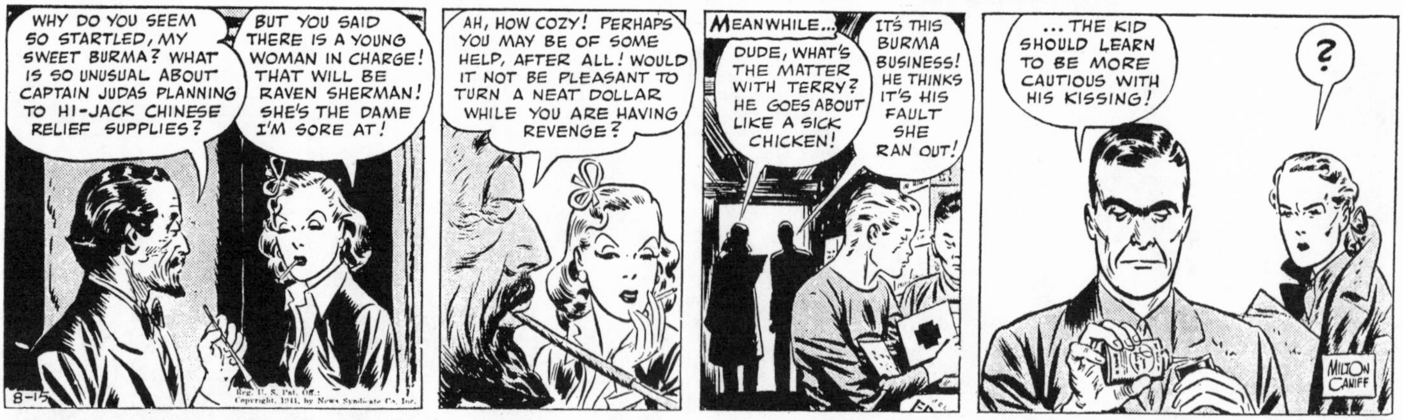
WHY DO YOU SEEM SO STARTLED, MY SWEET BURMA? WHAT IS SO UNUSUAL ABOUT CAPTAIN JUDAS PLANNING TO HI-JACK CHINESE RELIEF SUPPLIES?
BUT YOU SAID THERE IS A YOUNG WOMAN IN CHARGE! THAT WILL BE RAVEN SHERMAN! SHE'S THE DAME I'M SORE AT!
AH, HOW COZY! PERHAPS YOU MAY BE OF SOME HELP, AFTER ALL! WOULD IT NOT BE PLEASANT TO TURN A NEAT DOLLAR WHILE YOU ARE HAVING REVENGE?
MEANWHILE...
DUDE, WHAT'S THE MATTER WITH TERRY? HE GOES ABOUT LIKE A SICK CHICKEN!
IT'S THIS BURMA BUSINESS! HE THINKS IT'S HIS FAULT SHE RAN OUT!
... THE KID SHOULD LEARN TO BE MORE CAUTIOUS WITH HIS KISSING!
?
8-15
Reg. U. S. Pat. Off.: Copyright, 1941, by News Syndicate Co. Inc.
MILTON CANIFF

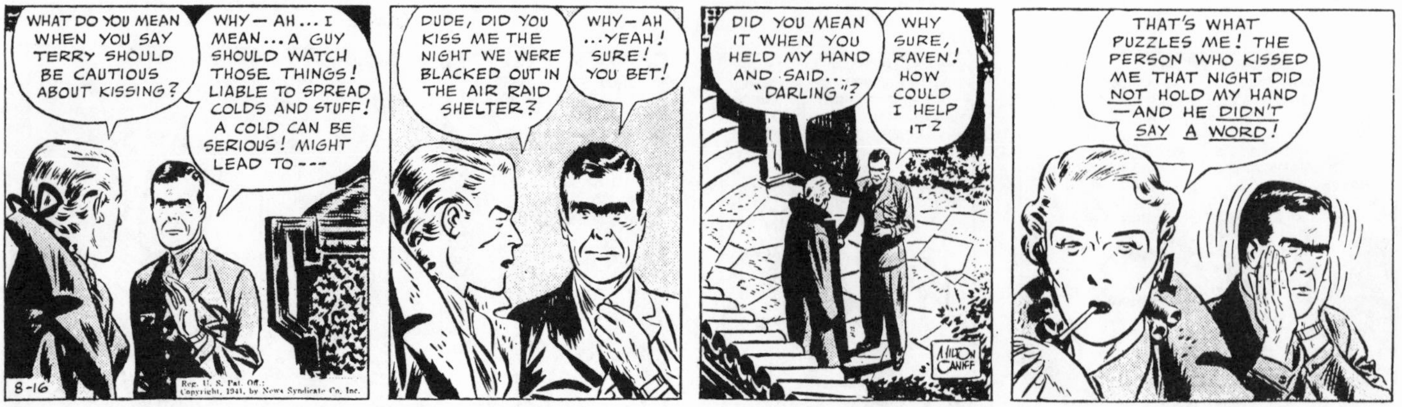
WHAT DO YOU MEAN WHEN YOU SAY TERRY SHOULD BE CAUTIOUS ABOUT KISSING?
WHY—AH... I MEAN... A GUY SHOULD WATCH THOSE THINGS! LIABLE TO SPREAD COLDS AND STUFF! A COLD CAN BE SERIOUS! MIGHT LEAD TO---
DUDE, DID YOU KISS ME THE NIGHT WE WERE BLACKED OUT IN THE AIR RAID SHELTER?
WHY—AH ...YEAH! SURE! YOU BET!
DID YOU MEAN IT WHEN YOU HELD MY HAND AND SAID... "DARLING"?
WHY SURE, RAVEN! HOW COULD I HELP IT?
THAT'S WHAT PUZZLES ME! THE PERSON WHO KISSED ME THAT NIGHT DID NOT HOLD MY HAND —AND HE DIDN'T SAY A WORD!
8-16
Reg. U. S. Pat. Off.: Copyright, 1941, by News Syndicate Co. Inc.
MILTON CANIFF

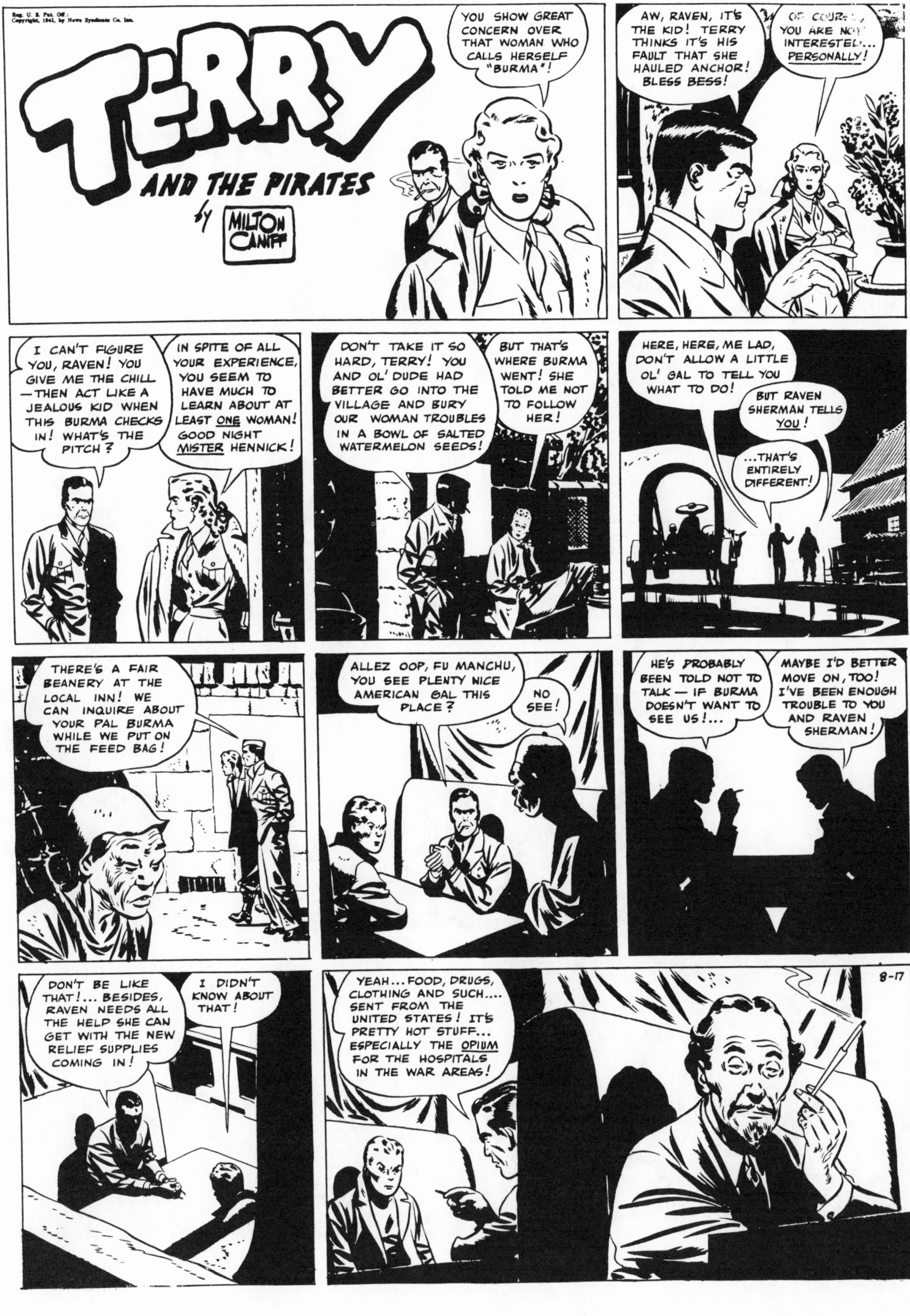
Reg. U. S. Pat. Off.:
Copyright, 1941, by News Syndicate Co. Inc.
TERRY AND THE PIRATES
by MILTON CANIFF
YOU SHOW GREAT CONCERN OVER THAT WOMAN WHO CALLS HERSELF "BURMA"!
AW, RAVEN, IT'S THE KID! TERRY THINKS IT'S HIS FAULT THAT SHE HAULED ANCHOR! BLESS BESS!
OF COURSE, YOU ARE NOT INTERESTED... PERSONALLY!
I CAN'T FIGURE YOU, RAVEN! YOU GIVE ME THE CHILL—THEN ACT LIKE A JEALOUS KID WHEN THIS BURMA CHECKS IN! WHAT'S THE PITCH?
IN SPITE OF ALL YOUR EXPERIENCE, YOU SEEM TO HAVE MUCH TO LEARN ABOUT AT LEAST ONE WOMAN! GOOD NIGHT MISTER HENNICK!
DON'T TAKE IT SO HARD, TERRY! YOU AND OL' DUDE HAD BETTER GO INTO THE VILLAGE AND BURY OUR WOMAN TROUBLES IN A BOWL OF SALTED WATERMELON SEEDS!
BUT THAT'S WHERE BURMA WENT! SHE TOLD ME NOT TO FOLLOW HER!
HERE, HERE, ME LAD, DON'T ALLOW A LITTLE OL' GAL TO TELL YOU WHAT TO DO!
BUT RAVEN SHERMAN TELLS YOU!
...THAT'S ENTIRELY DIFFERENT!
THERE'S A FAIR BEANERY AT THE LOCAL INN! WE CAN INQUIRE ABOUT YOUR PAL BURMA WHILE WE PUT ON THE FEED BAG!
ALLEZ OOP, FU MANCHU, YOU SEE PLENTY NICE AMERICAN GAL THIS PLACE?
NO SEE!
HE'S PROBABLY BEEN TOLD NOT TO TALK — IF BURMA DOESN'T WANT TO SEE US!...
MAYBE I'D BETTER MOVE ON, TOO! I'VE BEEN ENOUGH TROUBLE TO YOU AND RAVEN SHERMAN!
DON'T BE LIKE THAT!... BESIDES, RAVEN NEEDS ALL THE HELP SHE CAN GET WITH THE NEW RELIEF SUPPLIES COMING IN!
I DIDN'T KNOW ABOUT THAT!
YEAH... FOOD, DRUGS, CLOTHING AND SUCH.... SENT FROM THE UNITED STATES! IT'S PRETTY HOT STUFF... ESPECIALLY THE OPIUM FOR THE HOSPITALS IN THE WAR AREAS!
8-17

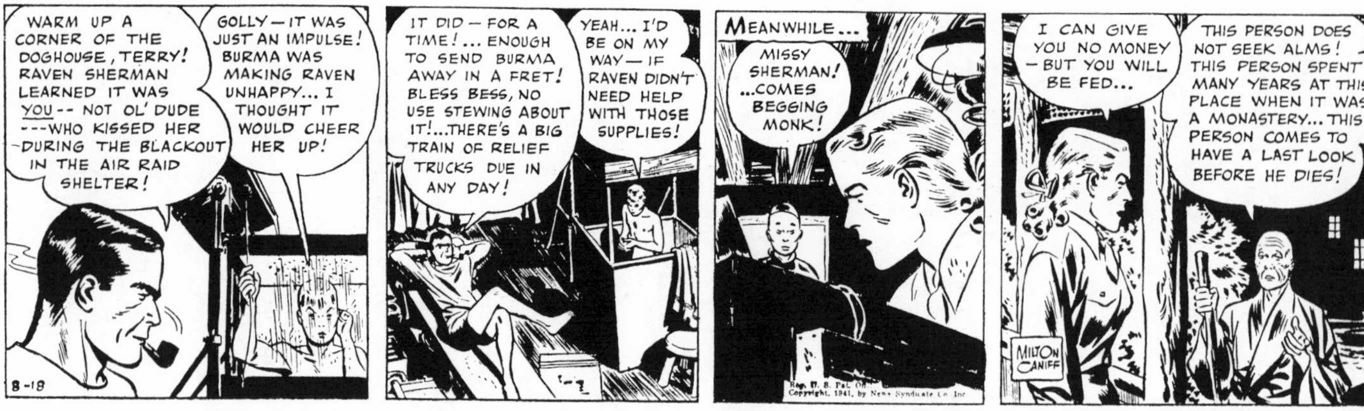
WARM UP A CORNER OF THE DOGHOUSE, TERRY! RAVEN SHERMAN LEARNED IT WAS YOU -- NOT OL' DUDE ---WHO KISSED HER -DURING THE BLACKOUT IN THE AIR RAID SHELTER!
GOLLY—IT WAS JUST AN IMPULSE! BURMA WAS MAKING RAVEN UNHAPPY... I THOUGHT IT WOULD CHEER HER UP!
8-18
IT DID—FOR A TIME!... ENOUGH TO SEND BURMA AWAY IN A FRET! BLESS BESS, NO USE STEWING ABOUT IT!...THERE'S A BIG TRAIN OF RELIEF TRUCKS DUE IN ANY DAY!
YEAH... I'D BE ON MY WAY—IF RAVEN DIDN'T NEED HELP WITH THOSE SUPPLIES!
MEANWHILE...
MISSY SHERMAN! ...COMES BEGGING MONK!
Reg. U. S. Pat. Off. Copyright, 1941, by News Syndicate Co. Inc.
I CAN GIVE YOU NO MONEY—BUT YOU WILL BE FED...
THIS PERSON DOES NOT SEEK ALMS! THIS PERSON SPENT MANY YEARS AT THIS PLACE WHEN IT WAS A MONASTERY... THIS PERSON COMES TO HAVE A LAST LOOK BEFORE HE DIES!
MILTON CANIFF

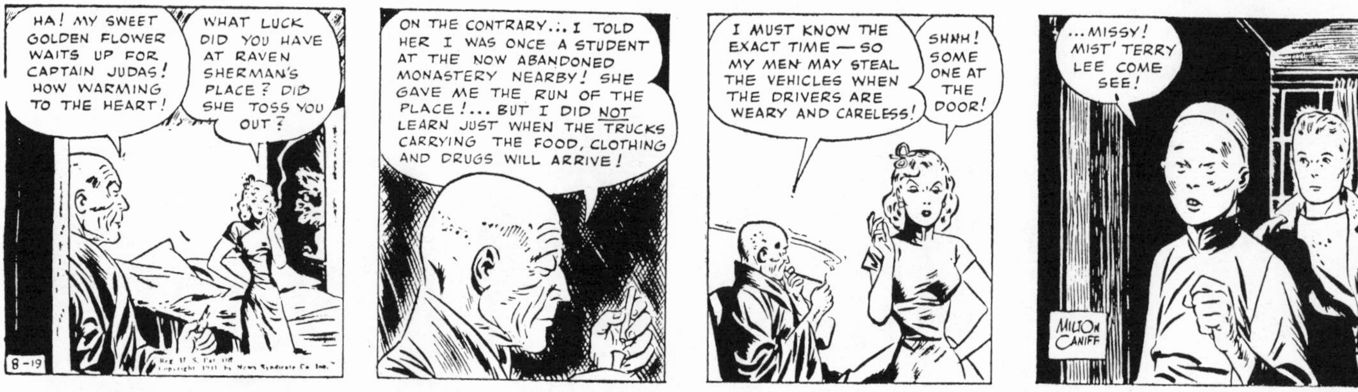
HA! MY SWEET GOLDEN FLOWER WAITS UP FOR CAPTAIN JUDAS! HOW WARMING TO THE HEART!
WHAT LUCK DID YOU HAVE AT RAVEN SHERMAN'S PLACE? DID SHE TOSS YOU OUT?
8-19
Reg. U. S. Pat. Off. Copyright, 1941, by News Syndicate Co. Inc.
ON THE CONTRARY... I TOLD HER I WAS ONCE A STUDENT AT THE NOW ABANDONED MONASTERY NEARBY! SHE GAVE ME THE RUN OF THE PLACE!... BUT I DID NOT LEARN JUST WHEN THE TRUCKS CARRYING THE FOOD, CLOTHING AND DRUGS WILL ARRIVE!
I MUST KNOW THE EXACT TIME—SO MY MEN MAY STEAL THE VEHICLES WHEN THE DRIVERS ARE WEARY AND CARELESS!
SHHH! SOME ONE AT THE DOOR!
...MISSY! MIST' TERRY LEE COME SEE!
MILTON CANIFF

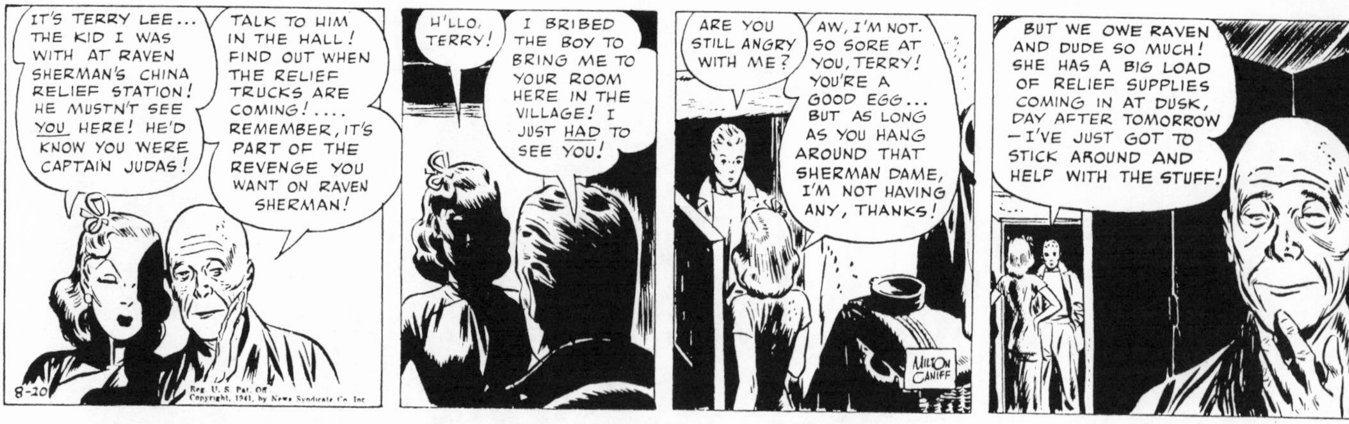
IT'S TERRY LEE... THE KID I WAS WITH AT RAVEN SHERMAN'S CHINA RELIEF STATION! HE MUSTN'T SEE YOU HERE! HE'D KNOW YOU WERE CAPTAIN JUDAS!
TALK TO HIM IN THE HALL! FIND OUT WHEN THE RELIEF TRUCKS ARE COMING!.... REMEMBER, IT'S PART OF THE REVENGE YOU WANT ON RAVEN SHERMAN!
8-20
Reg. U. S. Pat. Off. Copyright, 1941, by News Syndicate Co. Inc.
H'LLO, TERRY!
I BRIBED THE BOY TO BRING ME TO YOUR ROOM HERE IN THE VILLAGE! I JUST HAD TO SEE YOU!
ARE YOU STILL ANGRY WITH ME?
AW, I'M NOT SO SORE AT YOU, TERRY! YOU'RE A GOOD EGG... BUT AS LONG AS YOU HANG AROUND THAT SHERMAN DAME, I'M NOT HAVING ANY, THANKS!
MILTON CANIFF
BUT WE OWE RAVEN AND DUDE SO MUCH! SHE HAS A BIG LOAD OF RELIEF SUPPLIES COMING IN AT DUSK, DAY AFTER TOMORROW—I'VE JUST GOT TO STICK AROUND AND HELP WITH THE STUFF!

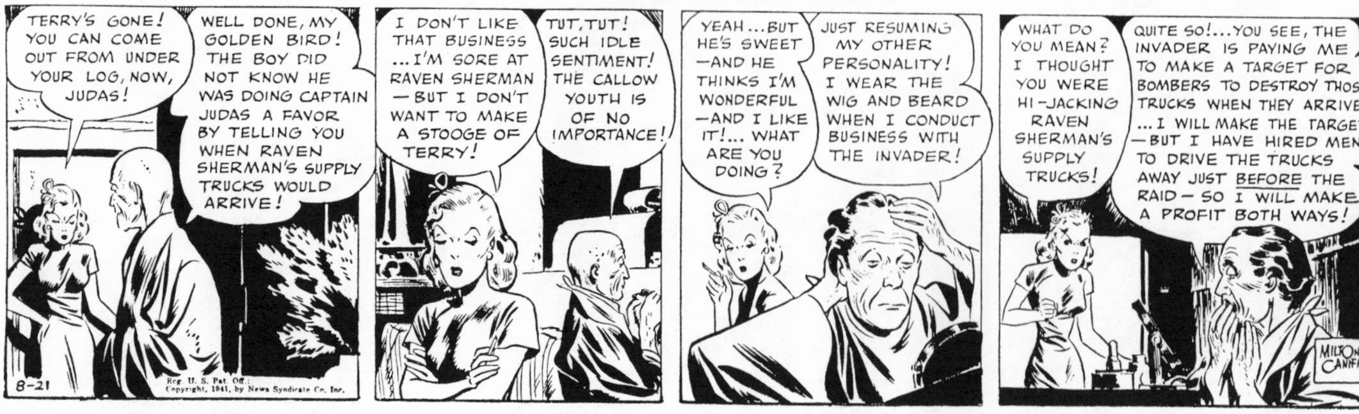
TERRY'S GONE! YOU CAN COME OUT FROM UNDER YOUR LOG, NOW, JUDAS!
WELL DONE, MY GOLDEN BIRD! THE BOY DID NOT KNOW HE WAS DOING CAPTAIN JUDAS A FAVOR BY TELLING YOU WHEN RAVEN SHERMAN'S SUPPLY TRUCKS WOULD ARRIVE!
8-21
Reg. U. S. Pat. Off. Copyright, 1941, by News Syndicate Co. Inc.
I DON'T LIKE THAT BUSINESS ...I'M SORE AT RAVEN SHERMAN—BUT I DON'T WANT TO MAKE A STOOGE OF TERRY!
TUT, TUT! SUCH IDLE SENTIMENT! THE CALLOW YOUTH IS OF NO IMPORTANCE!
YEAH... BUT HE'S SWEET—AND HE THINKS I'M WONDERFUL—AND I LIKE IT!... WHAT ARE YOU DOING?
JUST RESUMING MY OTHER PERSONALITY! I WEAR THE WIG AND BEARD WHEN I CONDUCT BUSINESS WITH THE INVADER!
WHAT DO YOU MEAN? I THOUGHT YOU WERE HI-JACKING RAVEN SHERMAN'S SUPPLY TRUCKS!
QUITE SO!... YOU SEE, THE INVADER IS PAYING ME TO MAKE A TARGET FOR BOMBERS TO DESTROY THOSE TRUCKS WHEN THEY ARRIVE! ...I WILL MAKE THE TARGET—BUT I HAVE HIRED MEN TO DRIVE THE TRUCKS AWAY JUST BEFORE THE RAID—SO I WILL MAKE A PROFIT BOTH WAYS!
MILTON CANIFF

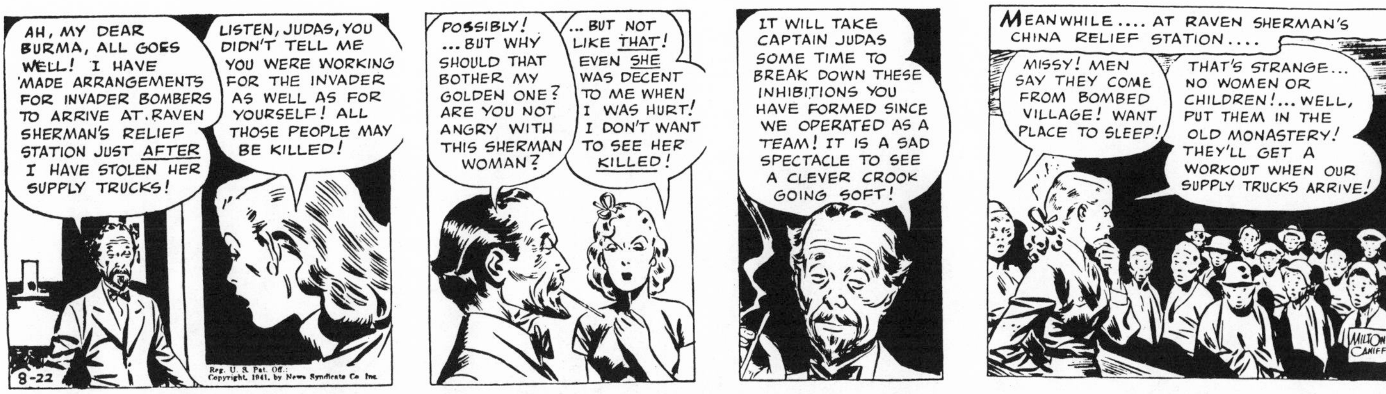
AH, MY DEAR BURMA, ALL GOES WELL! I HAVE MADE ARRANGEMENTS FOR INVADER BOMBERS TO ARRIVE AT RAVEN SHERMAN'S RELIEF STATION JUST AFTER I HAVE STOLEN HER SUPPLY TRUCKS!
LISTEN, JUDAS, YOU DIDN'T TELL ME YOU WERE WORKING FOR THE INVADER AS WELL AS FOR YOURSELF! ALL THOSE PEOPLE MAY BE KILLED!
8-22
Reg. U. S. Pat. Off.: Copyright, 1941, by News Syndicate Co. Inc.
POSSIBLY! ...BUT WHY SHOULD THAT BOTHER MY GOLDEN ONE? ARE YOU NOT ANGRY WITH THIS SHERMAN WOMAN?
...BUT NOT LIKE THAT! EVEN SHE WAS DECENT TO ME WHEN I WAS HURT! I DON'T WANT TO SEE HER KILLED!
IT WILL TAKE CAPTAIN JUDAS SOME TIME TO BREAK DOWN THESE INHIBITIONS YOU HAVE FORMED SINCE WE OPERATED AS A TEAM! IT IS A SAD SPECTACLE TO SEE A CLEVER CROOK GOING SOFT!
MEANWHILE.... AT RAVEN SHERMAN'S CHINA RELIEF STATION....
MISSY! MEN SAY THEY COME FROM BOMBED VILLAGE! WANT PLACE TO SLEEP!
THAT'S STRANGE... NO WOMEN OR CHILDREN!... WELL, PUT THEM IN THE OLD MONASTERY! THEY'LL GET A WORKOUT WHEN OUR SUPPLY TRUCKS ARRIVE!
MILTON CANIFF

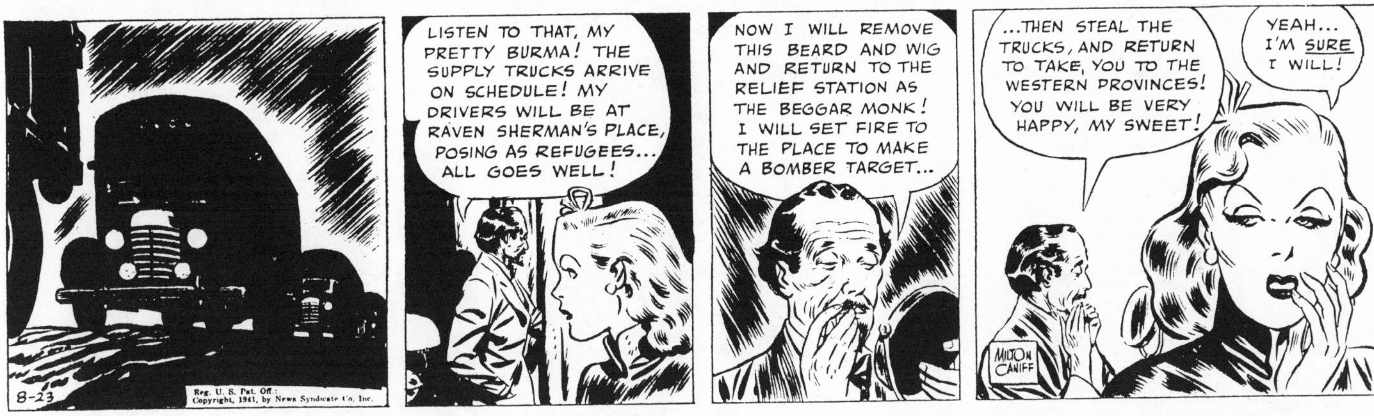
8-23
Reg. U. S. Pat. Off.: Copyright, 1941, by News Syndicate Co. Inc.
LISTEN TO THAT, MY PRETTY BURMA! THE SUPPLY TRUCKS ARRIVE ON SCHEDULE! MY DRIVERS WILL BE AT RAVEN SHERMAN'S PLACE, POSING AS REFUGEES... ALL GOES WELL!
NOW I WILL REMOVE THIS BEARD AND WIG AND RETURN TO THE RELIEF STATION AS THE BEGGAR MONK! I WILL SET FIRE TO THE PLACE TO MAKE A BOMBER TARGET...
...THEN STEAL THE TRUCKS, AND RETURN TO TAKE YOU TO THE WESTERN PROVINCES! YOU WILL BE VERY HAPPY, MY SWEET!
YEAH... I'M SURE I WILL!
MILTON CANIFF

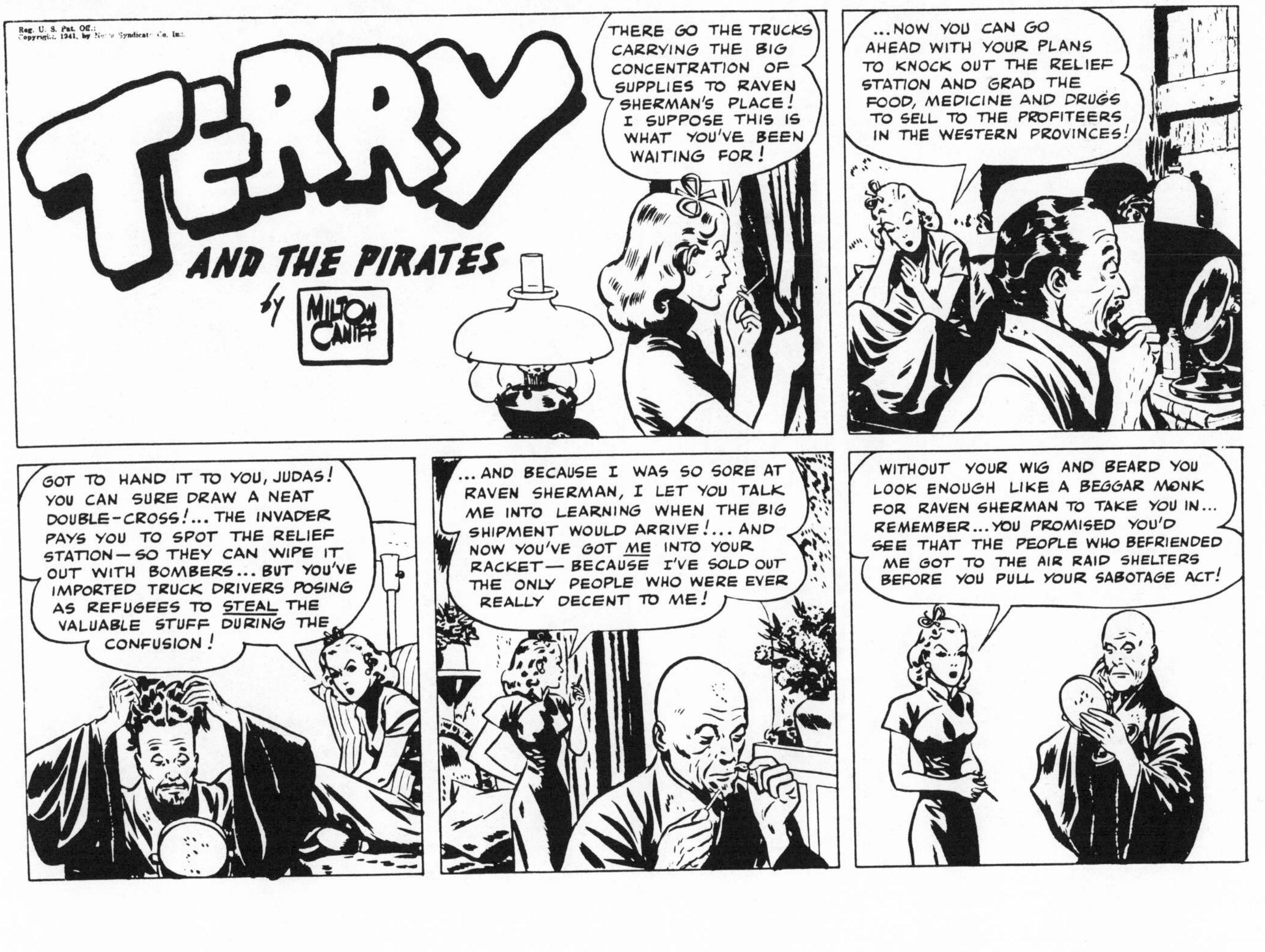
Reg. U. S. Pat. Off.: Copyright, 1941, by News Syndicate Co. Inc.
TERRY AND THE PIRATES
by MILTON CANIFF
THERE GO THE TRUCKS CARRYING THE BIG CONCENTRATION OF SUPPLIES TO RAVEN SHERMAN'S PLACE! I SUPPOSE THIS IS WHAT YOU'VE BEEN WAITING FOR!
...NOW YOU CAN GO AHEAD WITH YOUR PLANS TO KNOCK OUT THE RELIEF STATION AND GRAD THE FOOD, MEDICINE AND DRUGS TO SELL TO THE PROFITEERS IN THE WESTERN PROVINCES!
GOT TO HAND IT TO YOU, JUDAS! YOU CAN SURE DRAW A NEAT DOUBLE-CROSS!... THE INVADER PAYS YOU TO SPOT THE RELIEF STATION—SO THEY CAN WIPE IT OUT WITH BOMBERS... BUT YOU'VE IMPORTED TRUCK DRIVERS POSING AS REFUGEES TO STEAL THE VALUABLE STUFF DURING THE CONFUSION!
...AND BECAUSE I WAS SO SORE AT RAVEN SHERMAN, I LET YOU TALK ME INTO LEARNING WHEN THE BIG SHIPMENT WOULD ARRIVE!... AND NOW YOU'VE GOT ME INTO YOUR RACKET— BECAUSE I'VE SOLD OUT THE ONLY PEOPLE WHO WERE EVER REALLY DECENT TO ME!
WITHOUT YOUR WIG AND BEARD YOU LOOK ENOUGH LIKE A BEGGAR MONK FOR RAVEN SHERMAN TO TAKE YOU IN... REMEMBER... YOU PROMISED YOU'D SEE THAT THE PEOPLE WHO BEFRIENDED ME GOT TO THE AIR RAID SHELTERS BEFORE YOU PULL YOUR SABOTAGE ACT!

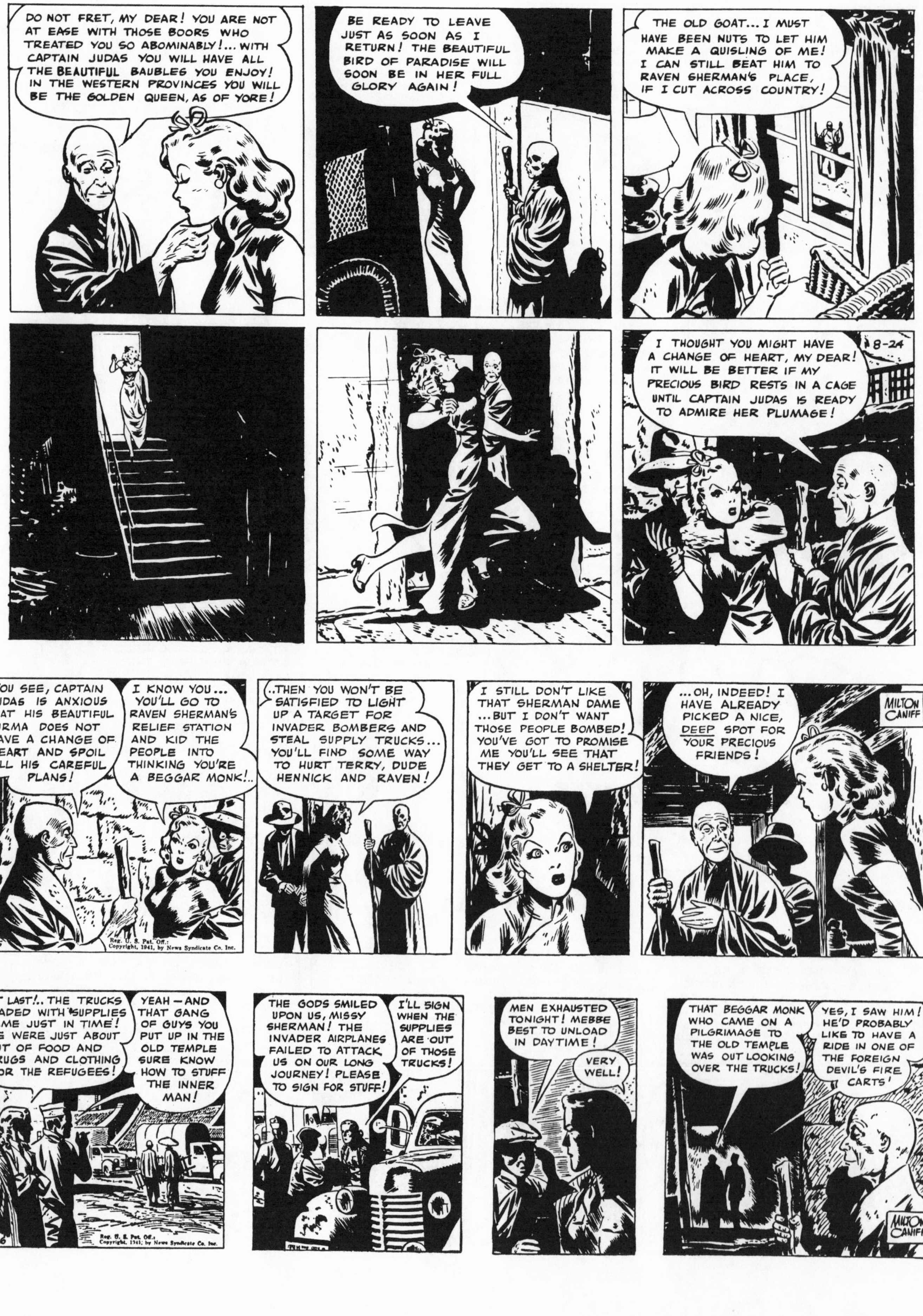
DO NOT FRET, MY DEAR! YOU ARE NOT AT EASE WITH THOSE BOORS WHO TREATED YOU SO ABOMINABLY!... WITH CAPTAIN JUDAS YOU WILL HAVE ALL THE BEAUTIFUL BAUBLES YOU ENJOY! IN THE WESTERN PROVINCES YOU WILL BE THE GOLDEN QUEEN, AS OF YORE!
BE READY TO LEAVE JUST AS SOON AS I RETURN! THE BEAUTIFUL BIRD OF PARADISE WILL SOON BE IN HER FULL GLORY AGAIN!
THE OLD GOAT... I MUST HAVE BEEN NUTS TO LET HIM MAKE A QUISLING OF ME! I CAN STILL BEAT HIM TO RAVEN SHERMAN'S PLACE, IF I CUT ACROSS COUNTRY!
8-24
I THOUGHT YOU MIGHT HAVE A CHANGE OF HEART, MY DEAR! IT WILL BE BETTER IF MY PRECIOUS BIRD RESTS IN A CAGE UNTIL CAPTAIN JUDAS IS READY TO ADMIRE HER PLUMAGE!
YOU SEE, CAPTAIN JUDAS IS ANXIOUS THAT HIS BEAUTIFUL BURMA DOES NOT HAVE A CHANGE OF HEART AND SPOIL ALL HIS CAREFUL PLANS!
I KNOW YOU... YOU'LL GO TO RAVEN SHERMAN'S RELIEF STATION AND KID THE PEOPLE INTO THINKING YOU'RE A BEGGAR MONK!..
8-25
Reg. U. S. Pat. Off.; Copyright, 1941, by News Syndicate Co. Inc.
..THEN YOU WON'T BE SATISFIED TO LIGHT UP A TARGET FOR INVADER BOMBERS AND STEAL SUPPLY TRUCKS... YOU'LL FIND SOME WAY TO HURT TERRY, DUDE HENNICK AND RAVEN!
I STILL DON'T LIKE THAT SHERMAN DAME ... BUT I DON'T WANT THOSE PEOPLE BOMBED! YOU'VE GOT TO PROMISE ME YOU'LL SEE THAT THEY GET TO A SHELTER!
...OH, INDEED! I HAVE ALREADY PICKED A NICE, DEEP SPOT FOR YOUR PRECIOUS FRIENDS!
MILTON CANIFF
AT LAST!.. THE TRUCKS LOADED WITH SUPPLIES CAME JUST IN TIME! WE WERE JUST ABOUT OUT OF FOOD AND DRUGS AND CLOTHING FOR THE REFUGEES!
YEAH—AND THAT GANG OF GUYS YOU PUT UP IN THE OLD TEMPLE SURE KNOW HOW TO STUFF THE INNER MAN!
8-26
Reg. U. S. Pat. Off.; Copyright, 1941, by News Syndicate Co. Inc.
THE GODS SMILED UPON US, MISSY SHERMAN! THE INVADER AIRPLANES FAILED TO ATTACK US ON OUR LONG JOURNEY! PLEASE TO SIGN FOR STUFF!
I'LL SIGN WHEN THE SUPPLIES ARE OUT OF THOSE TRUCKS!
MEN EXHAUSTED TONIGHT! MEBBE BEST TO UNLOAD IN DAYTIME!
VERY WELL!
THAT BEGGAR MONK WHO CAME ON A PILGRIMAGE TO THE OLD TEMPLE WAS OUT LOOKING OVER THE TRUCKS!
YES, I SAW HIM! HE'D PROBABLY LIKE TO HAVE A RIDE IN ONE OF THE FOREIGN DEVIL'S FIRE CARTS!
MILTON CANIFF

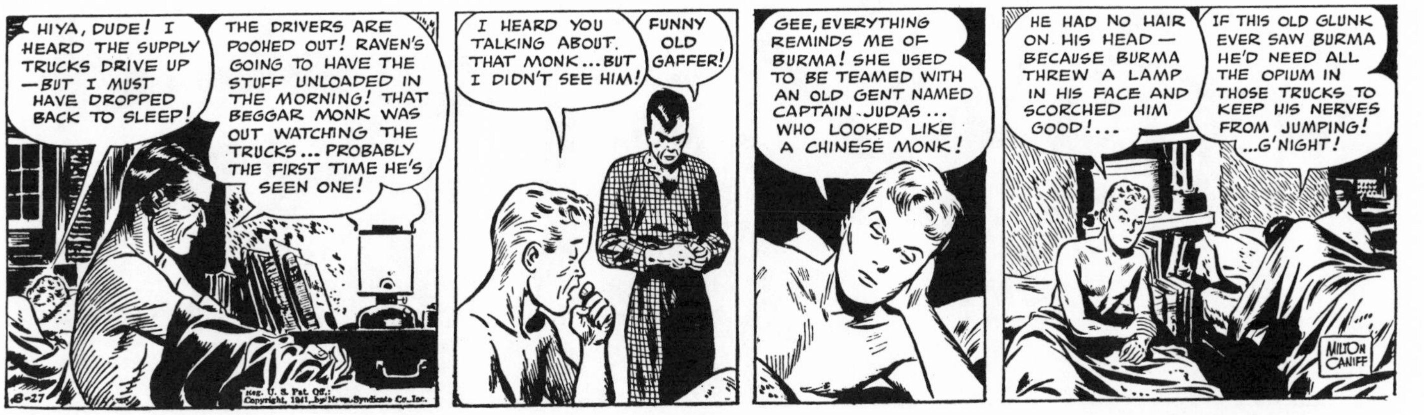
HIYA, DUDE! I HEARD THE SUPPLY TRUCKS DRIVE UP —BUT I MUST HAVE DROPPED BACK TO SLEEP!
THE DRIVERS ARE POOHED OUT! RAVEN'S GOING TO HAVE THE STUFF UNLOADED IN THE MORNING! THAT BEGGAR MONK WAS OUT WATCHING THE TRUCKS ... PROBABLY THE FIRST TIME HE'S SEEN ONE!
8-27
Reg. U. S. Pat. Off.; Copyright, 1941, by News Syndicate Co. Inc.
I HEARD YOU TALKING ABOUT THAT MONK ... BUT I DIDN'T SEE HIM!
FUNNY OLD GAFFER!
GEE, EVERYTHING REMINDS ME OF BURMA! SHE USED TO BE TEAMED WITH AN OLD GENT NAMED CAPTAIN JUDAS ... WHO LOOKED LIKE A CHINESE MONK!
HE HAD NO HAIR ON HIS HEAD — BECAUSE BURMA THREW A LAMP IN HIS FACE AND SCORCHED HIM GOOD! ...
IF THIS OLD GLUNK EVER SAW BURMA HE'D NEED ALL THE OPIUM IN THOSE TRUCKS TO KEEP HIS NERVES FROM JUMPING! ...G'NIGHT!
MILTON CANIFF

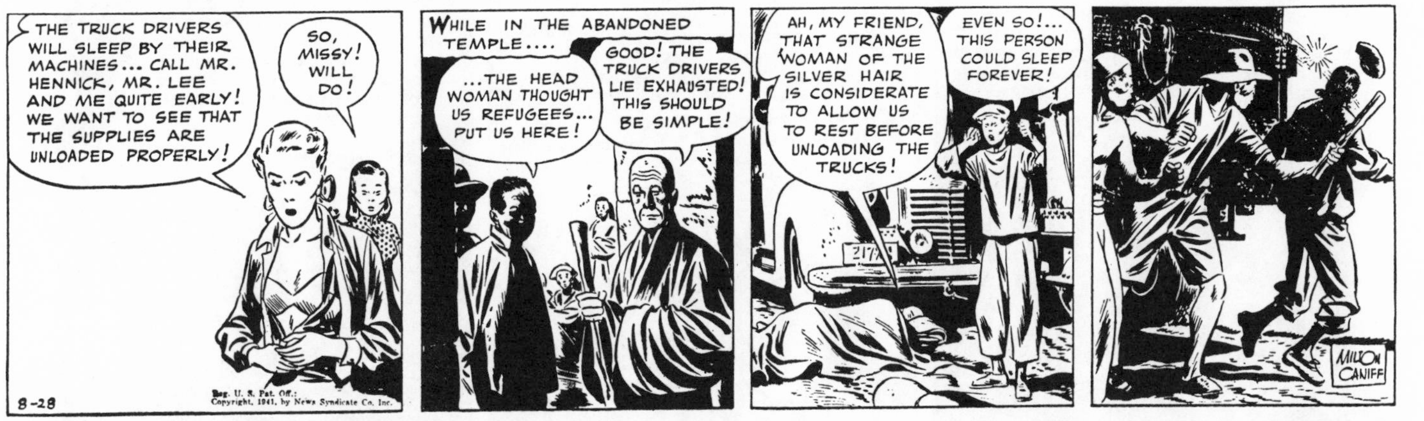
THE TRUCK DRIVERS WILL SLEEP BY THEIR MACHINES ... CALL MR. HENNICK, MR. LEE AND ME QUITE EARLY! WE WANT TO SEE THAT THE SUPPLIES ARE UNLOADED PROPERLY!
SO, MISSY! WILL DO!
8-28
Reg. U. S. Pat. Off.; Copyright, 1941, by News Syndicate Co. Inc.
WHILE IN THE ABANDONED TEMPLE....
...THE HEAD WOMAN THOUGHT US REFUGEES ... PUT US HERE!
GOOD! THE TRUCK DRIVERS LIE EXHAUSTED! THIS SHOULD BE SIMPLE!
AH, MY FRIEND, THAT STRANGE WOMAN OF THE SILVER HAIR IS CONSIDERATE TO ALLOW US TO REST BEFORE UNLOADING THE TRUCKS!
EVEN SO!... THIS PERSON COULD SLEEP FOREVER!
MILTON CANIFF

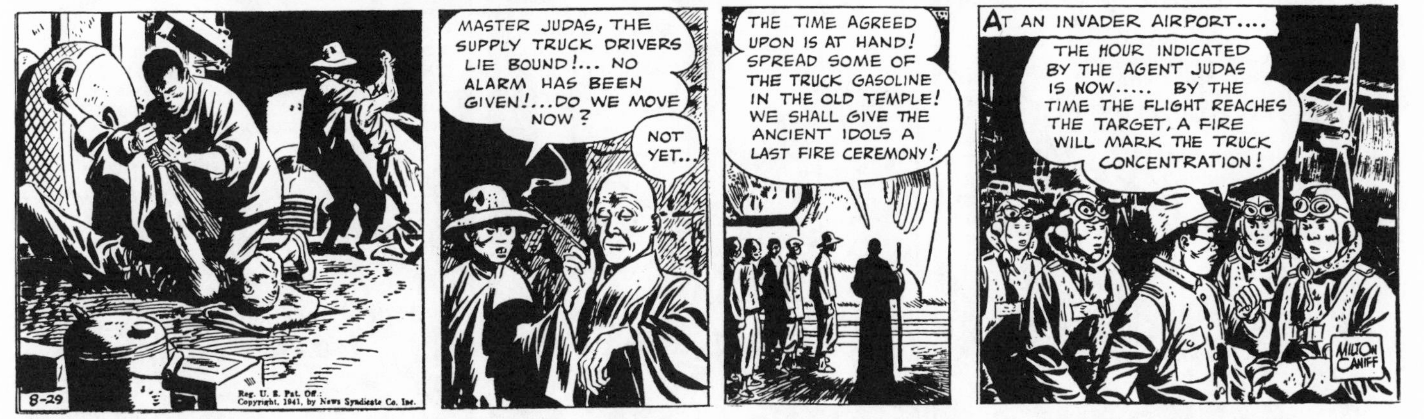
8-29
Reg. U. S. Pat. Off.; Copyright, 1941, by News Syndicate Co. Inc.
MASTER JUDAS, THE SUPPLY TRUCK DRIVERS LIE BOUND!... NO ALARM HAS BEEN GIVEN!...DO WE MOVE NOW ?
NOT YET...
THE TIME AGREED UPON IS AT HAND! SPREAD SOME OF THE TRUCK GASOLINE IN THE OLD TEMPLE! WE SHALL GIVE THE ANCIENT IDOLS A LAST FIRE CEREMONY!
AT AN INVADER AIRPORT....
THE HOUR INDICATED BY THE AGENT JUDAS IS NOW..... BY THE TIME THE FLIGHT REACHES THE TARGET, A FIRE WILL MARK THE TRUCK CONCENTRATION!
MILTON CANIFF

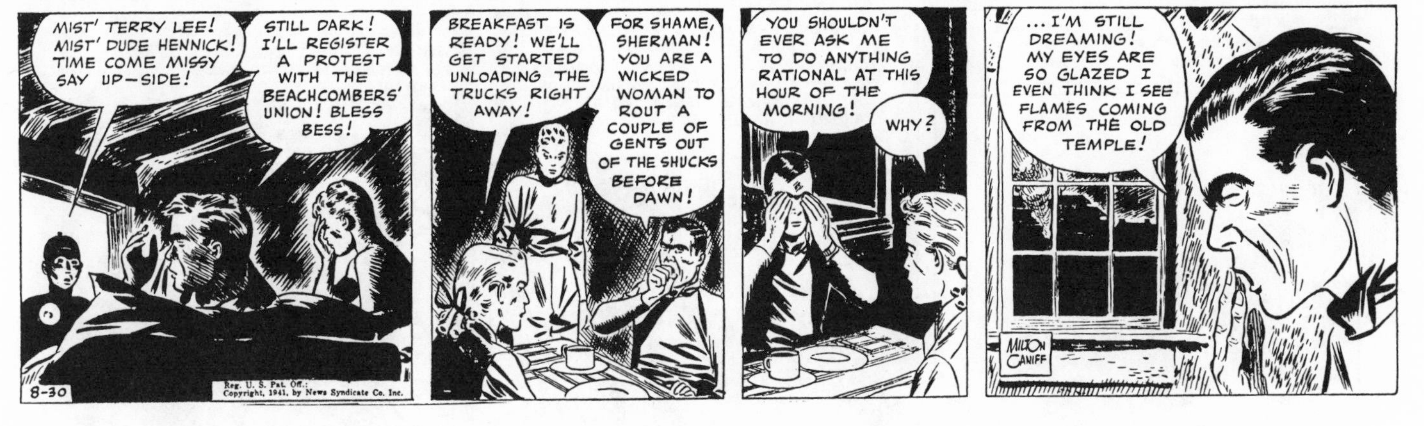
MIST' TERRY LEE! MIST' DUDE HENNICK! TIME COME MISSY SAY UP-SIDE!
STILL DARK! I'LL REGISTER A PROTEST WITH THE BEACHCOMBERS' UNION! BLESS BESS!
8-30
Reg. U. S. Pat. Off.; Copyright, 1941, by News Syndicate Co. Inc.
BREAKFAST IS READY! WE'LL GET STARTED UNLOADING THE TRUCKS RIGHT AWAY!
FOR SHAME, SHERMAN! YOU ARE A WICKED WOMAN TO ROUT A COUPLE OF GENTS OUT OF THE SHUCKS BEFORE DAWN!
YOU SHOULDN'T EVER ASK ME TO DO ANYTHING RATIONAL AT THIS HOUR OF THE MORNING!
WHY?
... I'M STILL DREAMING! MY EYES ARE SO GLAZED I EVEN THINK I SEE FLAMES COMING FROM THE OLD TEMPLE!
MILTON CANIFF

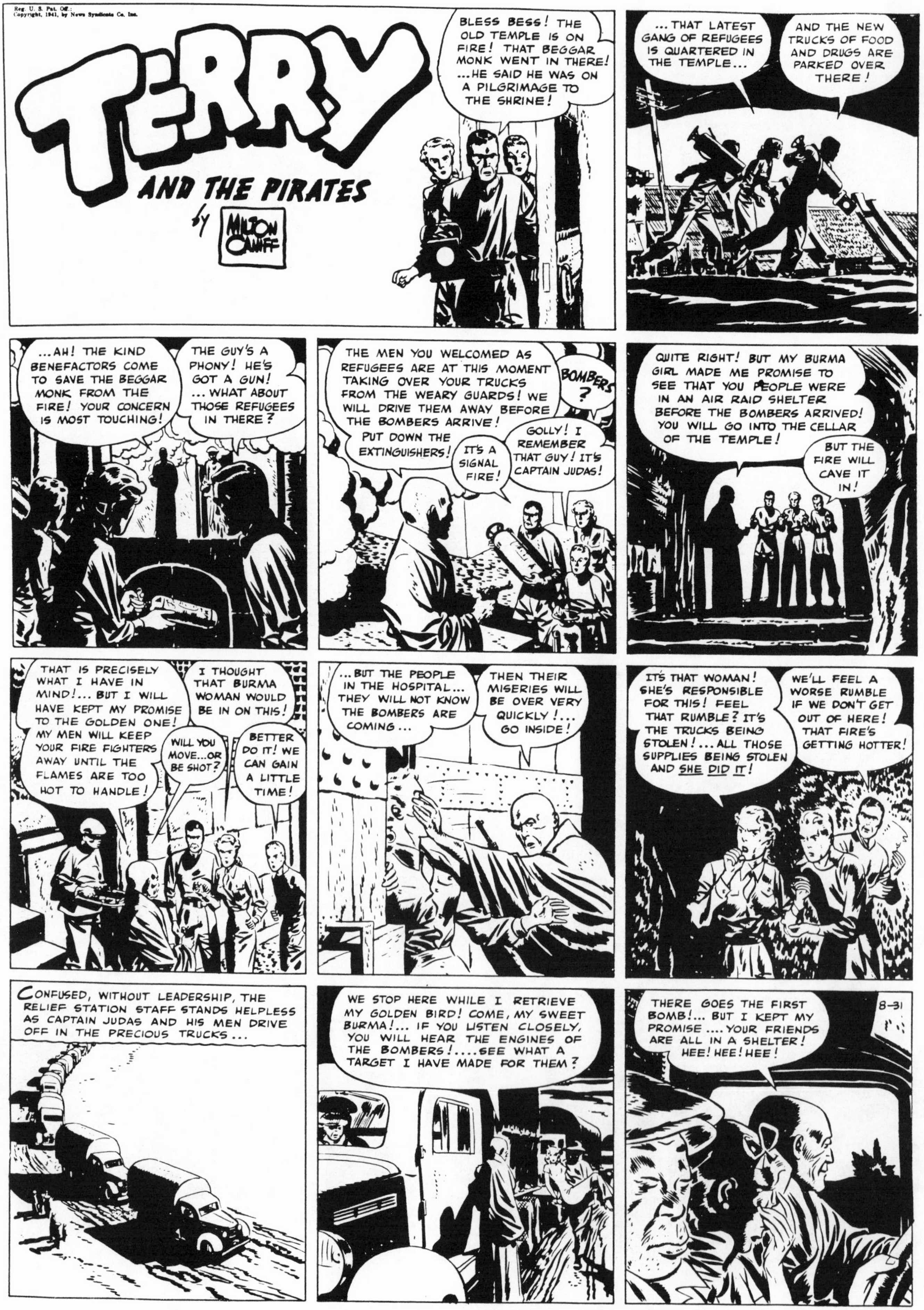

Reg. U. S. Pat. Off.: Copyright, 1941, by News Syndicate Co. Inc.
TERRY AND THE PIRATES
by MILTON CANIFF
BLESS BESS! THE OLD TEMPLE IS ON FIRE! THAT BEGGAR MONK WENT IN THERE! ...HE SAID HE WAS ON A PILGRIMAGE TO THE SHRINE!
...THAT LATEST GANG OF REFUGEES IS QUARTERED IN THE TEMPLE...
AND THE NEW TRUCKS OF FOOD AND DRUGS ARE PARKED OVER THERE!
...AH! THE KIND BENEFACTORS COME TO SAVE THE BEGGAR MONK FROM THE FIRE! YOUR CONCERN IS MOST TOUCHING!
THE GUY'S A PHONY! HE'S GOT A GUN! ... WHAT ABOUT THOSE REFUGEES IN THERE?
THE MEN YOU WELCOMED AS REFUGEES ARE AT THIS MOMENT TAKING OVER YOUR TRUCKS FROM THE WEARY GUARDS! WE WILL DRIVE THEM AWAY BEFORE THE BOMBERS ARRIVE!
BOMBERS?
PUT DOWN THE EXTINGUISHERS!
IT'S A SIGNAL FIRE!
GOLLY! I REMEMBER THAT GUY! IT'S CAPTAIN JUDAS!
QUITE RIGHT! BUT MY BURMA GIRL MADE ME PROMISE TO SEE THAT YOU PEOPLE WERE IN AN AIR RAID SHELTER BEFORE THE BOMBERS ARRIVED! YOU WILL GO INTO THE CELLAR OF THE TEMPLE!
BUT THE FIRE WILL CAVE IT IN!
THAT IS PRECISELY WHAT I HAVE IN MIND!... BUT I WILL HAVE KEPT MY PROMISE TO THE GOLDEN ONE! MY MEN WILL KEEP YOUR FIRE FIGHTERS AWAY UNTIL THE FLAMES ARE TOO HOT TO HANDLE!
I THOUGHT THAT BURMA WOMAN WOULD BE IN ON THIS!
WILL YOU MOVE...OR BE SHOT?
BETTER DO IT! WE CAN GAIN A LITTLE TIME!
...BUT THE PEOPLE IN THE HOSPITAL... THEY WILL NOT KNOW THE BOMBERS ARE COMING...
THEN THEIR MISERIES WILL BE OVER VERY QUICKLY!... GO INSIDE!
IT'S THAT WOMAN! SHE'S RESPONSIBLE FOR THIS! FEEL THAT RUMBLE? IT'S THE TRUCKS BEING STOLEN!... ALL THOSE SUPPLIES BEING STOLEN AND SHE DID IT!
WE'LL FEEL A WORSE RUMBLE IF WE DON'T GET OUT OF HERE! THAT FIRE'S GETTING HOTTER!
CONFUSED, WITHOUT LEADERSHIP, THE RELIEF STATION STAFF STANDS HELPLESS AS CAPTAIN JUDAS AND HIS MEN DRIVE OFF IN THE PRECIOUS TRUCKS...
WE STOP HERE WHILE I RETRIEVE MY GOLDEN BIRD! COME, MY SWEET BURMA!... IF YOU LISTEN CLOSELY, YOU WILL HEAR THE ENGINES OF THE BOMBERS!....SEE WHAT A TARGET I HAVE MADE FOR THEM?
8-31
THERE GOES THE FIRST BOMB!... BUT I KEPT MY PROMISE .... YOUR FRIENDS ARE ALL IN A SHELTER! HEE! HEE! HEE!

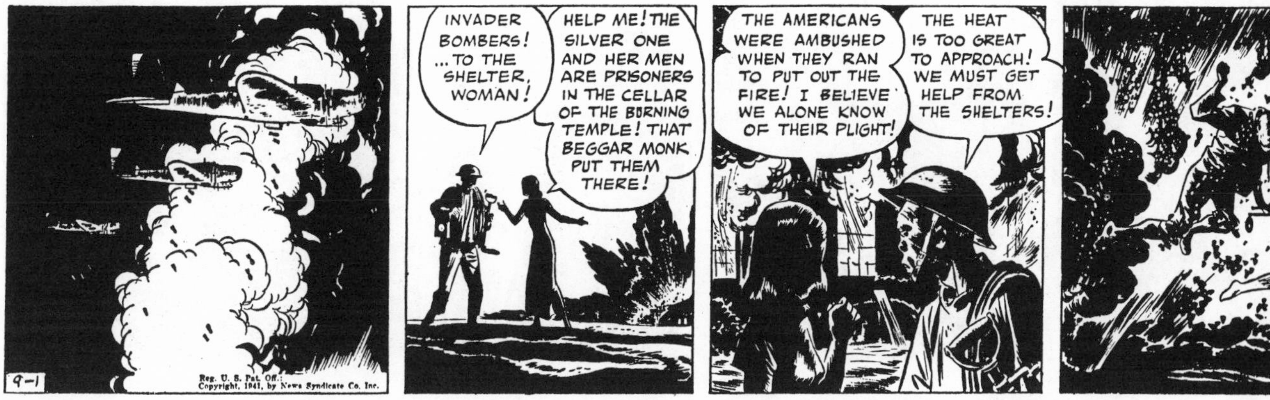
9-1
Reg. U. S. Pat. Off.: Copyright, 1941, by News Syndicate Co. Inc.
INVADER BOMBERS! ...TO THE SHELTER, WOMAN!
HELP ME! THE SILVER ONE AND HER MEN ARE PRISONERS IN THE CELLAR OF THE BURNING TEMPLE! THAT BEGGAR MONK PUT THEM THERE!
THE AMERICANS WERE AMBUSHED WHEN THEY RAN TO PUT OUT THE FIRE! I BELIEVE WE ALONE KNOW OF THEIR PLIGHT!
THE HEAT IS TOO GREAT TO APPROACH! WE MUST GET HELP FROM THE SHELTERS!
MILTON CANIFF

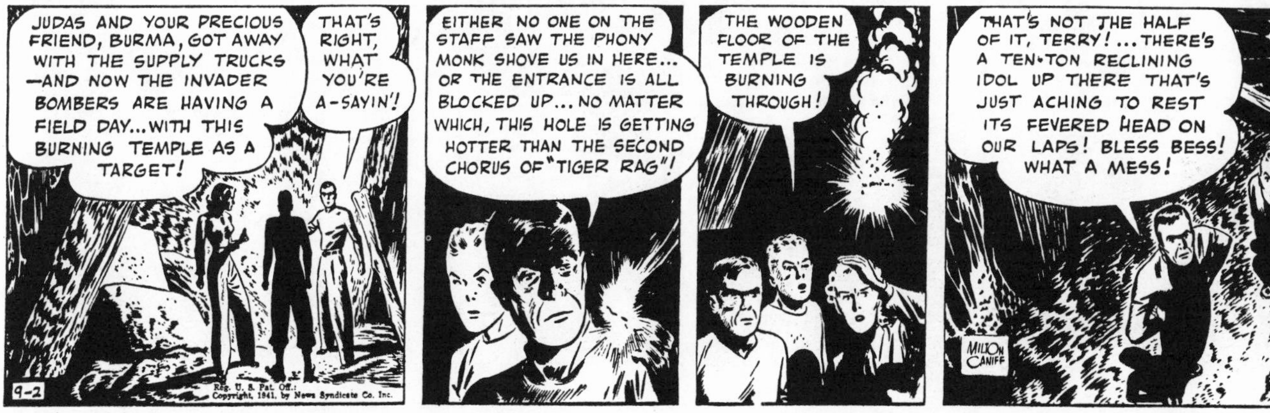
JUDAS AND YOUR PRECIOUS FRIEND, BURMA, GOT AWAY WITH THE SUPPLY TRUCKS —AND NOW THE INVADER BOMBERS ARE HAVING A FIELD DAY...WITH THIS BURNING TEMPLE AS A TARGET!
THAT'S RIGHT, WHAT YOU'RE A-SAYIN'!
9-2
Reg. U. S. Pat. Off.: Copyright, 1941, by News Syndicate Co. Inc.
EITHER NO ONE ON THE STAFF SAW THE PHONY MONK SHOVE US IN HERE... OR THE ENTRANCE IS ALL BLOCKED UP... NO MATTER WHICH, THIS HOLE IS GETTING HOTTER THAN THE SECOND CHORUS OF "TIGER RAG"!
THE WOODEN FLOOR OF THE TEMPLE IS BURNING THROUGH!
THAT'S NOT THE HALF OF IT, TERRY! ... THERE'S A TEN-TON RECLINING IDOL UP THERE THAT'S JUST ACHING TO REST ITS FEVERED HEAD ON OUR LAPS! BLESS BESS! WHAT A MESS!
MILTON CANIFF

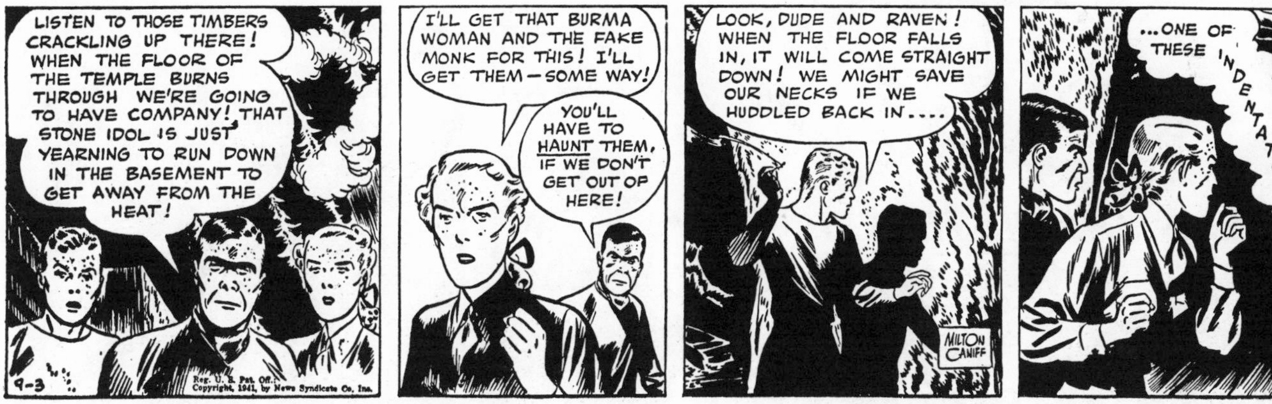
LISTEN TO THOSE TIMBERS CRACKLING UP THERE! WHEN THE FLOOR OF THE TEMPLE BURNS THROUGH WE'RE GOING TO HAVE COMPANY! THAT STONE IDOL IS JUST YEARNING TO RUN DOWN IN THE BASEMENT TO GET AWAY FROM THE HEAT!
9-3
Reg. U. S. Pat. Off.: Copyright, 1941, by News Syndicate Co. Inc.
I'LL GET THAT BURMA WOMAN AND THE FAKE MONK FOR THIS! I'LL GET THEM—SOME WAY!
YOU'LL HAVE TO HAUNT THEM, IF WE DON'T GET OUT OF HERE!
LOOK, DUDE AND RAVEN! WHEN THE FLOOR FALLS IN, IT WILL COME STRAIGHT DOWN! WE MIGHT SAVE OUR NECKS IF WE HUDDLED BACK IN....
MILTON CANIFF
...ONE OF THESE INDENTATIONS!!??

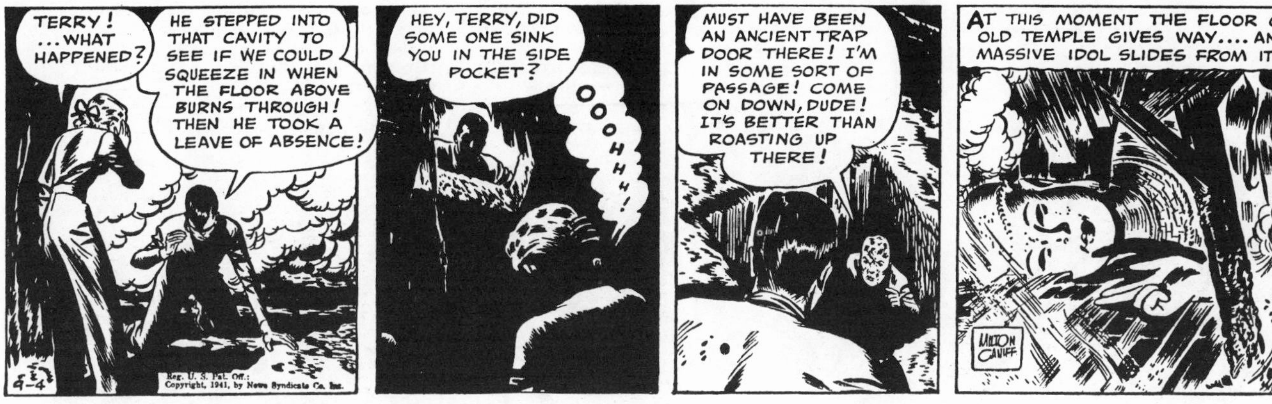
TERRY! ...WHAT HAPPENED?
HE STEPPED INTO THAT CAVITY TO SEE IF WE COULD SQUEEZE IN WHEN THE FLOOR ABOVE BURNS THROUGH! THEN HE TOOK A LEAVE OF ABSENCE!
9-4
Reg. U. S. Pat. Off.: Copyright, 1941, by News Syndicate Co. Inc.
HEY, TERRY, DID SOME ONE SINK YOU IN THE SIDE POCKET?
OOOHHH!
MUST HAVE BEEN AN ANCIENT TRAP DOOR THERE! I'M IN SOME SORT OF PASSAGE! COME ON DOWN, DUDE! IT'S BETTER THAN ROASTING UP THERE!
AT THIS MOMENT THE FLOOR OF THE OLD TEMPLE GIVES WAY.... AND THE MASSIVE IDOL SLIDES FROM ITS BASE...
MILTON CANIFF

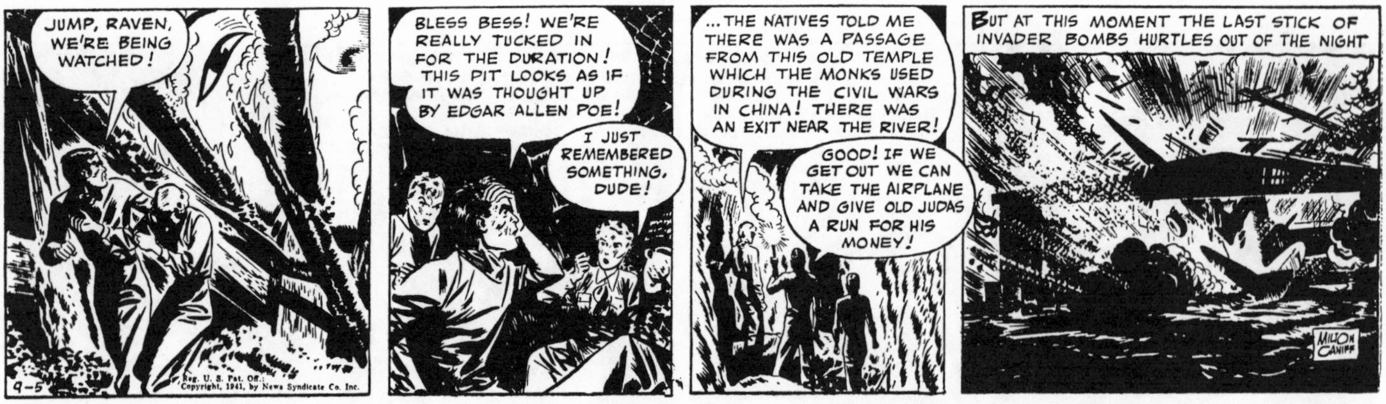
JUMP, RAVEN, WE'RE BEING WATCHED!
9-5
Reg. U. S. Pat. Off.: Copyright, 1941, by News Syndicate Co. Inc.
BLESS BESS! WE'RE REALLY TUCKED IN FOR THE DURATION! THIS PIT LOOKS AS IF IT WAS THOUGHT UP BY EDGAR ALLEN POE!
I JUST REMEMBERED SOMETHING, DUDE!
...THE NATIVES TOLD ME THERE WAS A PASSAGE FROM THIS OLD TEMPLE WHICH THE MONKS USED DURING THE CIVIL WARS IN CHINA! THERE WAS AN EXIT NEAR THE RIVER!
GOOD! IF WE GET OUT WE CAN TAKE THE AIRPLANE AND GIVE OLD JUDAS A RUN FOR HIS MONEY!
BUT AT THIS MOMENT THE LAST STICK OF INVADER BOMBS HURTLES OUT OF THE NIGHT
MILTON CANIFF

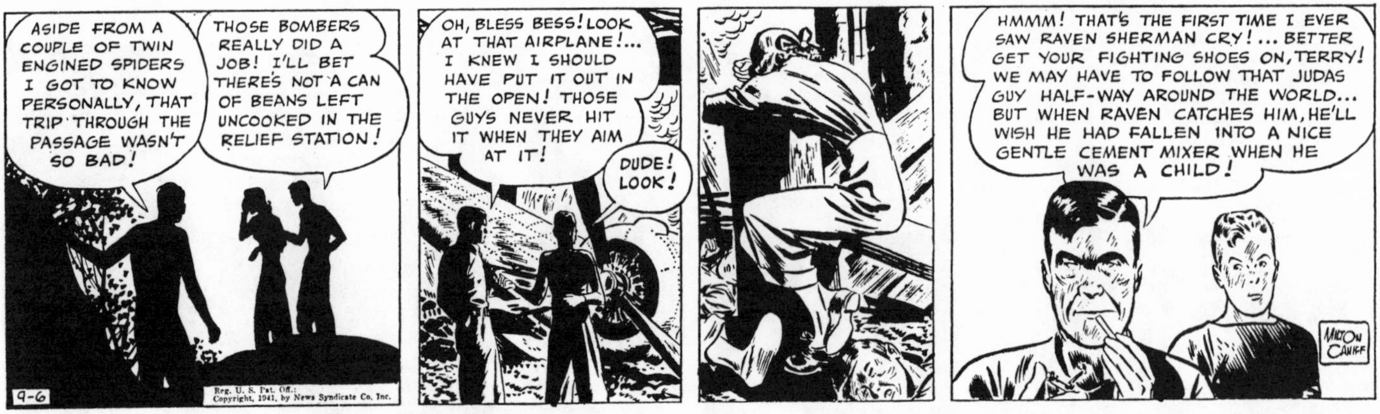
ASIDE FROM A COUPLE OF TWIN ENGINED SPIDERS I GOT TO KNOW PERSONALLY, THAT TRIP THROUGH THE PASSAGE WASN'T SO BAD!
THOSE BOMBERS REALLY DID A JOB! I'LL BET THERE'S NOT A CAN OF BEANS LEFT UNCOOKED IN THE RELIEF STATION!
9-6
Reg. U. S. Pat. Off.: Copyright, 1941, by News Syndicate Co. Inc.
OH, BLESS BESS! LOOK AT THAT AIRPLANE!... I KNEW I SHOULD HAVE PUT IT OUT IN THE OPEN! THOSE GUYS NEVER HIT IT WHEN THEY AIM AT IT!
DUDE! LOOK!
HMMM! THAT'S THE FIRST TIME I EVER SAW RAVEN SHERMAN CRY!... BETTER GET YOUR FIGHTING SHOES ON, TERRY! WE MAY HAVE TO FOLLOW THAT JUDAS GUY HALF-WAY AROUND THE WORLD... BUT WHEN RAVEN CATCHES HIM, HE'LL WISH HE HAD FALLEN INTO A NICE GENTLE CEMENT MIXER WHEN HE WAS A CHILD!
MILTON CANIFF

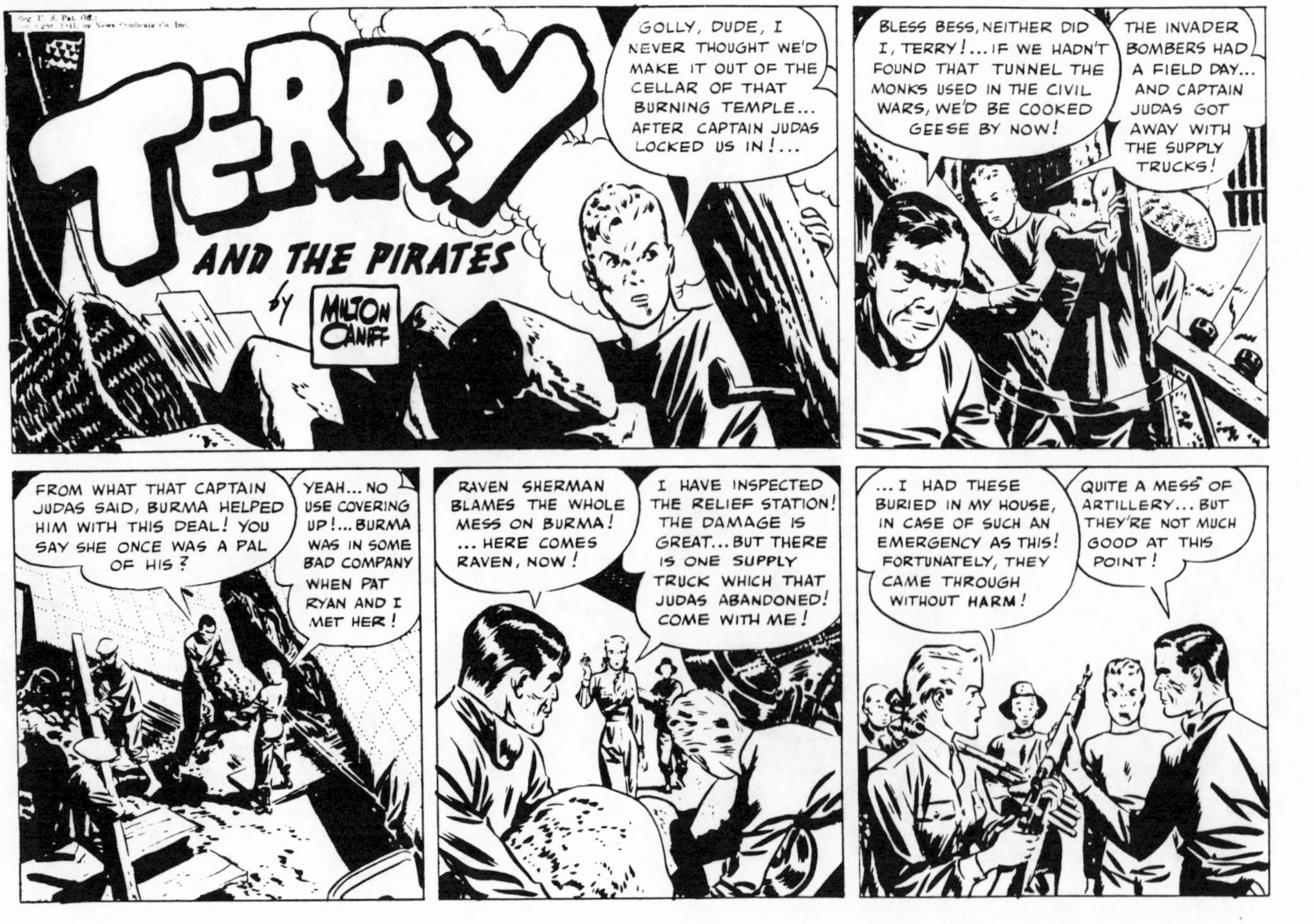
TERRY AND THE PIRATES by MILTON CANIFF
GOLLY, DUDE, I NEVER THOUGHT WE'D MAKE IT OUT OF THE CELLAR OF THAT BURNING TEMPLE... AFTER CAPTAIN JUDAS LOCKED US IN!...
BLESS BESS, NEITHER DID I, TERRY!... IF WE HADN'T FOUND THAT TUNNEL THE MONKS USED IN THE CIVIL WARS, WE'D BE COOKED GEESE BY NOW!
THE INVADER BOMBERS HAD A FIELD DAY... AND CAPTAIN JUDAS GOT AWAY WITH THE SUPPLY TRUCKS!
FROM WHAT THAT CAPTAIN JUDAS SAID, BURMA HELPED HIM WITH THIS DEAL! YOU SAY SHE ONCE WAS A PAL OF HIS?
YEAH... NO USE COVERING UP!... BURMA WAS IN SOME BAD COMPANY WHEN PAT RYAN AND I MET HER!
RAVEN SHERMAN BLAMES THE WHOLE MESS ON BURMA! ... HERE COMES RAVEN, NOW!
I HAVE INSPECTED THE RELIEF STATION! THE DAMAGE IS GREAT... BUT THERE IS ONE SUPPLY TRUCK WHICH THAT JUDAS ABANDONED! COME WITH ME!
... I HAD THESE BURIED IN MY HOUSE, IN CASE OF SUCH AN EMERGENCY AS THIS! FORTUNATELY, THEY CAME THROUGH WITHOUT HARM!
QUITE A MESS OF ARTILLERY... BUT THEY'RE NOT MUCH GOOD AT THIS POINT!

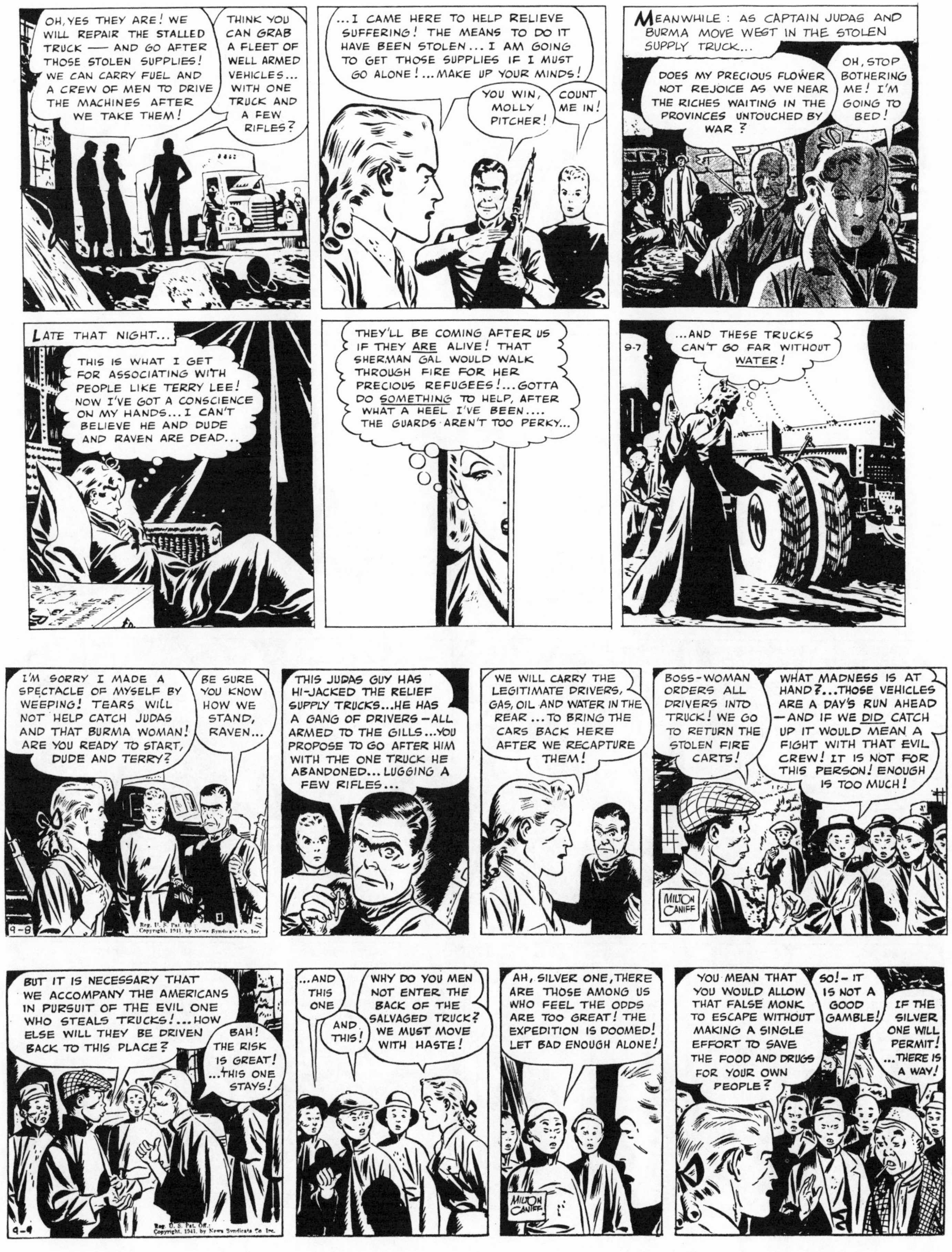
OH, YES THEY ARE! WE WILL REPAIR THE STALLED TRUCK — AND GO AFTER THOSE STOLEN SUPPLIES! WE CAN CARRY FUEL AND A CREW OF MEN TO DRIVE THE MACHINES AFTER WE TAKE THEM!
THINK YOU CAN GRAB A FLEET OF WELL ARMED VEHICLES... WITH ONE TRUCK AND A FEW RIFLES?
...I CAME HERE TO HELP RELIEVE SUFFERING! THE MEANS TO DO IT HAVE BEEN STOLEN... I AM GOING TO GET THOSE SUPPLIES IF I MUST GO ALONE! ...MAKE UP YOUR MINDS!
YOU WIN, MOLLY PITCHER!
COUNT ME IN!
MEANWHILE: AS CAPTAIN JUDAS AND BURMA MOVE WEST IN THE STOLEN SUPPLY TRUCK...
DOES MY PRECIOUS FLOWER NOT REJOICE AS WE NEAR THE RICHES WAITING IN THE PROVINCES UNTOUCHED BY WAR?
OH, STOP BOTHERING ME! I'M GOING TO BED!
LATE THAT NIGHT...
THIS IS WHAT I GET FOR ASSOCIATING WITH PEOPLE LIKE TERRY LEE! NOW I'VE GOT A CONSCIENCE ON MY HANDS... I CAN'T BELIEVE HE AND DUDE AND RAVEN ARE DEAD...
THEY'LL BE COMING AFTER US IF THEY ARE ALIVE! THAT SHERMAN GAL WOULD WALK THROUGH FIRE FOR HER PRECIOUS REFUGEES!... GOTTA DO SOMETHING TO HELP, AFTER WHAT A HEEL I'VE BEEN.... THE GUARDS AREN'T TOO PERKY...
9-7
...AND THESE TRUCKS CAN'T GO FAR WITHOUT WATER!
I'M SORRY I MADE A SPECTACLE OF MYSELF BY WEEPING! TEARS WILL NOT HELP CATCH JUDAS AND THAT BURMA WOMAN! ARE YOU READY TO START, DUDE AND TERRY?
BE SURE YOU KNOW HOW WE STAND, RAVEN...
9-8
THIS JUDAS GUY HAS HI-JACKED THE RELIEF SUPPLY TRUCKS... HE HAS A GANG OF DRIVERS — ALL ARMED TO THE GILLS... YOU PROPOSE TO GO AFTER HIM WITH THE ONE TRUCK HE ABANDONED... LUGGING A FEW RIFLES...
WE WILL CARRY THE LEGITIMATE DRIVERS, GAS, OIL AND WATER IN THE REAR... TO BRING THE CARS BACK HERE AFTER WE RECAPTURE THEM!
BOSS-WOMAN ORDERS ALL DRIVERS INTO TRUCK! WE GO TO RETURN THE STOLEN FIRE CARTS!
WHAT MADNESS IS AT HAND?... THOSE VEHICLES ARE A DAY'S RUN AHEAD — AND IF WE DID CATCH UP IT WOULD MEAN A FIGHT WITH THAT EVIL CREW! IT IS NOT FOR THIS PERSON! ENOUGH IS TOO MUCH!
MILTON CANIFF
BUT IT IS NECESSARY THAT WE ACCOMPANY THE AMERICANS IN PURSUIT OF THE EVIL ONE WHO STEALS TRUCKS!... HOW ELSE WILL THEY BE DRIVEN BACK TO THIS PLACE?
BAH! THE RISK IS GREAT! ...THIS ONE STAYS!
9-9
Reg. U. S. Pat. Off.: Copyright, 1941, by News Syndicate Co. Inc.
...AND THIS ONE
AND THIS!
WHY DO YOU MEN NOT ENTER THE BACK OF THE SALVAGED TRUCK? WE MUST MOVE WITH HASTE!
AH, SILVER ONE, THERE ARE THOSE AMONG US WHO FEEL THE ODDS ARE TOO GREAT! THE EXPEDITION IS DOOMED! LET BAD ENOUGH ALONE!
MILTON CANIFF
YOU MEAN THAT YOU WOULD ALLOW THAT FALSE MONK TO ESCAPE WITHOUT MAKING A SINGLE EFFORT TO SAVE THE FOOD AND DRUGS FOR YOUR OWN PEOPLE?
SO! — IT IS NOT A GOOD GAMBLE!
IF THE SILVER ONE WILL PERMIT! ...THERE IS A WAY!

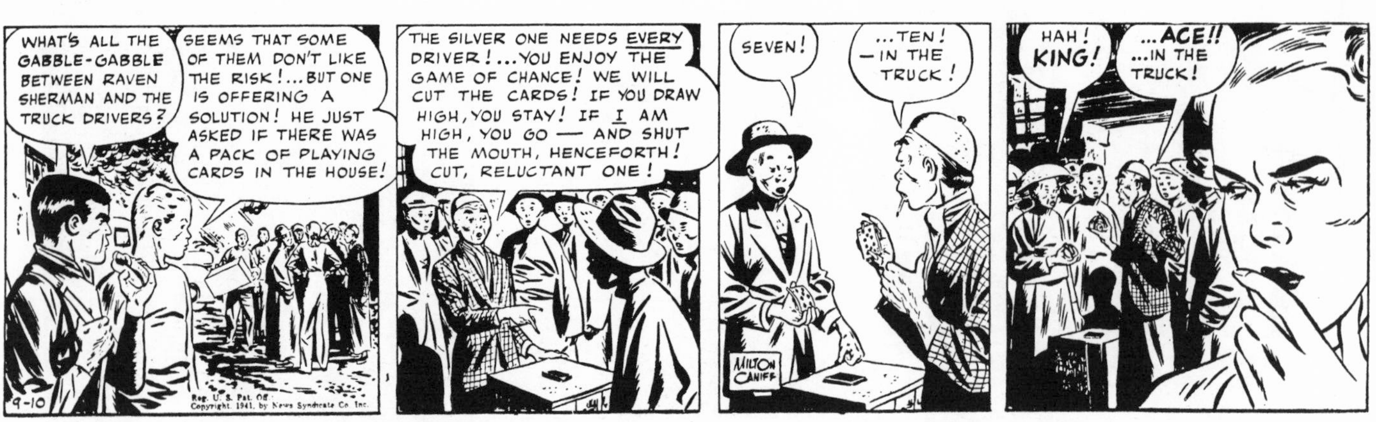
WHAT'S ALL THE GABBLE-GABBLE BETWEEN RAVEN SHERMAN AND THE TRUCK DRIVERS?
SEEMS THAT SOME OF THEM DON'T LIKE THE RISK!...BUT ONE IS OFFERING A SOLUTION! HE JUST ASKED IF THERE WAS A PACK OF PLAYING CARDS IN THE HOUSE!
9-10
Reg. U. S. Pat. Off.: Copyright, 1941, by News Syndicate Co. Inc.
THE SILVER ONE NEEDS EVERY DRIVER!...YOU ENJOY THE GAME OF CHANCE! WE WILL CUT THE CARDS! IF YOU DRAW HIGH, YOU STAY! IF I AM HIGH, YOU GO — AND SHUT THE MOUTH, HENCEFORTH! CUT, RELUCTANT ONE!
SEVEN!
...TEN! — IN THE TRUCK!
MILTON CANIFF
HAH! KING!
...ACE!! ...IN THE TRUCK!

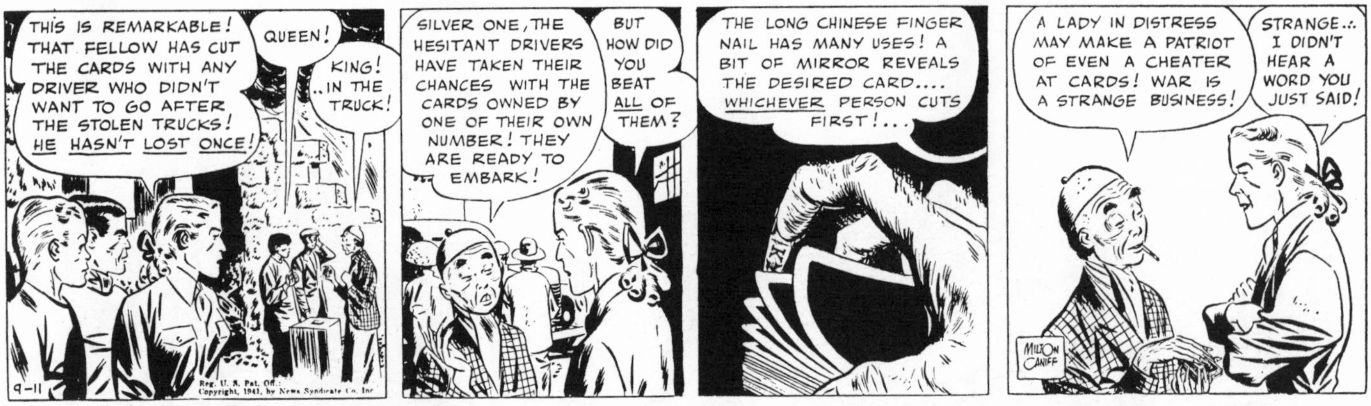
THIS IS REMARKABLE! THAT FELLOW HAS CUT THE CARDS WITH ANY DRIVER WHO DIDN'T WANT TO GO AFTER THE STOLEN TRUCKS! HE HASN'T LOST ONCE!
QUEEN!
KING! ..IN THE TRUCK!
9-11
Reg. U. S. Pat. Off.: Copyright, 1941, by News Syndicate Co. Inc.
SILVER ONE, THE HESITANT DRIVERS HAVE TAKEN THEIR CHANCES WITH THE CARDS OWNED BY ONE OF THEIR OWN NUMBER! THEY ARE READY TO EMBARK!
BUT HOW DID YOU BEAT ALL OF THEM?
THE LONG CHINESE FINGER NAIL HAS MANY USES! A BIT OF MIRROR REVEALS THE DESIRED CARD.... WHICHEVER PERSON CUTS FIRST!...
A LADY IN DISTRESS MAY MAKE A PATRIOT OF EVEN A CHEATER AT CARDS! WAR IS A STRANGE BUSINESS!
STRANGE... I DIDN'T HEAR A WORD YOU JUST SAID!
MILTON CANIFF

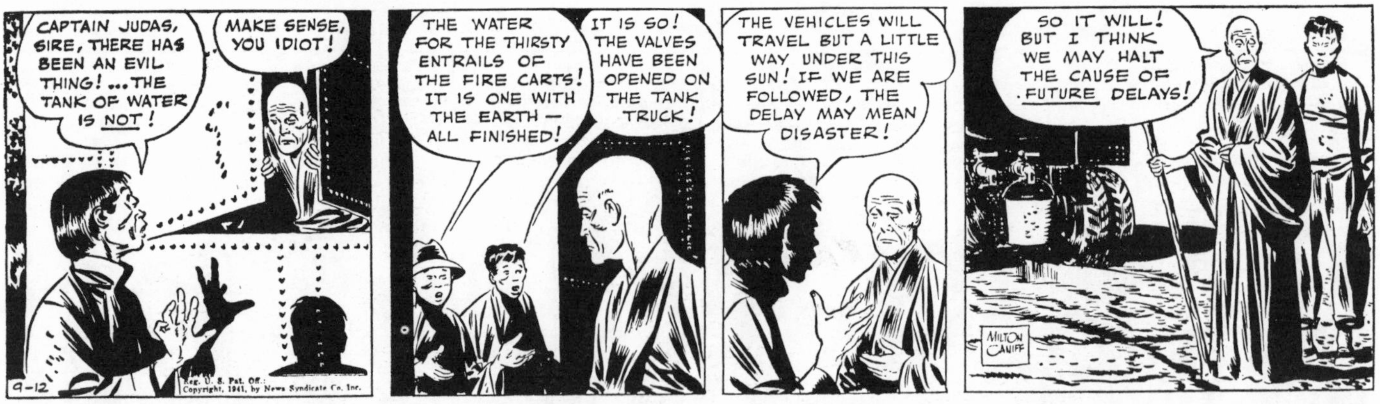
CAPTAIN JUDAS, SIRE, THERE HAS BEEN AN EVIL THING!...THE TANK OF WATER IS NOT!
MAKE SENSE, YOU IDIOT!
9-12
Reg. U. S. Pat. Off.: Copyright, 1941, by News Syndicate Co. Inc.
THE WATER FOR THE THIRSTY ENTRAILS OF THE FIRE CARTS! IT IS ONE WITH THE EARTH — ALL FINISHED!
IT IS SO! THE VALVES HAVE BEEN OPENED ON THE TANK TRUCK!
THE VEHICLES WILL TRAVEL BUT A LITTLE WAY UNDER THIS SUN! IF WE ARE FOLLOWED, THE DELAY MAY MEAN DISASTER!
SO IT WILL! BUT I THINK WE MAY HALT THE CAUSE OF FUTURE DELAYS!
MILTON CANIFF

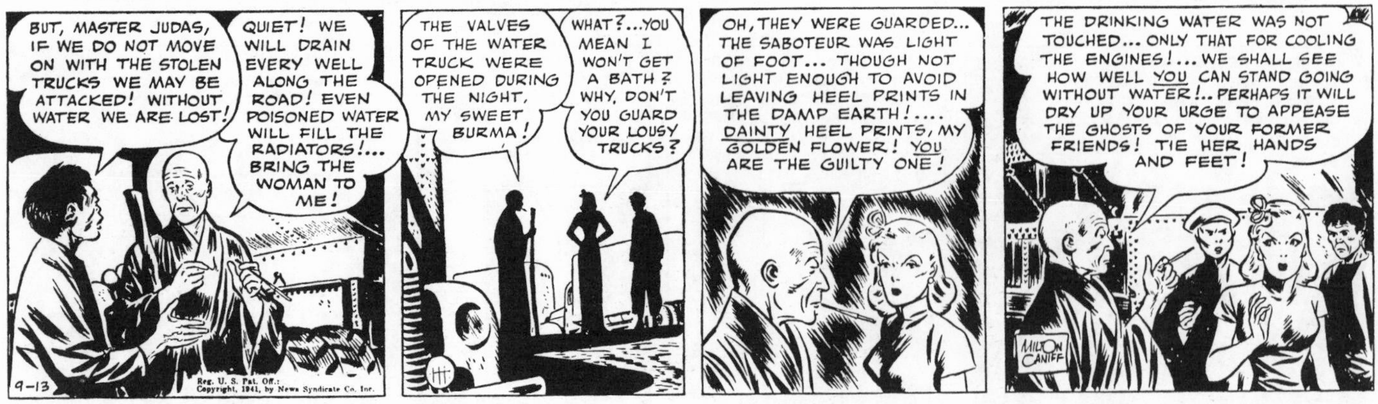
BUT, MASTER JUDAS, IF WE DO NOT MOVE ON WITH THE STOLEN TRUCKS WE MAY BE ATTACKED! WITHOUT WATER WE ARE LOST!
QUIET! WE WILL DRAIN EVERY WELL ALONG THE ROAD! EVEN POISONED WATER WILL FILL THE RADIATORS!... BRING THE WOMAN TO ME!
9-13
Reg. U. S. Pat. Off.: Copyright, 1941, by News Syndicate Co. Inc.
THE VALVES OF THE WATER TRUCK WERE OPENED DURING THE NIGHT, MY SWEET BURMA!
WHAT?...YOU MEAN I WON'T GET A BATH? WHY, DON'T YOU GUARD YOUR LOUSY TRUCKS?
OH, THEY WERE GUARDED... THE SABOTEUR WAS LIGHT OF FOOT... THOUGH NOT LIGHT ENOUGH TO AVOID LEAVING HEEL PRINTS IN THE DAMP EARTH!.... DAINTY HEEL PRINTS, MY GOLDEN FLOWER! YOU ARE THE GUILTY ONE!
THE DRINKING WATER WAS NOT TOUCHED... ONLY THAT FOR COOLING THE ENGINES!... WE SHALL SEE HOW WELL YOU CAN STAND GOING WITHOUT WATER!.. PERHAPS IT WILL DRY UP YOUR URGE TO APPEASE THE GHOSTS OF YOUR FORMER FRIENDS! TIE HER HANDS AND FEET!
MILTON CANIFF

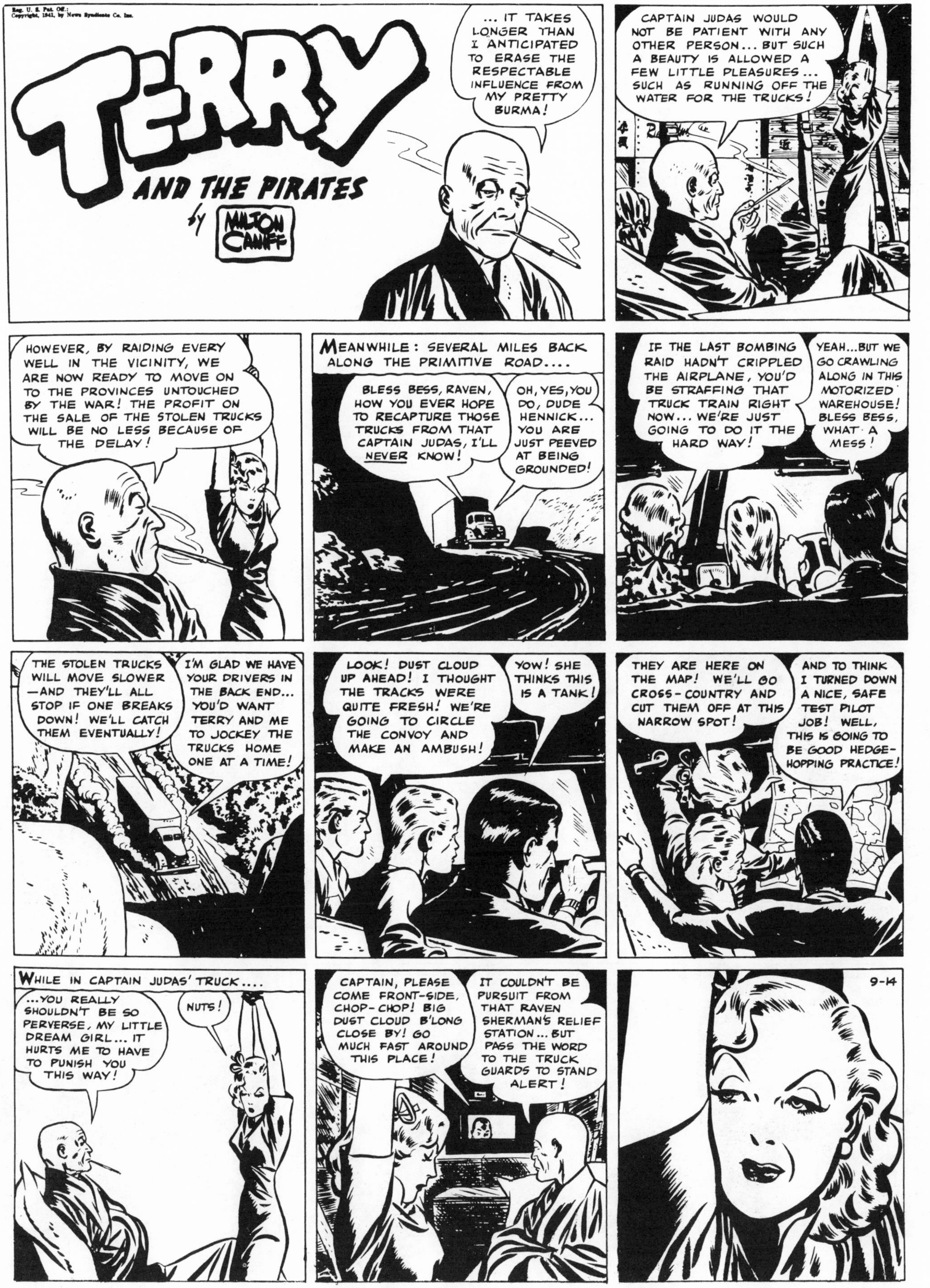

Reg. U. S. Pat. Off.: Copyright, 1941, by News Syndicate Co. Inc.
TERRY AND THE PIRATES
by MILTON CANIFF
... IT TAKES LONGER THAN I ANTICIPATED TO ERASE THE RESPECTABLE INFLUENCE FROM MY PRETTY BURMA!
CAPTAIN JUDAS WOULD NOT BE PATIENT WITH ANY OTHER PERSON... BUT SUCH A BEAUTY IS ALLOWED A FEW LITTLE PLEASURES... SUCH AS RUNNING OFF THE WATER FOR THE TRUCKS!
HOWEVER, BY RAIDING EVERY WELL IN THE VICINITY, WE ARE NOW READY TO MOVE ON TO THE PROVINCES UNTOUCHED BY THE WAR! THE PROFIT ON THE SALE OF THE STOLEN TRUCKS WILL BE NO LESS BECAUSE OF THE DELAY!
MEANWHILE: SEVERAL MILES BACK ALONG THE PRIMITIVE ROAD....
BLESS BESS, RAVEN, HOW YOU EVER HOPE TO RECAPTURE THOSE TRUCKS FROM THAT CAPTAIN JUDAS, I'LL NEVER KNOW!
OH, YES, YOU DO, DUDE HENNICK... YOU ARE JUST PEEVED AT BEING GROUNDED!
IF THE LAST BOMBING RAID HADN'T CRIPPLED THE AIRPLANE, YOU'D BE STRAFFING THAT TRUCK TRAIN RIGHT NOW... WE'RE JUST GOING TO DO IT THE HARD WAY!
YEAH...BUT WE GO CRAWLING ALONG IN THIS MOTORIZED WAREHOUSE! BLESS BESS, WHAT A MESS!
THE STOLEN TRUCKS WILL MOVE SLOWER —AND THEY'LL ALL STOP IF ONE BREAKS DOWN! WE'LL CATCH THEM EVENTUALLY!
I'M GLAD WE HAVE YOUR DRIVERS IN THE BACK END... YOU'D WANT TERRY AND ME TO JOCKEY THE TRUCKS HOME ONE AT A TIME!
LOOK! DUST CLOUD UP AHEAD! I THOUGHT THE TRACKS WERE QUITE FRESH! WE'RE GOING TO CIRCLE THE CONVOY AND MAKE AN AMBUSH!
YOW! SHE THINKS THIS IS A TANK!
THEY ARE HERE ON THE MAP! WE'LL GO CROSS-COUNTRY AND CUT THEM OFF AT THIS NARROW SPOT!
AND TO THINK I TURNED DOWN A NICE, SAFE TEST PILOT JOB! WELL, THIS IS GOING TO BE GOOD HEDGE-HOPPING PRACTICE!
WHILE IN CAPTAIN JUDAS' TRUCK....
...YOU REALLY SHOULDN'T BE SO PERVERSE, MY LITTLE DREAM GIRL... IT HURTS ME TO HAVE TO PUNISH YOU THIS WAY!
NUTS!
CAPTAIN, PLEASE COME FRONT-SIDE, CHOP-CHOP! BIG DUST CLOUD B'LONG CLOSE BY! GO MUCH FAST AROUND THIS PLACE!
IT COULDN'T BE PURSUIT FROM THAT RAVEN SHERMAN'S RELIEF STATION... BUT PASS THE WORD TO THE TRUCK GUARDS TO STAND ALERT!
9-14

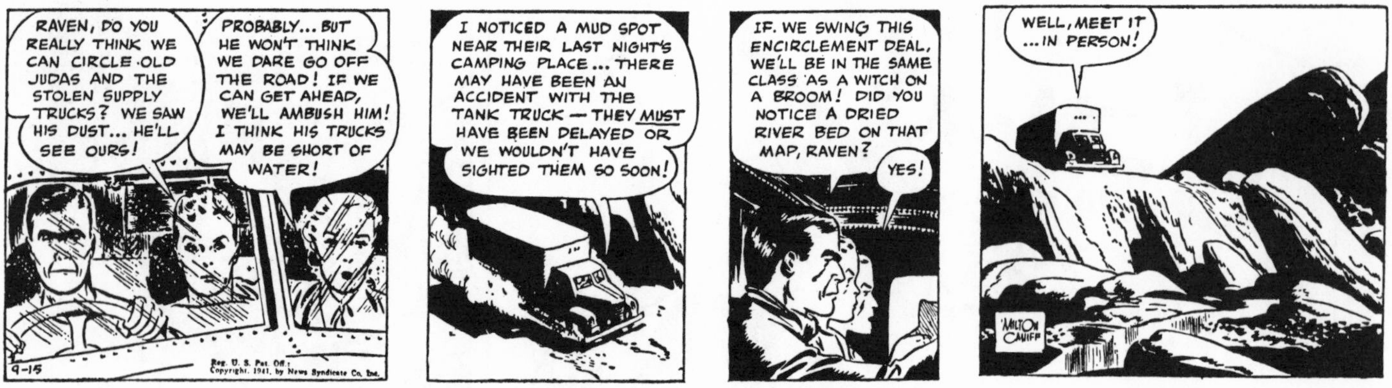
RAVEN, DO YOU REALLY THINK WE CAN CIRCLE OLD JUDAS AND THE STOLEN SUPPLY TRUCKS? WE SAW HIS DUST... HE'LL SEE OURS!
PROBABLY... BUT HE WON'T THINK WE DARE GO OFF THE ROAD! IF WE CAN GET AHEAD, WE'LL AMBUSH HIM! I THINK HIS TRUCKS MAY BE SHORT OF WATER!
9-15
Reg. U. S. Pat. Off.: Copyright, 1941, by News Syndicate Co. Inc.
I NOTICED A MUD SPOT NEAR THEIR LAST NIGHT'S CAMPING PLACE... THERE MAY HAVE BEEN AN ACCIDENT WITH THE TANK TRUCK — THEY MUST HAVE BEEN DELAYED OR WE WOULDN'T HAVE SIGHTED THEM SO SOON!
IF WE SWING THIS ENCIRCLEMENT DEAL, WE'LL BE IN THE SAME CLASS AS A WITCH ON A BROOM! DID YOU NOTICE A DRIED RIVER BED ON THAT MAP, RAVEN?
YES!
WELL, MEET IT ...IN PERSON!
MILTON CANIFF
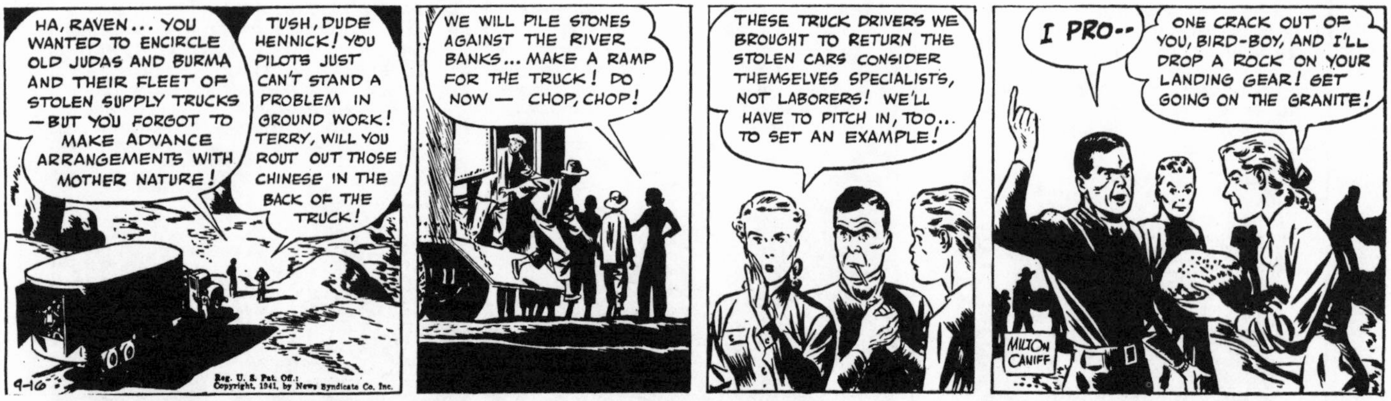
HA, RAVEN... YOU WANTED TO ENCIRCLE OLD JUDAS AND BURMA AND THEIR FLEET OF STOLEN SUPPLY TRUCKS — BUT YOU FORGOT TO MAKE ADVANCE ARRANGEMENTS WITH MOTHER NATURE!
TUSH, DUDE HENNICK! YOU PILOTS JUST CAN'T STAND A PROBLEM IN GROUND WORK! TERRY, WILL YOU ROUT OUT THOSE CHINESE IN THE BACK OF THE TRUCK!
9-16
Reg. U. S. Pat. Off.: Copyright, 1941, by News Syndicate Co. Inc.
WE WILL PILE STONES AGAINST THE RIVER BANKS... MAKE A RAMP FOR THE TRUCK! DO NOW — CHOP, CHOP!
THESE TRUCK DRIVERS WE BROUGHT TO RETURN THE STOLEN CARS CONSIDER THEMSELVES SPECIALISTS, NOT LABORERS! WE'LL HAVE TO PITCH IN, TOO... TO SET AN EXAMPLE!
I PRO--
ONE CRACK OUT OF YOU, BIRD-BOY, AND I'LL DROP A ROCK ON YOUR LANDING GEAR! GET GOING ON THE GRANITE!
MILTON CANIFF
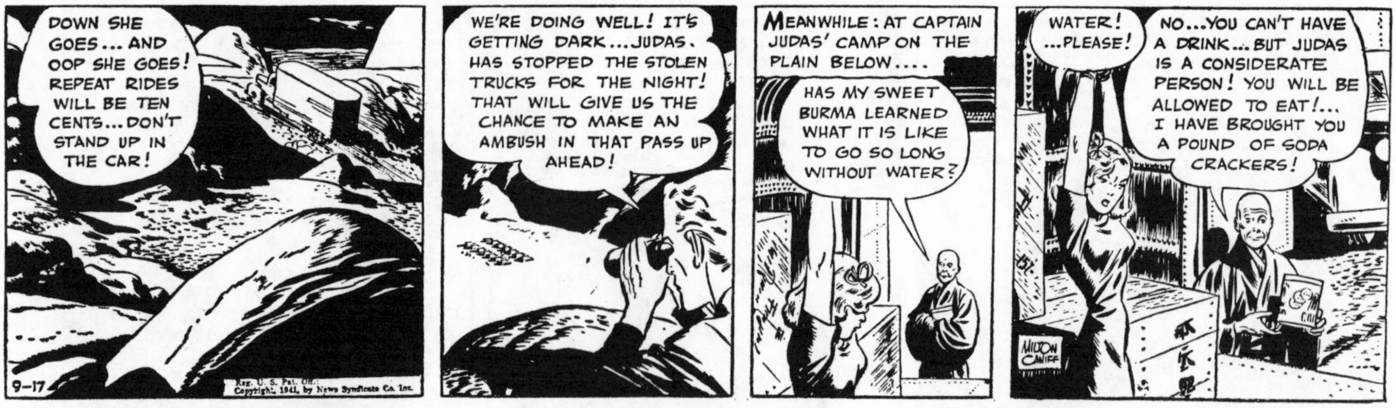
DOWN SHE GOES... AND OOP SHE GOES! REPEAT RIDES WILL BE TEN CENTS... DON'T STAND UP IN THE CAR!
9-17
Reg. U. S. Pat. Off.: Copyright, 1941, by News Syndicate Co. Inc.
WE'RE DOING WELL! IT'S GETTING DARK... JUDAS HAS STOPPED THE STOLEN TRUCKS FOR THE NIGHT! THAT WILL GIVE US THE CHANCE TO MAKE AN AMBUSH IN THAT PASS UP AHEAD!
MEANWHILE: AT CAPTAIN JUDAS' CAMP ON THE PLAIN BELOW....
HAS MY SWEET BURMA LEARNED WHAT IT IS LIKE TO GO SO LONG WITHOUT WATER?
WATER! ...PLEASE!
NO...YOU CAN'T HAVE A DRINK... BUT JUDAS IS A CONSIDERATE PERSON! YOU WILL BE ALLOWED TO EAT!... I HAVE BROUGHT YOU A POUND OF SODA CRACKERS!
MILTON CANIFF
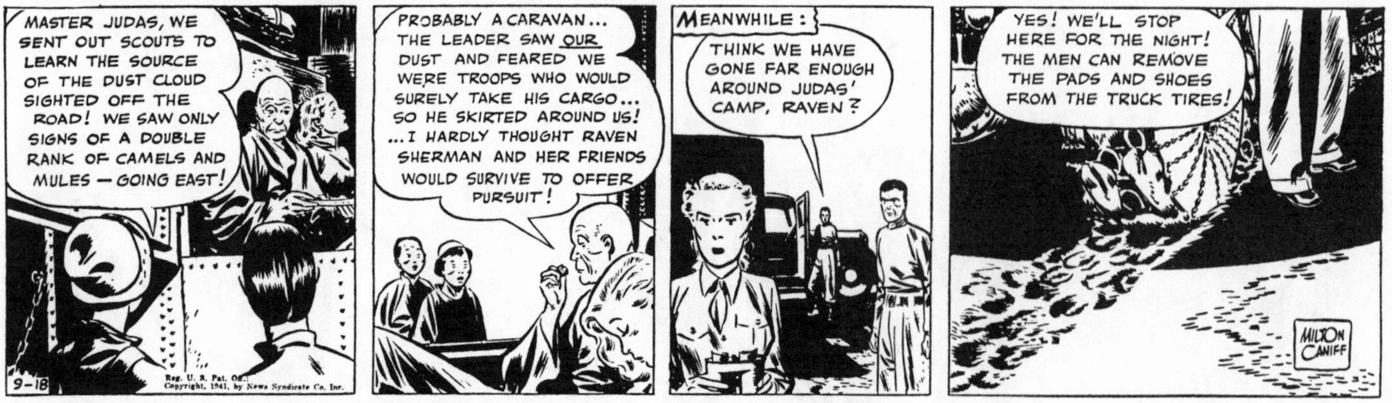
MASTER JUDAS, WE SENT OUT SCOUTS TO LEARN THE SOURCE OF THE DUST CLOUD SIGHTED OFF THE ROAD! WE SAW ONLY SIGNS OF A DOUBLE RANK OF CAMELS AND MULES — GOING EAST!
9-18
Reg. U. S. Pat. Off.: Copyright, 1941, by News Syndicate Co. Inc.
PROBABLY A CARAVAN... THE LEADER SAW OUR DUST AND FEARED WE WERE TROOPS WHO WOULD SURELY TAKE HIS CARGO... SO HE SKIRTED AROUND US! ...I HARDLY THOUGHT RAVEN SHERMAN AND HER FRIENDS WOULD SURVIVE TO OFFER PURSUIT!
MEANWHILE:
THINK WE HAVE GONE FAR ENOUGH AROUND JUDAS' CAMP, RAVEN?
YES! WE'LL STOP HERE FOR THE NIGHT! THE MEN CAN REMOVE THE PADS AND SHOES FROM THE TRUCK TIRES!
MILTON CANIFF

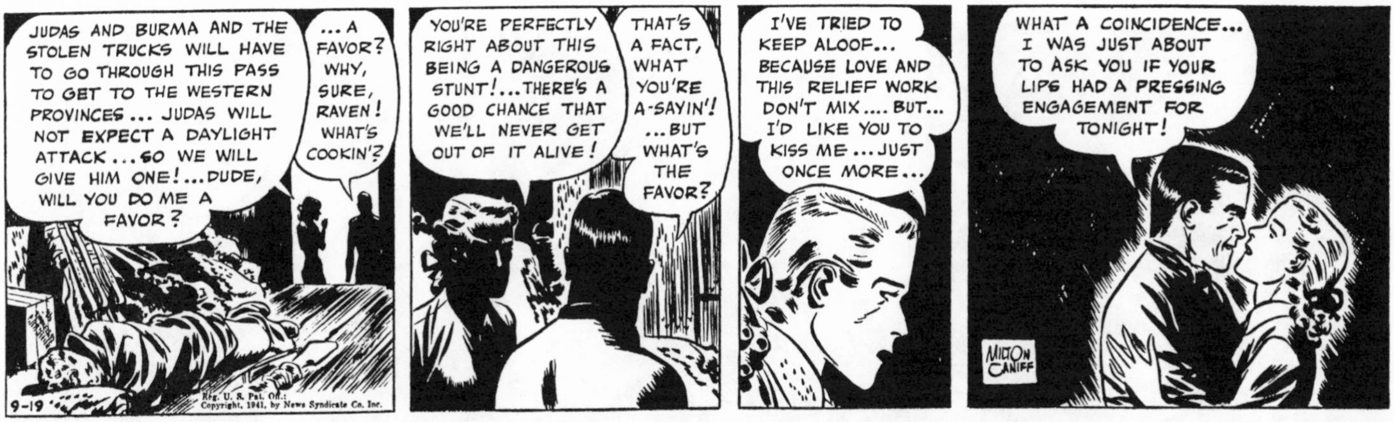
JUDAS AND BURMA AND THE STOLEN TRUCKS WILL HAVE TO GO THROUGH THIS PASS TO GET TO THE WESTERN PROVINCES ... JUDAS WILL NOT EXPECT A DAYLIGHT ATTACK ... SO WE WILL GIVE HIM ONE! ... DUDE, WILL YOU DO ME A FAVOR?
... A FAVOR? WHY, SURE, RAVEN! WHAT'S COOKIN'?
YOU'RE PERFECTLY RIGHT ABOUT THIS BEING A DANGEROUS STUNT! ... THERE'S A GOOD CHANCE THAT WE'LL NEVER GET OUT OF IT ALIVE!
THAT'S A FACT, WHAT YOU'RE A-SAYIN'! ... BUT WHAT'S THE FAVOR?
I'VE TRIED TO KEEP ALOOF ... BECAUSE LOVE AND THIS RELIEF WORK DON'T MIX .... BUT ... I'D LIKE YOU TO KISS ME ... JUST ONCE MORE ...
WHAT A COINCIDENCE ... I WAS JUST ABOUT TO ASK YOU IF YOUR LIPS HAD A PRESSING ENGAGEMENT FOR TONIGHT!
9-19
Reg. U. S. Pat. Off.: Copyright, 1941, by News Syndicate Co. Inc.
MILTON CANIFF

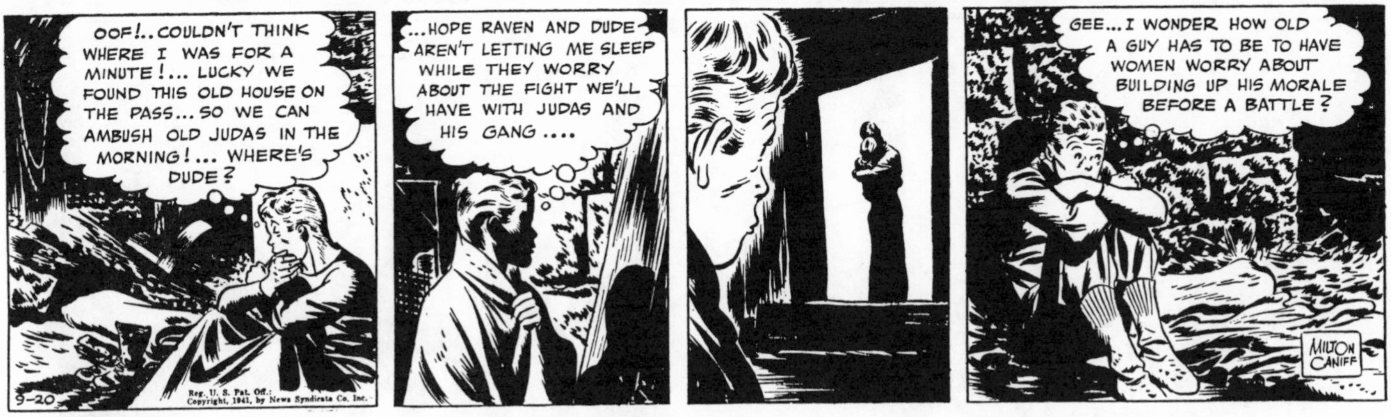
OOF! .. COULDN'T THINK WHERE I WAS FOR A MINUTE! ... LUCKY WE FOUND THIS OLD HOUSE ON THE PASS ... SO WE CAN AMBUSH OLD JUDAS IN THE MORNING! ... WHERE'S DUDE?
... HOPE RAVEN AND DUDE AREN'T LETTING ME SLEEP WHILE THEY WORRY ABOUT THE FIGHT WE'LL HAVE WITH JUDAS AND HIS GANG ....
GEE ... I WONDER HOW OLD A GUY HAS TO BE TO HAVE WOMEN WORRY ABOUT BUILDING UP HIS MORALE BEFORE A BATTLE?
9-20
Reg. U. S. Pat. Off.: Copyright, 1941, by News Syndicate Co. Inc.
MILTON CANIFF

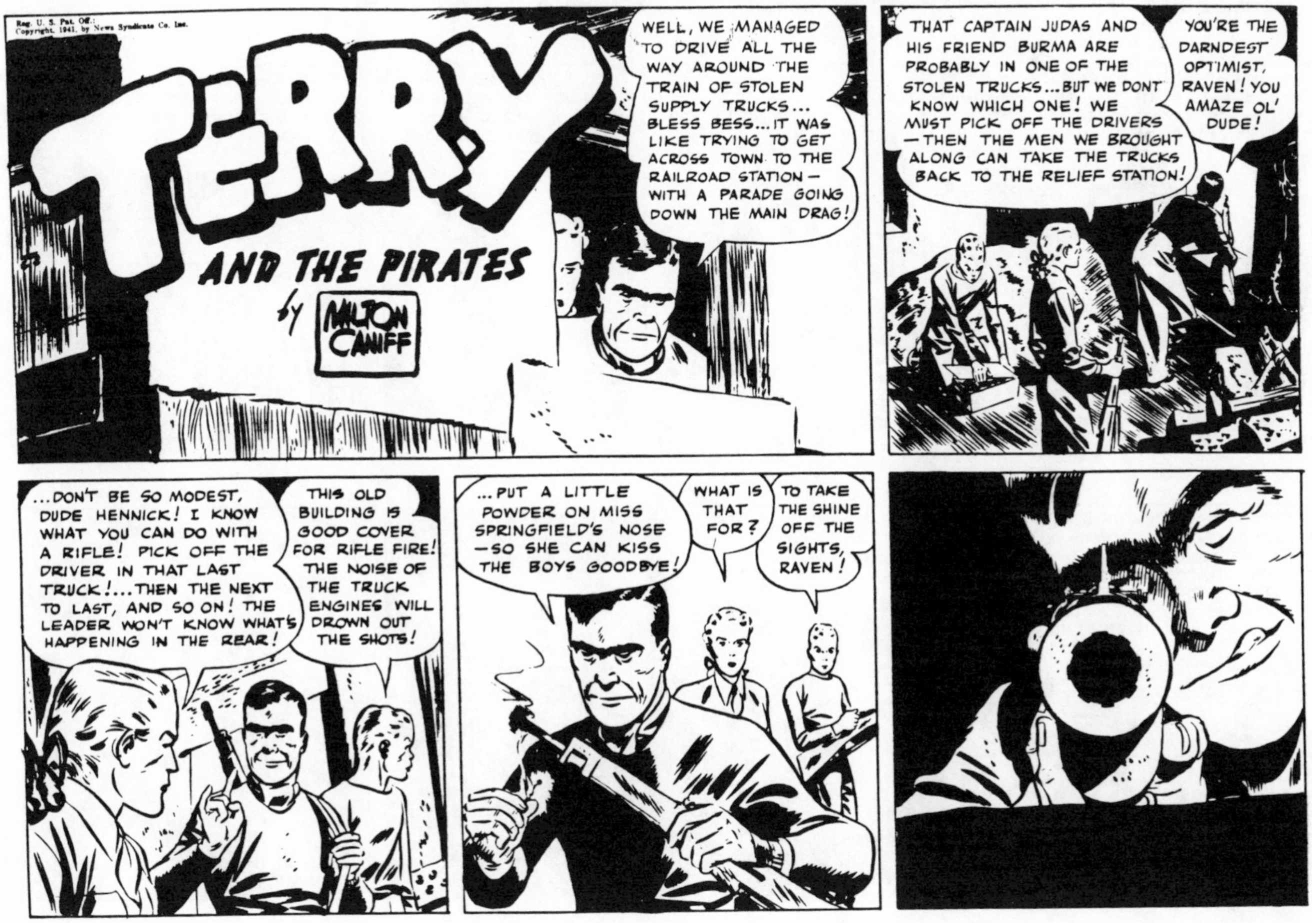
Reg. U. S. Pat. Off.: Copyright, 1941, by News Syndicate Co. Inc.
TERRY AND THE PIRATES by MILTON CANIFF
WELL, WE MANAGED TO DRIVE ALL THE WAY AROUND THE TRAIN OF STOLEN SUPPLY TRUCKS ... BLESS BESS ... IT WAS LIKE TRYING TO GET ACROSS TOWN TO THE RAILROAD STATION — WITH A PARADE GOING DOWN THE MAIN DRAG!
THAT CAPTAIN JUDAS AND HIS FRIEND BURMA ARE PROBABLY IN ONE OF THE STOLEN TRUCKS ... BUT WE DONT KNOW WHICH ONE! WE MUST PICK OFF THE DRIVERS — THEN THE MEN WE BROUGHT ALONG CAN TAKE THE TRUCKS BACK TO THE RELIEF STATION!
YOU'RE THE DARNDEST OPTIMIST, RAVEN! YOU AMAZE OL' DUDE!
... DON'T BE SO MODEST, DUDE HENNICK! I KNOW WHAT YOU CAN DO WITH A RIFLE! PICK OFF THE DRIVER IN THAT LAST TRUCK! ... THEN THE NEXT TO LAST, AND SO ON! THE LEADER WON'T KNOW WHAT'S HAPPENING IN THE REAR!
THIS OLD BUILDING IS GOOD COVER FOR RIFLE FIRE! THE NOISE OF THE TRUCK ENGINES WILL DROWN OUT THE SHOTS!
... PUT A LITTLE POWDER ON MISS SPRINGFIELD'S NOSE — SO SHE CAN KISS THE BOYS GOODBYE!
WHAT IS THAT FOR?
TO TAKE THE SHINE OFF THE SIGHTS, RAVEN!

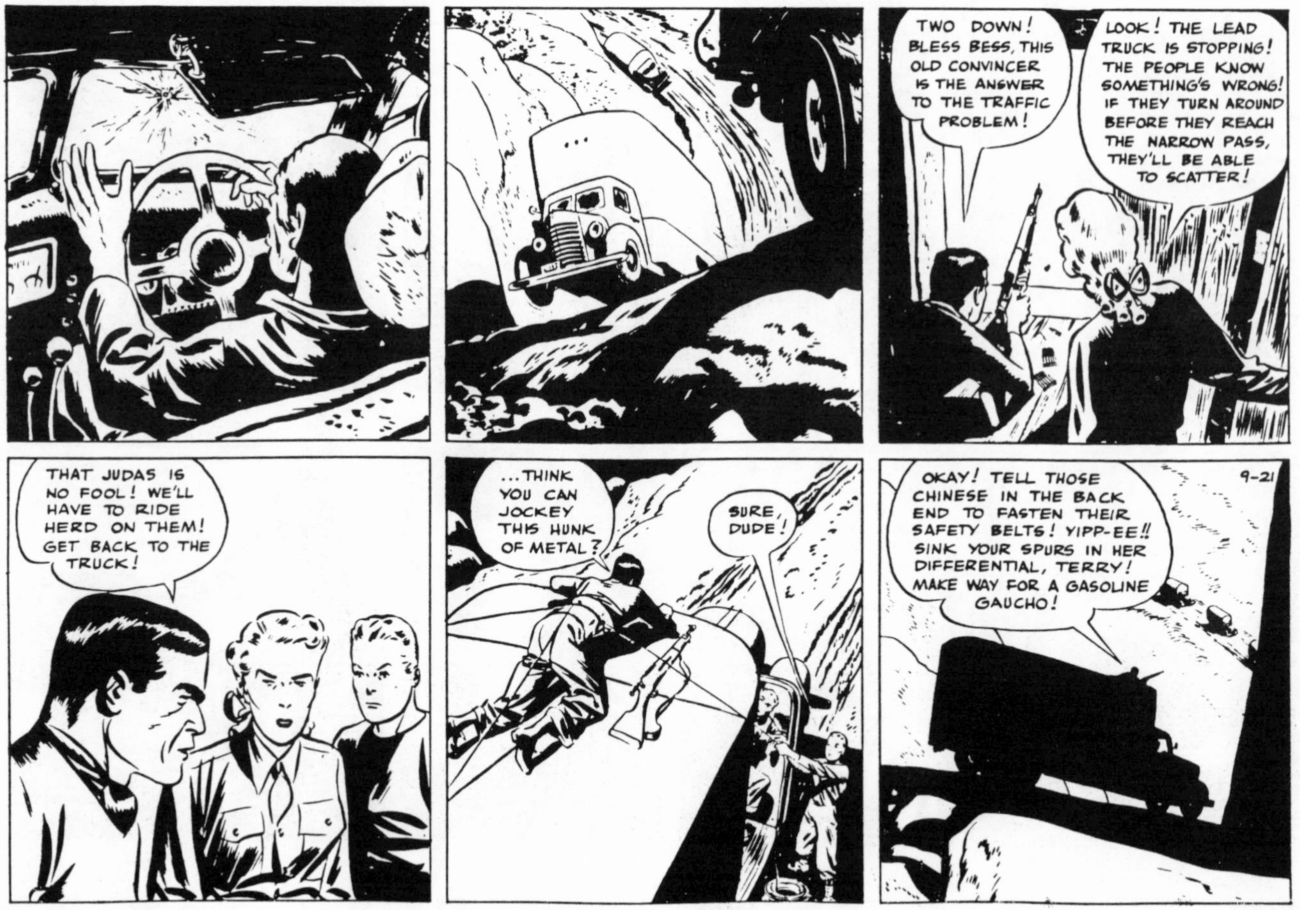
TWO DOWN! BLESS BESS, THIS OLD CONVINCER IS THE ANSWER TO THE TRAFFIC PROBLEM!
LOOK! THE LEAD TRUCK IS STOPPING! THE PEOPLE KNOW SOMETHING'S WRONG! IF THEY TURN AROUND BEFORE THEY REACH THE NARROW PASS, THEY'LL BE ABLE TO SCATTER!
THAT JUDAS IS NO FOOL! WE'LL HAVE TO RIDE HERD ON THEM! GET BACK TO THE TRUCK!
...THINK YOU CAN JOCKEY THIS HUNK OF METAL?
SURE, DUDE!
9-21
OKAY! TELL THOSE CHINESE IN THE BACK END TO FASTEN THEIR SAFETY BELTS! YIPP-EE!! SINK YOUR SPURS IN HER DIFFERENTIAL, TERRY! MAKE WAY FOR A GASOLINE GAUCHO!

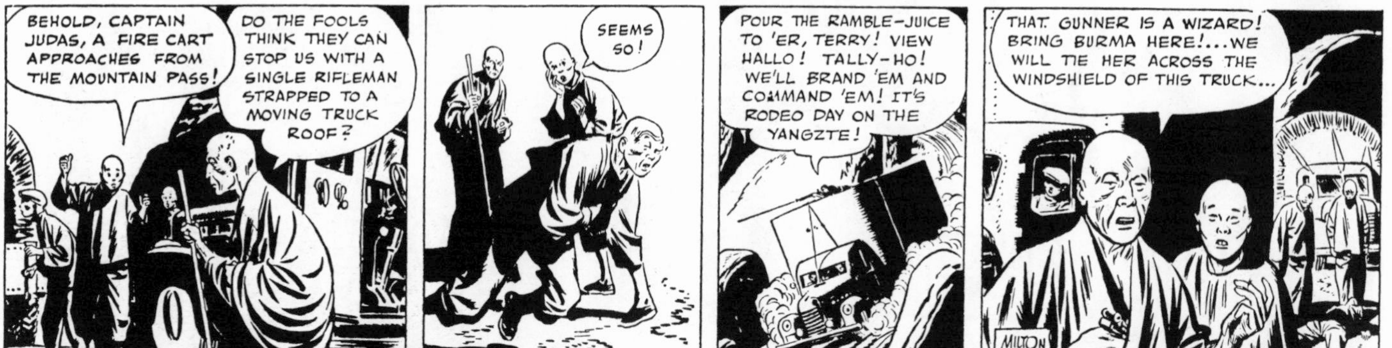
BEHOLD, CAPTAIN JUDAS, A FIRE CART APPROACHES FROM THE MOUNTAIN PASS!
DO THE FOOLS THINK THEY CAN STOP US WITH A SINGLE RIFLEMAN STRAPPED TO A MOVING TRUCK ROOF?
9-22
SEEMS SO!
Reg. U. S. Pat. Off.: Copyright, 1941, by News Syndicate Co. Inc.
POUR THE RAMBLE-JUICE TO 'ER, TERRY! VIEW HALLO! TALLY-HO! WE'LL BRAND 'EM AND COMMAND 'EM! IT'S RODEO DAY ON THE YANGZTE!
THAT GUNNER IS A WIZARD! BRING BURMA HERE!...WE WILL TIE HER ACROSS THE WINDSHIELD OF THIS TRUCK...
MILTON CANIFF

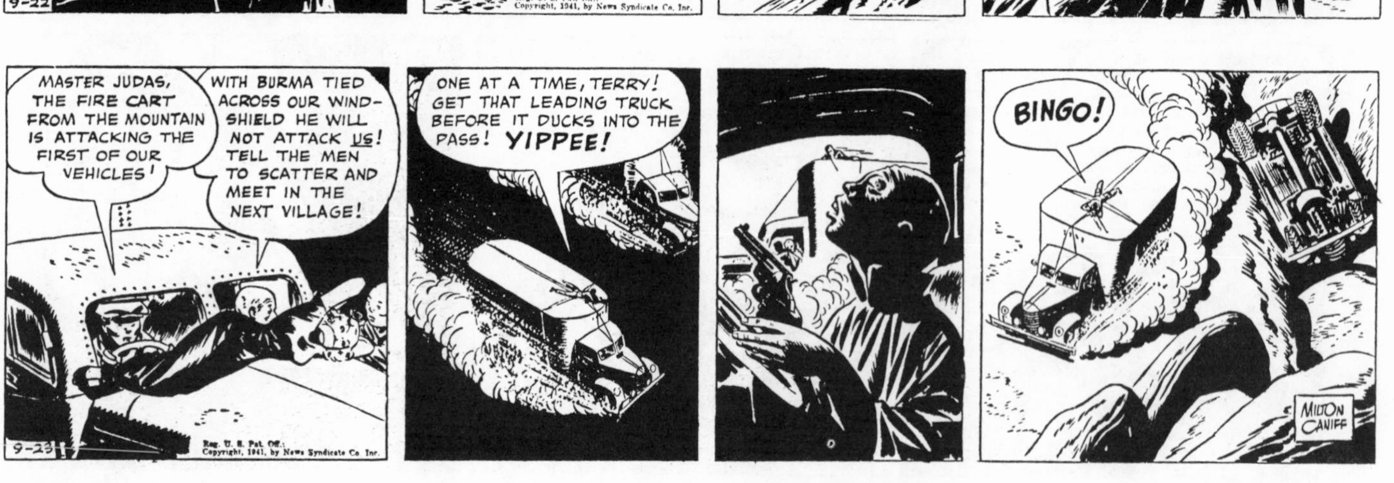
MASTER JUDAS, THE FIRE CART FROM THE MOUNTAIN IS ATTACKING THE FIRST OF OUR VEHICLES!
WITH BURMA TIED ACROSS OUR WINDSHIELD HE WILL NOT ATTACK US! TELL THE MEN TO SCATTER AND MEET IN THE NEXT VILLAGE!
9-23
Reg. U. S. Pat. Off.: Copyright, 1941, by News Syndicate Co. Inc.
ONE AT A TIME, TERRY! GET THAT LEADING TRUCK BEFORE IT DUCKS INTO THE PASS! YIPPEE!
BINGO!
MILTON CANIFF

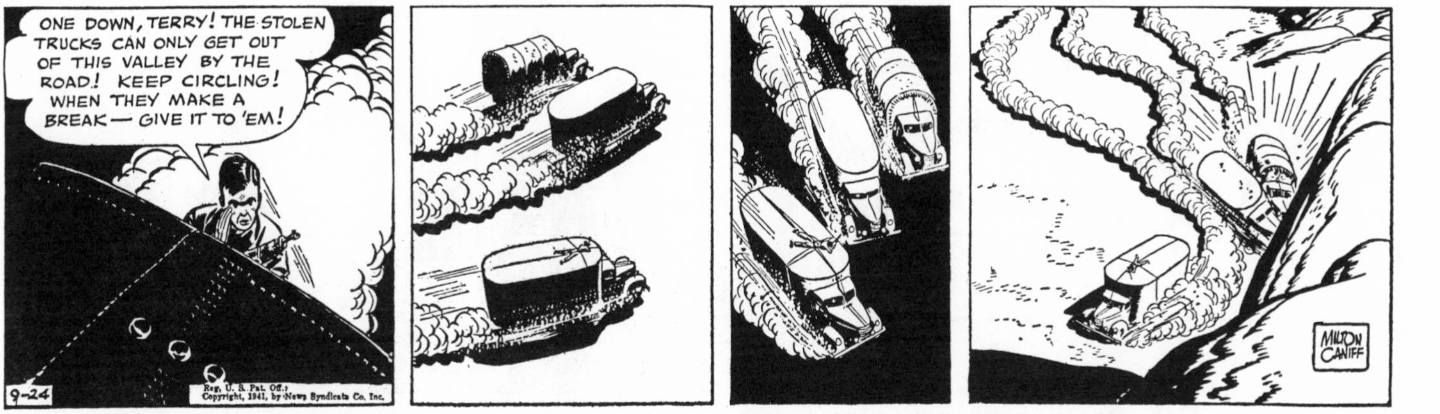
ONE DOWN, TERRY! THE STOLEN TRUCKS CAN ONLY GET OUT OF THIS VALLEY BY THE ROAD! KEEP CIRCLING! WHEN THEY MAKE A BREAK — GIVE IT TO 'EM!
9-24
Reg. U. S. Pat. Off.; Copyright, 1941, by News Syndicate Co. Inc.
MILTON CANIFF

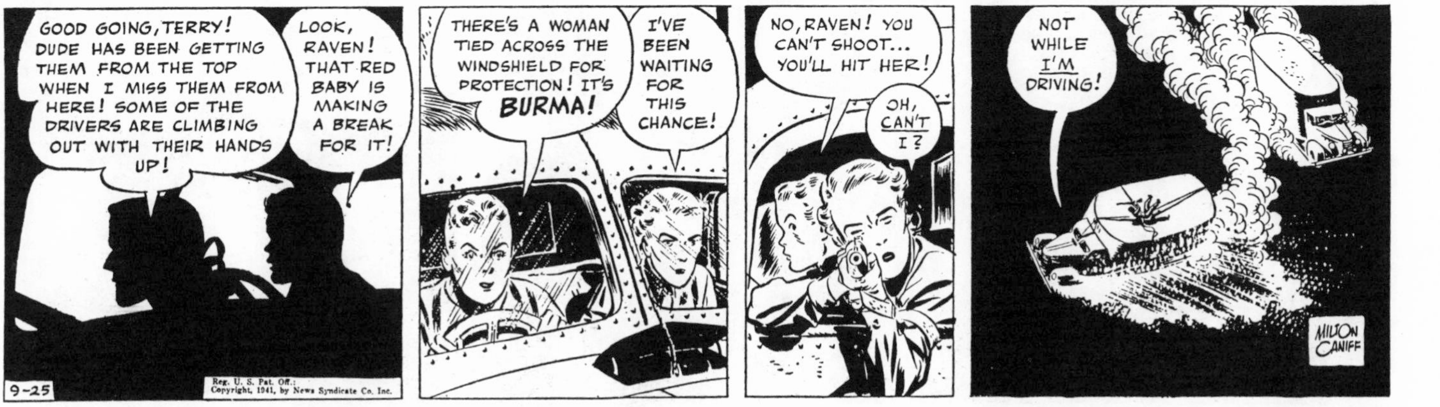
GOOD GOING, TERRY! DUDE HAS BEEN GETTING THEM FROM THE TOP WHEN I MISS THEM FROM HERE! SOME OF THE DRIVERS ARE CLIMBING OUT WITH THEIR HANDS UP!
LOOK, RAVEN! THAT RED BABY IS MAKING A BREAK FOR IT!
9-25
Reg. U. S. Pat. Off.; Copyright, 1941, by News Syndicate Co. Inc.
THERE'S A WOMAN TIED ACROSS THE WINDSHIELD FOR PROTECTION! IT'S BURMA!
I'VE BEEN WAITING FOR THIS CHANCE!
NO, RAVEN! YOU CAN'T SHOOT... YOU'LL HIT HER!
OH, CAN'T I?
NOT WHILE I'M DRIVING!
MILTON CANIFF

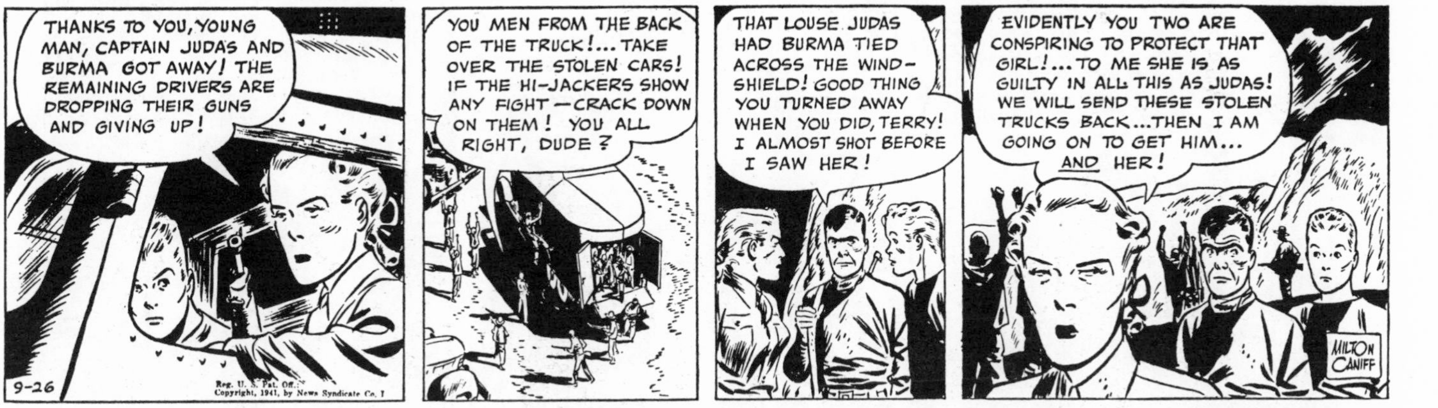
THANKS TO YOU, YOUNG MAN, CAPTAIN JUDAS AND BURMA GOT AWAY! THE REMAINING DRIVERS ARE DROPPING THEIR GUNS AND GIVING UP!
9-26
Reg. U. S. Pat. Off.; Copyright, 1941, by News Syndicate Co. I
YOU MEN FROM THE BACK OF THE TRUCK!... TAKE OVER THE STOLEN CARS! IF THE HI-JACKERS SHOW ANY FIGHT — CRACK DOWN ON THEM! YOU ALL RIGHT, DUDE?
THAT LOUSE JUDAS HAD BURMA TIED ACROSS THE WIND-SHIELD! GOOD THING YOU TURNED AWAY WHEN YOU DID, TERRY! I ALMOST SHOT BEFORE I SAW HER!
EVIDENTLY YOU TWO ARE CONSPIRING TO PROTECT THAT GIRL!... TO ME SHE IS AS GUILTY IN ALL THIS AS JUDAS! WE WILL SEND THESE STOLEN TRUCKS BACK... THEN I AM GOING ON TO GET HIM... AND HER!
MILTON CANIFF

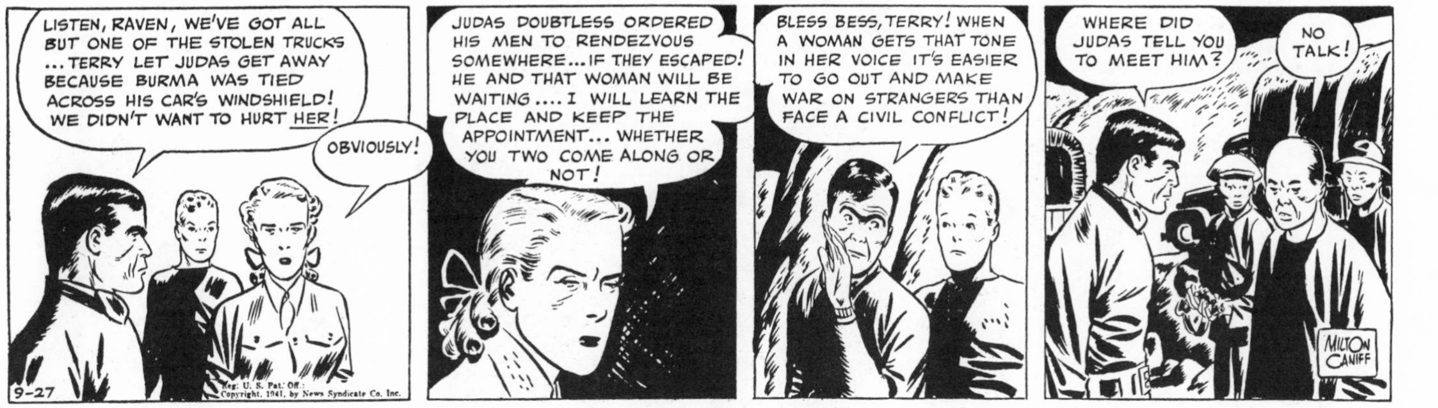
LISTEN, RAVEN, WE'VE GOT ALL BUT ONE OF THE STOLEN TRUCKS ... TERRY LET JUDAS GET AWAY BECAUSE BURMA WAS TIED ACROSS HIS CAR'S WINDSHIELD! WE DIDN'T WANT TO HURT HER!
OBVIOUSLY!
9-27
Reg. U. S. Pat. Off.; Copyright, 1941, by News Syndicate Co. Inc.
JUDAS DOUBTLESS ORDERED HIS MEN TO RENDEZVOUS SOMEWHERE... IF THEY ESCAPED! HE AND THAT WOMAN WILL BE WAITING.... I WILL LEARN THE PLACE AND KEEP THE APPOINTMENT... WHETHER YOU TWO COME ALONG OR NOT!
BLESS BESS, TERRY! WHEN A WOMAN GETS THAT TONE IN HER VOICE IT'S EASIER TO GO OUT AND MAKE WAR ON STRANGERS THAN FACE A CIVIL CONFLICT!
WHERE DID JUDAS TELL YOU TO MEET HIM?
NO TALK!
MILTON CANIFF

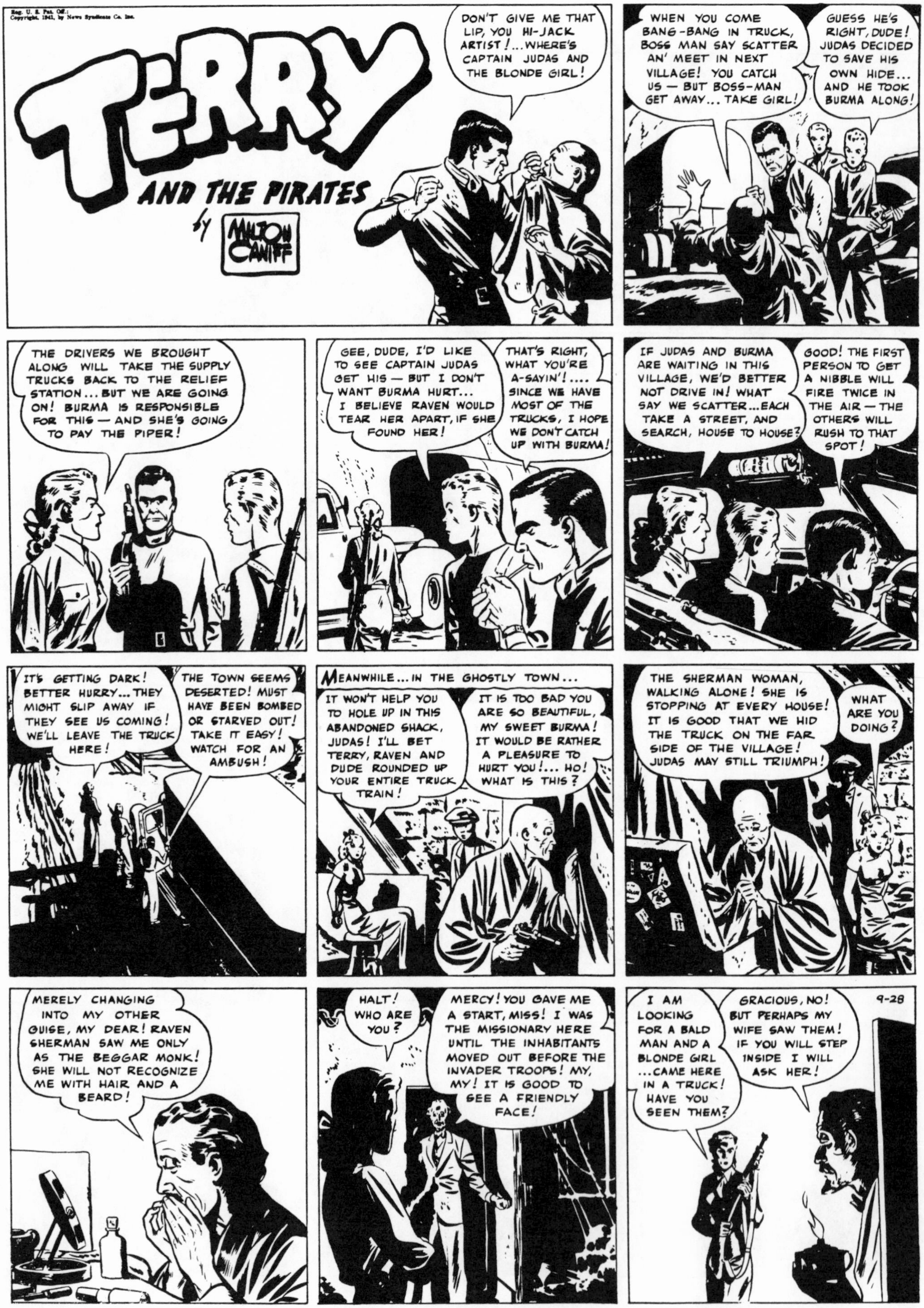
Reg. U. S. Pat. Off.;
Copyright, 1941, by News Syndicate Co. Inc.
TERRY AND THE PIRATES
by MILTON CANIFF
DON'T GIVE ME THAT LIP, YOU HI-JACK ARTIST! ... WHERE'S CAPTAIN JUDAS AND THE BLONDE GIRL!
WHEN YOU COME BANG-BANG IN TRUCK, BOSS MAN SAY SCATTER AN' MEET IN NEXT VILLAGE! YOU CATCH US — BUT BOSS-MAN GET AWAY... TAKE GIRL!
GUESS HE'S RIGHT, DUDE! JUDAS DECIDED TO SAVE HIS OWN HIDE... AND HE TOOK BURMA ALONG!
THE DRIVERS WE BROUGHT ALONG WILL TAKE THE SUPPLY TRUCKS BACK TO THE RELIEF STATION... BUT WE ARE GOING ON! BURMA IS RESPONSIBLE FOR THIS — AND SHE'S GOING TO PAY THE PIPER!
GEE, DUDE, I'D LIKE TO SEE CAPTAIN JUDAS GET HIS — BUT I DON'T WANT BURMA HURT... I BELIEVE RAVEN WOULD TEAR HER APART, IF SHE FOUND HER!
THAT'S RIGHT, WHAT YOU'RE A-SAYIN'! .... SINCE WE HAVE MOST OF THE TRUCKS, I HOPE WE DON'T CATCH UP WITH BURMA!
IF JUDAS AND BURMA ARE WAITING IN THIS VILLAGE, WE'D BETTER NOT DRIVE IN! WHAT SAY WE SCATTER... EACH TAKE A STREET, AND SEARCH, HOUSE TO HOUSE?
GOOD! THE FIRST PERSON TO GET A NIBBLE WILL FIRE TWICE IN THE AIR — THE OTHERS WILL RUSH TO THAT SPOT!
IT'S GETTING DARK! BETTER HURRY... THEY MIGHT SLIP AWAY IF THEY SEE US COMING! WE'LL LEAVE THE TRUCK HERE!
THE TOWN SEEMS DESERTED! MUST HAVE BEEN BOMBED OR STARVED OUT! TAKE IT EASY! WATCH FOR AN AMBUSH!
MEANWHILE... IN THE GHOSTLY TOWN...
IT WON'T HELP YOU TO HOLE UP IN THIS ABANDONED SHACK, JUDAS! I'LL BET TERRY, RAVEN AND DUDE ROUNDED UP YOUR ENTIRE TRUCK TRAIN!
IT IS TOO BAD YOU ARE SO BEAUTIFUL, MY SWEET BURMA! IT WOULD BE RATHER A PLEASURE TO HURT YOU! ... HO! WHAT IS THIS?
THE SHERMAN WOMAN, WALKING ALONE! SHE IS STOPPING AT EVERY HOUSE! IT IS GOOD THAT WE HID THE TRUCK ON THE FAR SIDE OF THE VILLAGE! JUDAS MAY STILL TRIUMPH!
WHAT ARE YOU DOING?
MERELY CHANGING INTO MY OTHER GUISE, MY DEAR! RAVEN SHERMAN SAW ME ONLY AS THE BEGGAR MONK! SHE WILL NOT RECOGNIZE ME WITH HAIR AND A BEARD!
HALT! WHO ARE YOU?
MERCY! YOU GAVE ME A START, MISS! I WAS THE MISSIONARY HERE UNTIL THE INHABITANTS MOVED OUT BEFORE THE INVADER TROOPS! MY, MY! IT IS GOOD TO SEE A FRIENDLY FACE!
9-28
I AM LOOKING FOR A BALD MAN AND A BLONDE GIRL ...CAME HERE IN A TRUCK! HAVE YOU SEEN THEM?
GRACIOUS, NO! BUT PERHAPS MY WIFE SAW THEM! IF YOU WILL STEP INSIDE I WILL ASK HER!

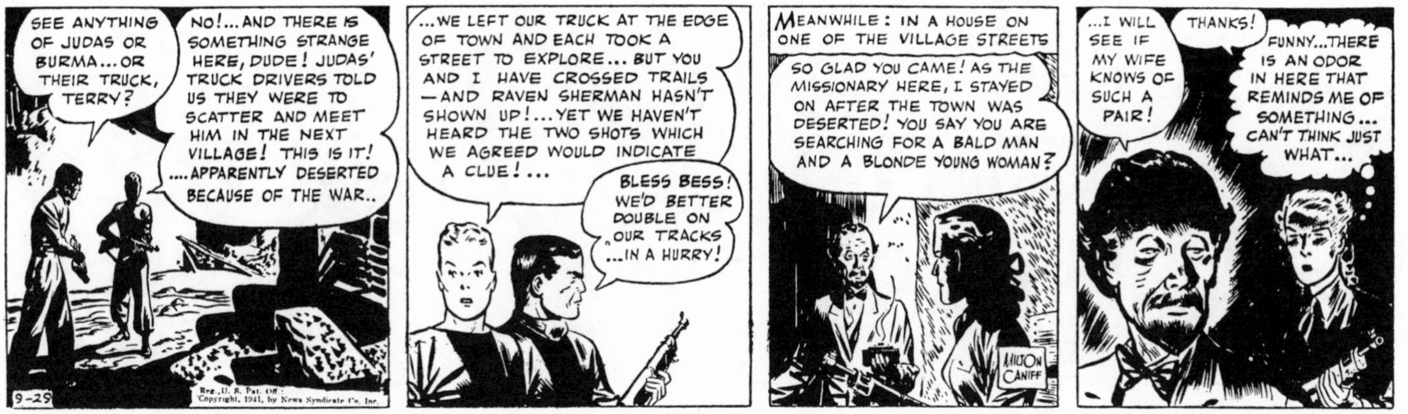
SEE ANYTHING OF JUDAS OR BURMA... OR THEIR TRUCK, TERRY?
NO!... AND THERE IS SOMETHING STRANGE HERE, DUDE! JUDAS' TRUCK DRIVERS TOLD US THEY WERE TO SCATTER AND MEET HIM IN THE NEXT VILLAGE! THIS IS IT! ....APPARENTLY DESERTED BECAUSE OF THE WAR..
9-29
Reg. U. S. Pat. Off.: Copyright, 1941, by News Syndicate Co. Inc.
...WE LEFT OUR TRUCK AT THE EDGE OF TOWN AND EACH TOOK A STREET TO EXPLORE... BUT YOU AND I HAVE CROSSED TRAILS —AND RAVEN SHERMAN HASN'T SHOWN UP!... YET WE HAVEN'T HEARD THE TWO SHOTS WHICH WE AGREED WOULD INDICATE A CLUE!...
BLESS BESS! WE'D BETTER DOUBLE ON OUR TRACKS ...IN A HURRY!
MEANWHILE: IN A HOUSE ON ONE OF THE VILLAGE STREETS
SO GLAD YOU CAME! AS THE MISSIONARY HERE, I STAYED ON AFTER THE TOWN WAS DESERTED! YOU SAY YOU ARE SEARCHING FOR A BALD MAN AND A BLONDE YOUNG WOMAN?
MILTON CANIFF
...I WILL SEE IF MY WIFE KNOWS OF SUCH A PAIR!
THANKS!
FUNNY...THERE IS AN ODOR IN HERE THAT REMINDS ME OF SOMETHING... CAN'T THINK JUST WHAT...

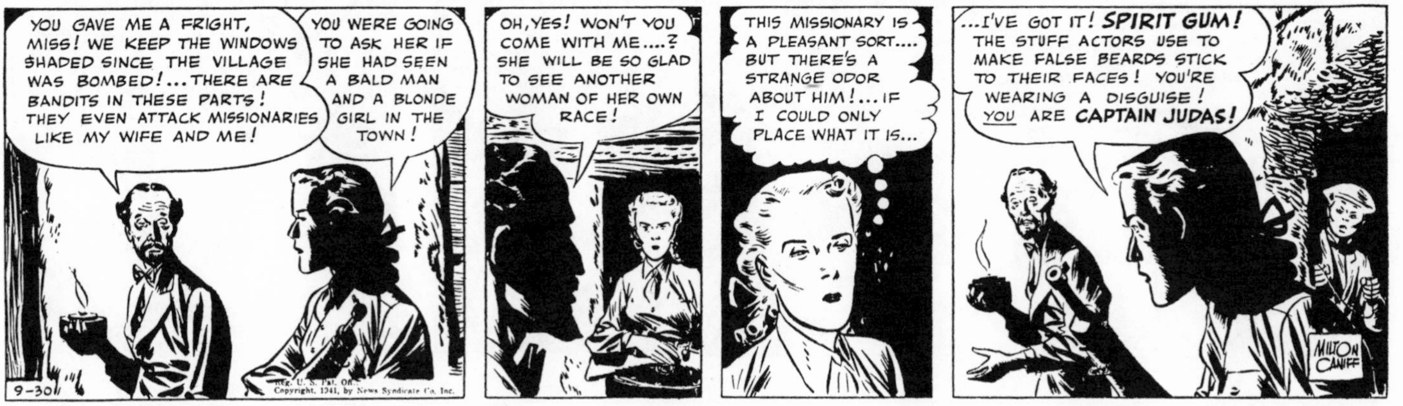
YOU GAVE ME A FRIGHT, MISS! WE KEEP THE WINDOWS SHADED SINCE THE VILLAGE WAS BOMBED!... THERE ARE BANDITS IN THESE PARTS! THEY EVEN ATTACK MISSIONARIES LIKE MY WIFE AND ME!
YOU WERE GOING TO ASK HER IF SHE HAD SEEN A BALD MAN AND A BLONDE GIRL IN THE TOWN!
9-30
Reg. U. S. Pat. Off.: Copyright, 1941, by News Syndicate Co. Inc.
OH, YES! WON'T YOU COME WITH ME....? SHE WILL BE SO GLAD TO SEE ANOTHER WOMAN OF HER OWN RACE!
THIS MISSIONARY IS A PLEASANT SORT.... BUT THERE'S A STRANGE ODOR ABOUT HIM!... IF I COULD ONLY PLACE WHAT IT IS...
...I'VE GOT IT! SPIRIT GUM! THE STUFF ACTORS USE TO MAKE FALSE BEARDS STICK TO THEIR FACES! YOU'RE WEARING A DISGUISE! YOU ARE CAPTAIN JUDAS!
MILTON CANIFF

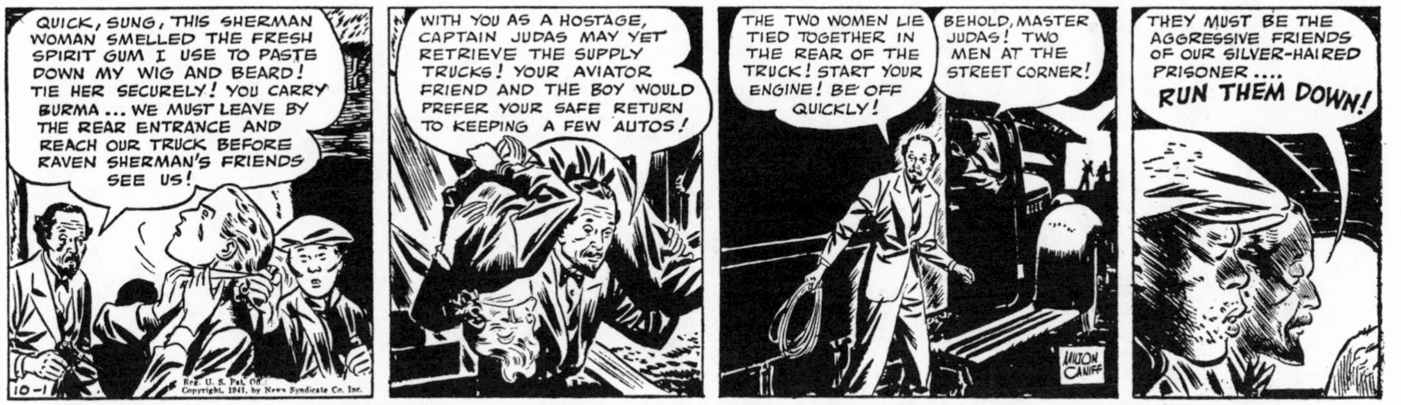
QUICK, SUNG, THIS SHERMAN WOMAN SMELLED THE FRESH SPIRIT GUM I USE TO PASTE DOWN MY WIG AND BEARD! TIE HER SECURELY! YOU CARRY BURMA... WE MUST LEAVE BY THE REAR ENTRANCE AND REACH OUR TRUCK BEFORE RAVEN SHERMAN'S FRIENDS SEE US!
10-1
Reg. U. S. Pat. Off.: Copyright, 1941, by News Syndicate Co. Inc.
WITH YOU AS A HOSTAGE, CAPTAIN JUDAS MAY YET RETRIEVE THE SUPPLY TRUCKS! YOUR AVIATOR FRIEND AND THE BOY WOULD PREFER YOUR SAFE RETURN TO KEEPING A FEW AUTOS!
THE TWO WOMEN LIE TIED TOGETHER IN THE REAR OF THE TRUCK! START YOUR ENGINE! BE OFF QUICKLY!
BEHOLD, MASTER JUDAS! TWO MEN AT THE STREET CORNER!
MILTON CANIFF
THEY MUST BE THE AGGRESSIVE FRIENDS OF OUR SILVER-HAIRED PRISONER....
RUN THEM DOWN!

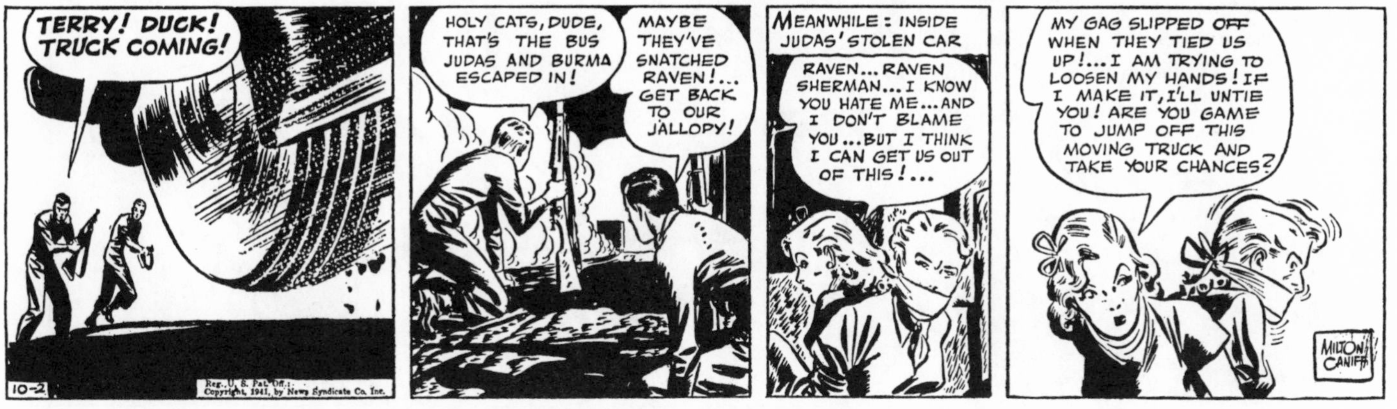
TERRY! DUCK! TRUCK COMING!
10-2
Reg. U. S. Pat. Off.: Copyright, 1941, by News Syndicate Co. Inc.
HOLY CATS, DUDE, THAT'S THE BUS JUDAS AND BURMA ESCAPED IN!
MAYBE THEY'VE SNATCHED RAVEN!... GET BACK TO OUR JALLOPY!
MEANWHILE: INSIDE JUDAS' STOLEN CAR
RAVEN... RAVEN SHERMAN... I KNOW YOU HATE ME... AND I DON'T BLAME YOU... BUT I THINK I CAN GET US OUT OF THIS!...
MY GAG SLIPPED OFF WHEN THEY TIED US UP!... I AM TRYING TO LOOSEN MY HANDS! IF I MAKE IT, I'LL UNTIE YOU! ARE YOU GAME TO JUMP OFF THIS MOVING TRUCK AND TAKE YOUR CHANCES?
MILTON CANIFF

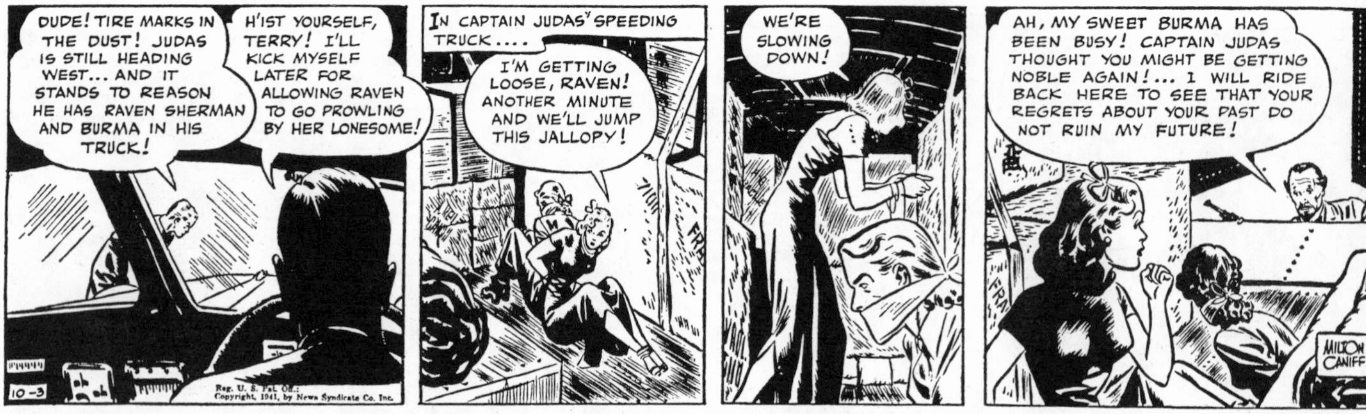
DUDE! TIRE MARKS IN THE DUST! JUDAS IS STILL HEADING WEST... AND IT STANDS TO REASON HE HAS RAVEN SHERMAN AND BURMA IN HIS TRUCK!
H'IST YOURSELF, TERRY! I'LL KICK MYSELF LATER FOR ALLOWING RAVEN TO GO PROWLING BY HER LONESOME!
10-3
Reg. U. S. Pat. Off.: Copyright, 1941, by News Syndicate Co. Inc.
IN CAPTAIN JUDAS' SPEEDING TRUCK....
I'M GETTING LOOSE, RAVEN! ANOTHER MINUTE AND WE'LL JUMP THIS JALLOPY!
WE'RE SLOWING DOWN!
AH, MY SWEET BURMA HAS BEEN BUSY! CAPTAIN JUDAS THOUGHT YOU MIGHT BE GETTING NOBLE AGAIN!... I WILL RIDE BACK HERE TO SEE THAT YOUR REGRETS ABOUT YOUR PAST DO NOT RUIN MY FUTURE!
MILTON CANIFF

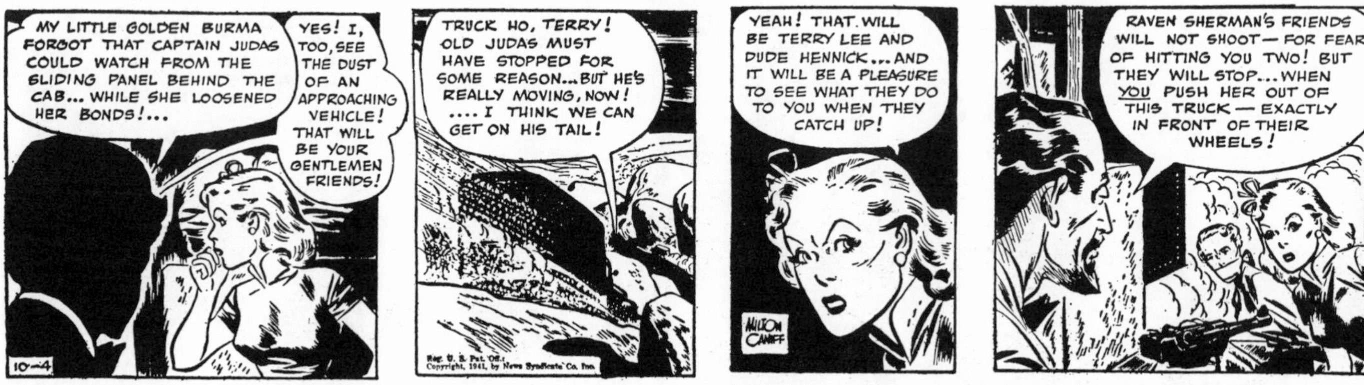
MY LITTLE GOLDEN BURMA FORGOT THAT CAPTAIN JUDAS COULD WATCH FROM THE SLIDING PANEL BEHIND THE CAB... WHILE SHE LOOSENED HER BONDS!...
YES! I, TOO, SEE THE DUST OF AN APPROACHING VEHICLE! THAT WILL BE YOUR GENTLEMEN FRIENDS!
10-4
TRUCK HO, TERRY! OLD JUDAS MUST HAVE STOPPED FOR SOME REASON... BUT HE'S REALLY MOVING, NOW! .... I THINK WE CAN GET ON HIS TAIL!
Reg. U. S. Pat. Off.: Copyright, 1941, by News Syndicate Co. Inc.
YEAH! THAT WILL BE TERRY LEE AND DUDE HENNICK... AND IT WILL BE A PLEASURE TO SEE WHAT THEY DO TO YOU WHEN THEY CATCH UP!
MILTON CANIFF
RAVEN SHERMAN'S FRIENDS WILL NOT SHOOT — FOR FEAR OF HITTING YOU TWO! BUT THEY WILL STOP... WHEN YOU PUSH HER OUT OF THIS TRUCK — EXACTLY IN FRONT OF THEIR WHEELS!

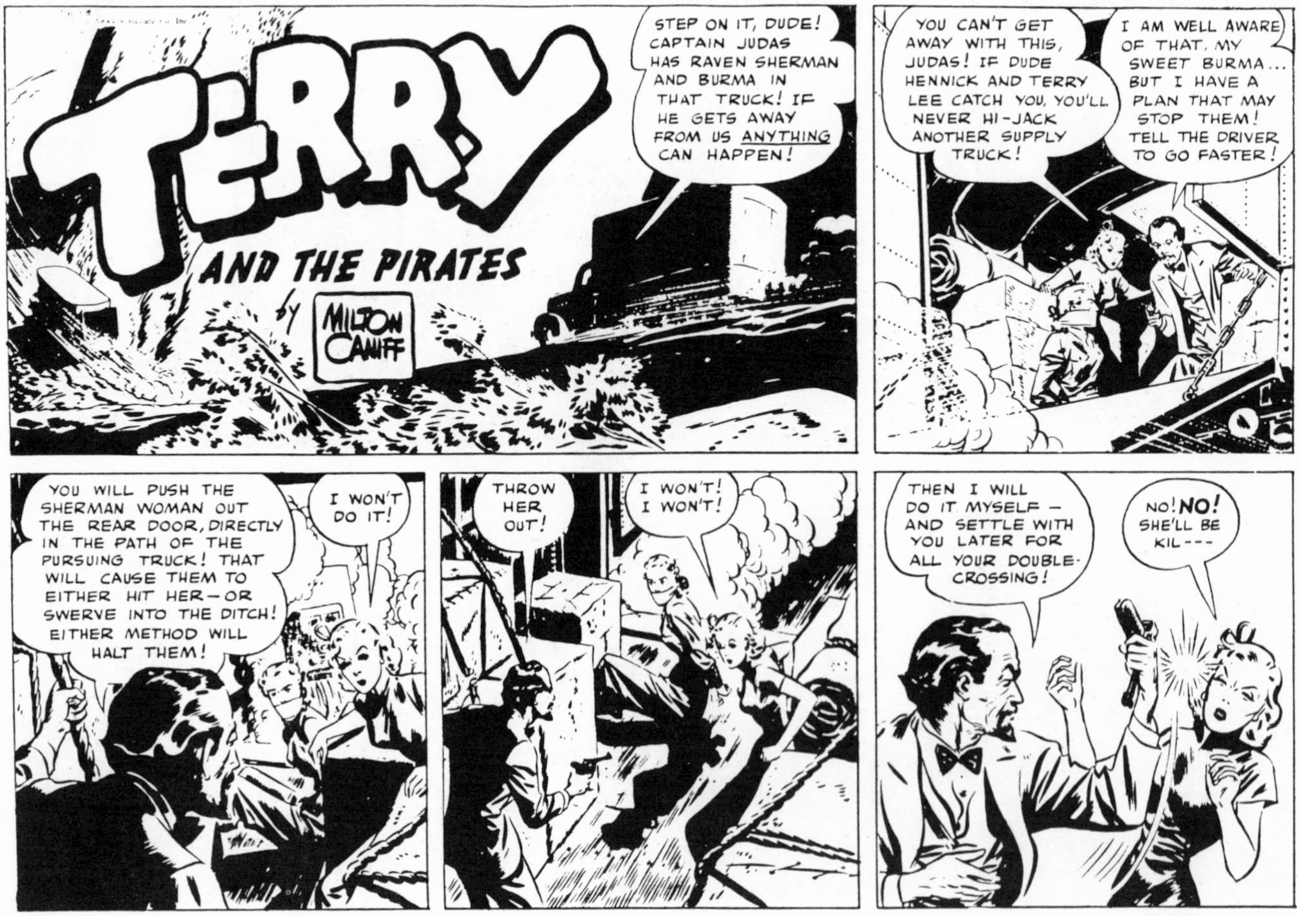
TERRY AND THE PIRATES
by MILTON CANIFF
STEP ON IT, DUDE! CAPTAIN JUDAS HAS RAVEN SHERMAN AND BURMA IN THAT TRUCK! IF HE GETS AWAY FROM US ANYTHING CAN HAPPEN!
YOU CAN'T GET AWAY WITH THIS, JUDAS! IF DUDE HENNICK AND TERRY LEE CATCH YOU, YOU'LL NEVER HI-JACK ANOTHER SUPPLY TRUCK!
I AM WELL AWARE OF THAT, MY SWEET BURMA... BUT I HAVE A PLAN THAT MAY STOP THEM! TELL THE DRIVER TO GO FASTER!
YOU WILL PUSH THE SHERMAN WOMAN OUT THE REAR DOOR, DIRECTLY IN THE PATH OF THE PURSUING TRUCK! THAT WILL CAUSE THEM TO EITHER HIT HER — OR SWERVE INTO THE DITCH! EITHER METHOD WILL HALT THEM!
I WON'T DO IT!
THROW HER OUT!
I WON'T! I WON'T!
THEN I WILL DO IT MYSELF — AND SETTLE WITH YOU LATER FOR ALL YOUR DOUBLE-CROSSING!
NO! NO! SHE'LL BE KIL---

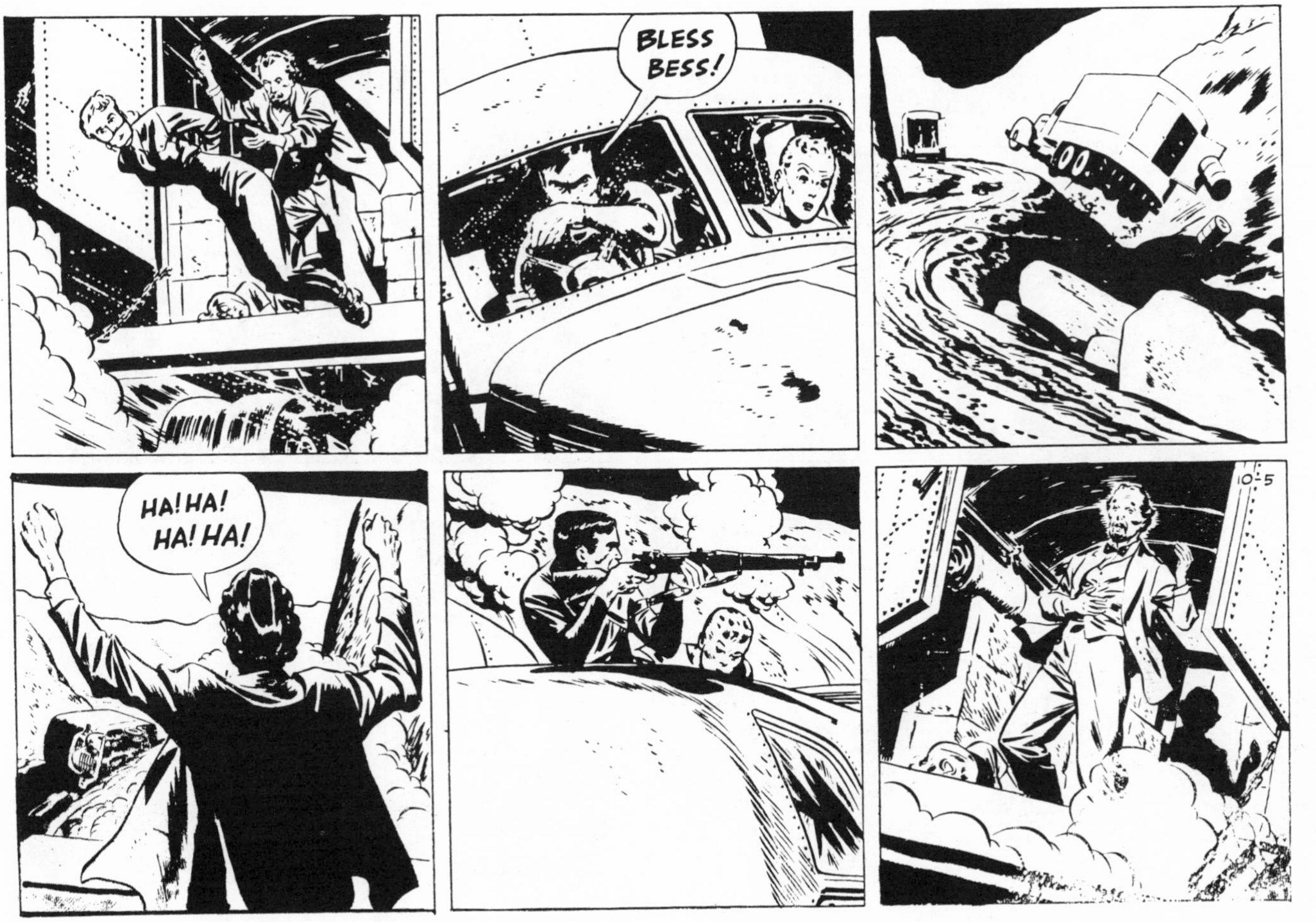
BLESS BESS!
HA! HA! HA! HA!
10-5

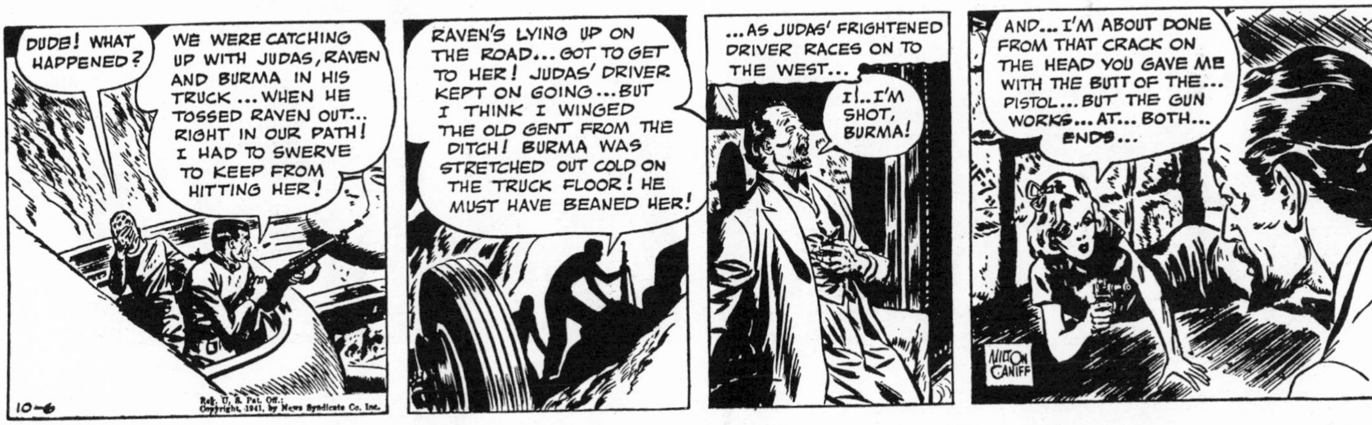
DUDE! WHAT HAPPENED?
WE WERE CATCHING UP WITH JUDAS, RAVEN AND BURMA IN HIS TRUCK ... WHEN HE TOSSED RAVEN OUT... RIGHT IN OUR PATH! I HAD TO SWERVE TO KEEP FROM HITTING HER!
RAVEN'S LYING UP ON THE ROAD... GOT TO GET TO HER! JUDAS' DRIVER KEPT ON GOING... BUT I THINK I WINGED THE OLD GENT FROM THE DITCH! BURMA WAS STRETCHED OUT COLD ON THE TRUCK FLOOR! HE MUST HAVE BEANED HER!
...AS JUDAS' FRIGHTENED DRIVER RACES ON TO THE WEST...
I!..I'M SHOT, BURMA!
AND... I'M ABOUT DONE FROM THAT CRACK ON THE HEAD YOU GAVE ME WITH THE BUTT OF THE... PISTOL... BUT THE GUN WORKS... AT... BOTH... ENDS...
MILTON CANIFF
10-6
Reg. U. S. & Pat. Off.; Copyright, 1941, by News Syndicate Co. Inc.

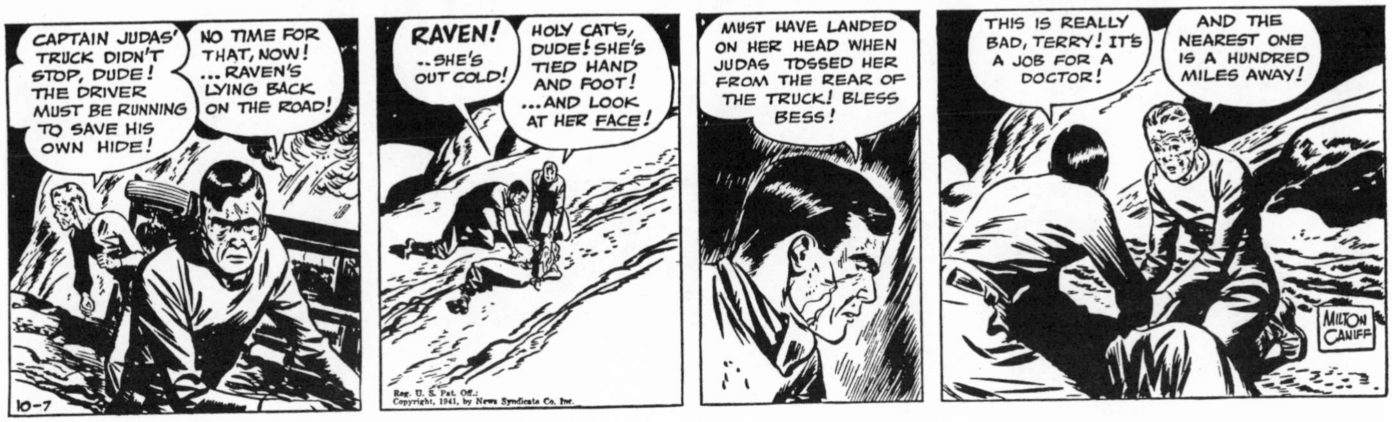
CAPTAIN JUDAS' TRUCK DIDN'T STOP, DUDE! THE DRIVER MUST BE RUNNING TO SAVE HIS OWN HIDE!
NO TIME FOR THAT, NOW! ...RAVEN'S LYING BACK ON THE ROAD!
RAVEN! ..SHE'S OUT COLD!
HOLY CAT'S, DUDE! SHE'S TIED HAND AND FOOT! ...AND LOOK AT HER FACE!
MUST HAVE LANDED ON HER HEAD WHEN JUDAS TOSSED HER FROM THE REAR OF THE TRUCK! BLESS BESS!
THIS IS REALLY BAD, TERRY! IT'S A JOB FOR A DOCTOR!
AND THE NEAREST ONE IS A HUNDRED MILES AWAY!
MILTON CANIFF
10-7
Reg. U. S. Pat. Off.; Copyright, 1941, by News Syndicate Co. Inc.

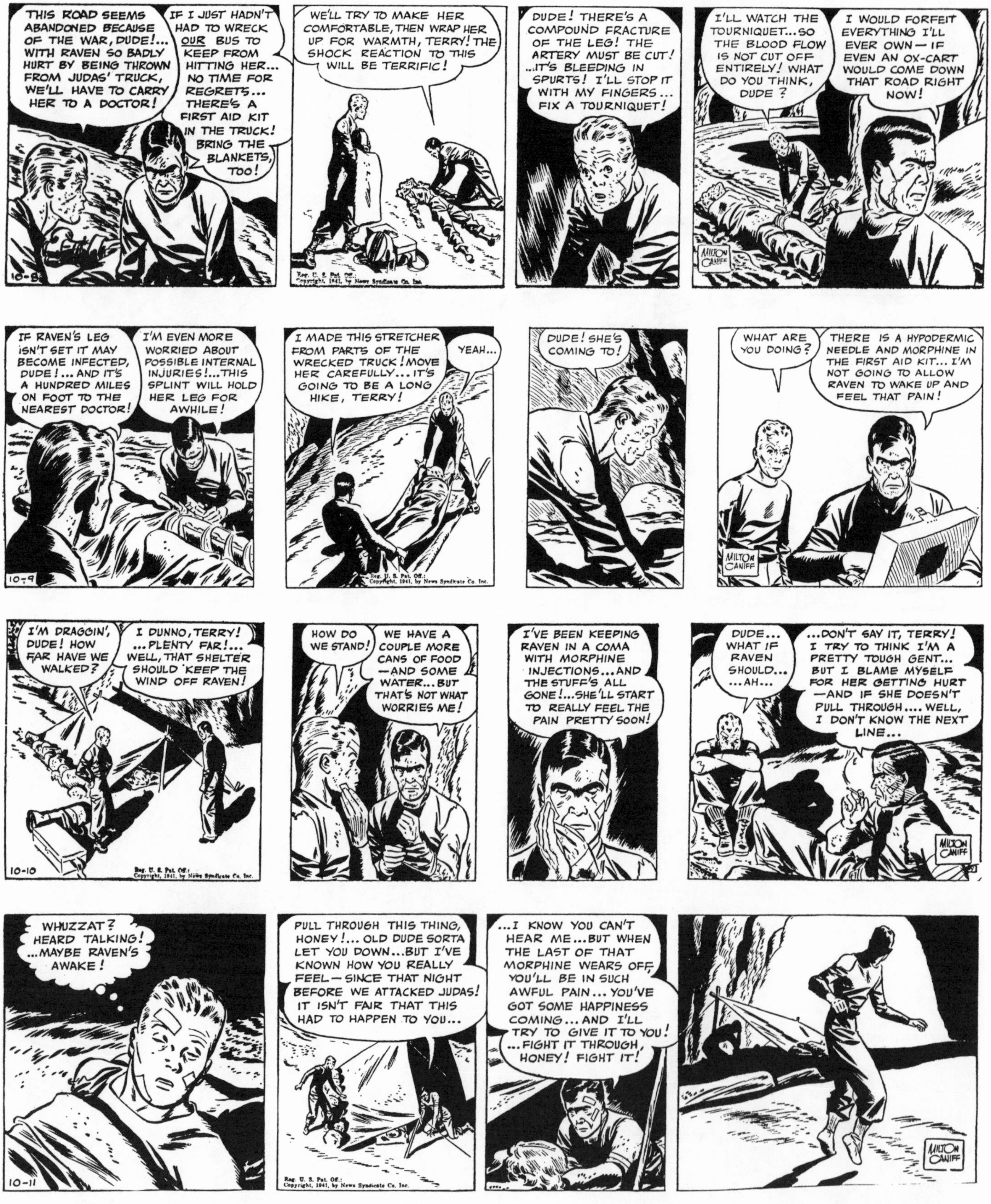
THIS ROAD SEEMS ABANDONED BECAUSE OF THE WAR, DUDE!... WITH RAVEN SO BADLY HURT BY BEING THROWN FROM JUDAS' TRUCK, WE'LL HAVE TO CARRY HER TO A DOCTOR!
IF I JUST HADN'T HAD TO WRECK OUR BUS TO KEEP FROM HITTING HER... NO TIME FOR REGRETS... THERE'S A FIRST AID KIT IN THE TRUCK! BRING THE BLANKETS, TOO!
10-8
WE'LL TRY TO MAKE HER COMFORTABLE, THEN WRAP HER UP FOR WARMTH, TERRY! THE SHOCK REACTION TO THIS WILL BE TERRIFIC!
Reg. U. S. Pat. Off.: Copyright, 1941, by News Syndicate Co. Inc.
DUDE! THERE'S A COMPOUND FRACTURE OF THE LEG! THE ARTERY MUST BE CUT! ...IT'S BLEEDING IN SPURTS! I'LL STOP IT WITH MY FINGERS... FIX A TOURNIQUET!
I'LL WATCH THE TOURNIQUET... SO THE BLOOD FLOW IS NOT CUT OFF ENTIRELY! WHAT DO YOU THINK, DUDE?
I WOULD FORFEIT EVERYTHING I'LL EVER OWN — IF EVEN AN OX-CART WOULD COME DOWN THAT ROAD RIGHT NOW!
MILTON CANIFF
IF RAVEN'S LEG ISN'T SET IT MAY BECOME INFECTED, DUDE!... AND IT'S A HUNDRED MILES ON FOOT TO THE NEAREST DOCTOR!
I'M EVEN MORE WORRIED ABOUT POSSIBLE INTERNAL INJURIES!... THIS SPLINT WILL HOLD HER LEG FOR AWHILE!
10-9
I MADE THIS STRETCHER FROM PARTS OF THE WRECKED TRUCK! MOVE HER CAREFULLY... IT'S GOING TO BE A LONG HIKE, TERRY!
YEAH...
Reg. U. S. Pat. Off.: Copyright, 1941, by News Syndicate Co. Inc.
DUDE! SHE'S COMING TO!
WHAT ARE YOU DOING?
THERE IS A HYPODERMIC NEEDLE AND MORPHINE IN THE FIRST AID KIT... I'M NOT GOING TO ALLOW RAVEN TO WAKE UP AND FEEL THAT PAIN!
MILTON CANIFF
I'M DRAGGIN', DUDE! HOW FAR HAVE WE WALKED?
I DUNNO, TERRY! ...PLENTY FAR!... WELL, THAT SHELTER SHOULD KEEP THE WIND OFF RAVEN!
10-10
Reg. U. S. Pat. Off.: Copyright, 1941, by News Syndicate Co. Inc.
HOW DO WE STAND?
WE HAVE A COUPLE MORE CANS OF FOOD —AND SOME WATER... BUT THAT'S NOT WHAT WORRIES ME!
I'VE BEEN KEEPING RAVEN IN A COMA WITH MORPHINE INJECTIONS... AND THE STUFF'S ALL GONE!... SHE'LL START TO REALLY FEEL THE PAIN PRETTY SOON!
DUDE... WHAT IF RAVEN SHOULD... ...AH...
...DON'T SAY IT, TERRY! I TRY TO THINK I'M A PRETTY TOUGH GENT... BUT I BLAME MYSELF FOR HER GETTING HURT —AND IF SHE DOESN'T PULL THROUGH.... WELL, I DON'T KNOW THE NEXT LINE...
MILTON CANIFF
WHUZZAT? HEARD TALKING! ...MAYBE RAVEN'S AWAKE!
10-11
PULL THROUGH THIS THING, HONEY!... OLD DUDE SORTA LET YOU DOWN... BUT I'VE KNOWN HOW YOU REALLY FEEL — SINCE THAT NIGHT BEFORE WE ATTACKED JUDAS! IT ISN'T FAIR THAT THIS HAD TO HAPPEN TO YOU...
Reg. U. S. Pat. Off.: Copyright, 1941, by News Syndicate Co. Inc.
...I KNOW YOU CAN'T HEAR ME... BUT WHEN THE LAST OF THAT MORPHINE WEARS OFF YOU'LL BE IN SUCH AWFUL PAIN... YOU'VE GOT SOME HAPPINESS COMING... AND I'LL TRY TO GIVE IT TO YOU! ...FIGHT IT THROUGH, HONEY! FIGHT IT!
MILTON CANIFF

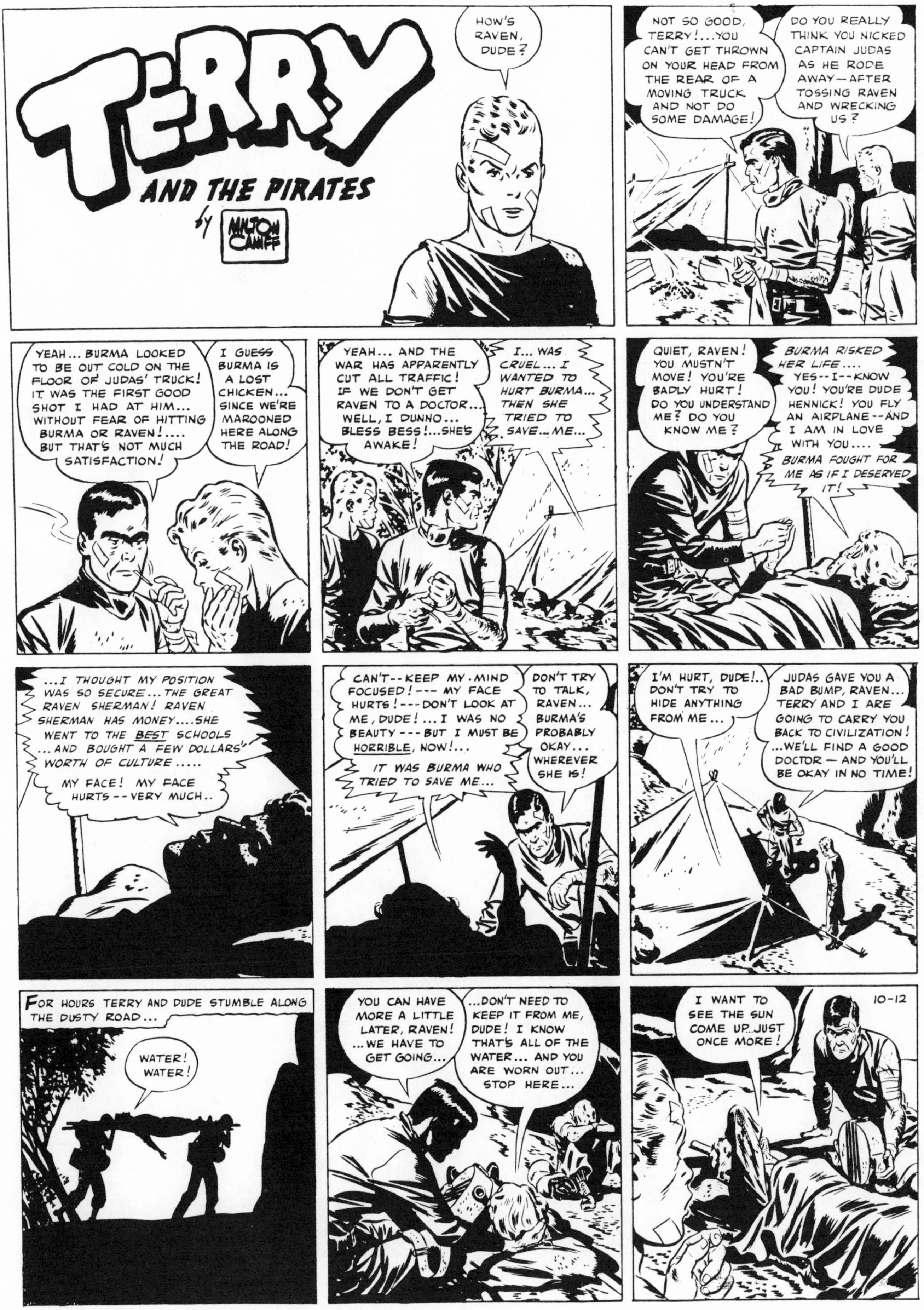
TERRY AND THE PIRATES
by MILTON CANIFF
HOW'S RAVEN, DUDE?
NOT SO GOOD, TERRY!...YOU CAN'T GET THROWN ON YOUR HEAD FROM THE REAR OF A MOVING TRUCK AND NOT DO SOME DAMAGE!
DO YOU REALLY THINK YOU NICKED CAPTAIN JUDAS AS HE RODE AWAY—AFTER TOSSING RAVEN AND WRECKING US?
YEAH ... BURMA LOOKED TO BE OUT COLD ON THE FLOOR OF JUDAS' TRUCK! IT WAS THE FIRST GOOD SHOT I HAD AT HIM... WITHOUT FEAR OF HITTING BURMA OR RAVEN!.... BUT THAT'S NOT MUCH SATISFACTION!
I GUESS BURMA IS A LOST CHICKEN... SINCE WE'RE MAROONED HERE ALONG THE ROAD!
YEAH... AND THE WAR HAS APPARENTLY CUT ALL TRAFFIC! IF WE DON'T GET RAVEN TO A DOCTOR... WELL, I DUNNO... BLESS BESS!...SHE'S AWAKE!
I... WAS CRUEL... I WANTED TO HURT BURMA... THEN SHE TRIED TO SAVE... ME...
QUIET, RAVEN! YOU MUSTN'T MOVE! YOU'RE BADLY HURT! DO YOU UNDERSTAND ME? DO YOU KNOW ME?
BURMA RISKED HER LIFE.... YES--I--KNOW YOU! YOU'RE DUDE HENNICK! YOU FLY AN AIRPLANE--AND I AM IN LOVE WITH YOU....
BURMA FOUGHT FOR ME AS IF I DESERVED IT!
...I THOUGHT MY POSITION WAS SO SECURE... THE GREAT RAVEN SHERMAN! RAVEN SHERMAN HAS MONEY....SHE WENT TO THE BEST SCHOOLS ...AND BOUGHT A FEW DOLLARS' WORTH OF CULTURE .....
MY FACE! MY FACE HURTS--VERY MUCH..
CAN'T--KEEP MY MIND FOCUSED!--- MY FACE HURTS!---DON'T LOOK AT ME, DUDE!...I WAS NO BEAUTY---BUT I MUST BE HORRIBLE, NOW!...
IT WAS BURMA WHO TRIED TO SAVE ME....
DON'T TRY TO TALK, RAVEN... BURMA'S PROBABLY OKAY... WHEREVER SHE IS!
I'M HURT, DUDE!.. DON'T TRY TO HIDE ANYTHING FROM ME...
JUDAS GAVE YOU A BAD BUMP, RAVEN... TERRY AND I ARE GOING TO CARRY YOU BACK TO CIVILIZATION! ...WE'LL FIND A GOOD DOCTOR — AND YOU'LL BE OKAY IN NO TIME!
FOR HOURS TERRY AND DUDE STUMBLE ALONG THE DUSTY ROAD...
WATER! WATER!
YOU CAN HAVE MORE A LITTLE LATER, RAVEN! ...WE HAVE TO GET GOING...
...DON'T NEED TO KEEP IT FROM ME, DUDE! I KNOW THAT'S ALL OF THE WATER... AND YOU ARE WORN OUT... STOP HERE...
10-12
I WANT TO SEE THE SUN COME UP...JUST ONCE MORE!

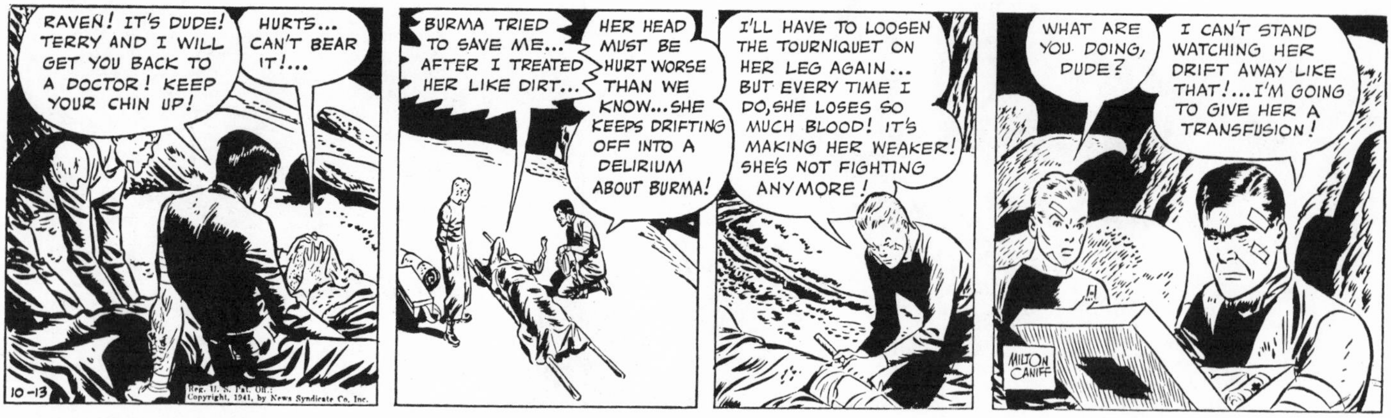
RAVEN! IT'S DUDE! TERRY AND I WILL GET YOU BACK TO A DOCTOR! KEEP YOUR CHIN UP!
HURTS... CAN'T BEAR IT!...
BURMA TRIED TO SAVE ME... AFTER I TREATED HER LIKE DIRT...
HER HEAD MUST BE HURT WORSE THAN WE KNOW... SHE KEEPS DRIFTING OFF INTO A DELIRIUM ABOUT BURMA!
I'LL HAVE TO LOOSEN THE TOURNIQUET ON HER LEG AGAIN... BUT EVERY TIME I DO, SHE LOSES SO MUCH BLOOD! IT'S MAKING HER WEAKER! SHE'S NOT FIGHTING ANYMORE!
WHAT ARE YOU DOING, DUDE?
I CAN'T STAND WATCHING HER DRIFT AWAY LIKE THAT!... I'M GOING TO GIVE HER A TRANSFUSION!
MILTON CANIFF
10-13
Reg. U. S. Pat. Off.; Copyright, 1941, by News Syndicate Co. Inc.

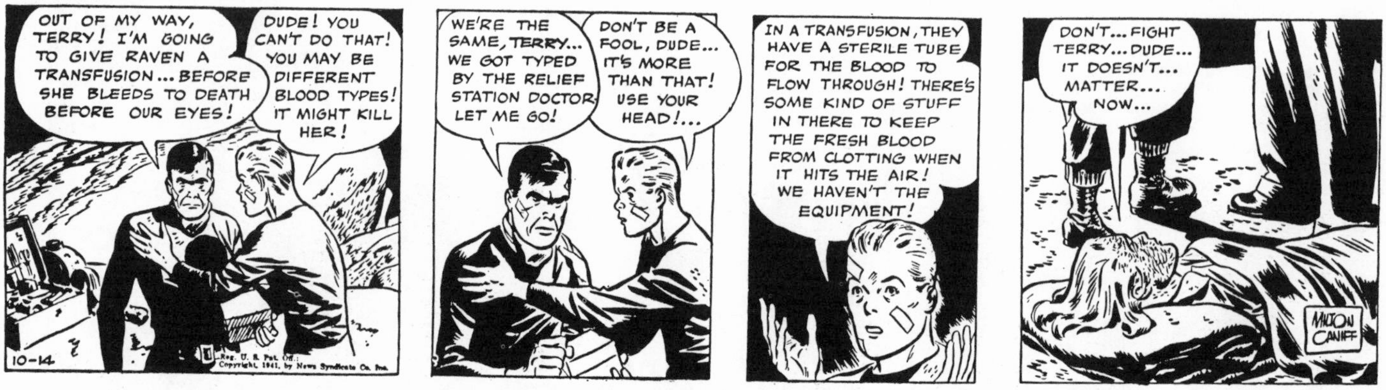
OUT OF MY WAY, TERRY! I'M GOING TO GIVE RAVEN A TRANSFUSION... BEFORE SHE BLEEDS TO DEATH BEFORE OUR EYES!
DUDE! YOU CAN'T DO THAT! YOU MAY BE DIFFERENT BLOOD TYPES! IT MIGHT KILL HER!
WE'RE THE SAME, TERRY... WE GOT TYPED BY THE RELIEF STATION DOCTOR. LET ME GO!
DON'T BE A FOOL, DUDE... IT'S MORE THAN THAT! USE YOUR HEAD!...
IN A TRANSFUSION, THEY HAVE A STERILE TUBE FOR THE BLOOD TO FLOW THROUGH! THERE'S SOME KIND OF STUFF IN THERE TO KEEP THE FRESH BLOOD FROM CLOTTING WHEN IT HITS THE AIR! WE HAVEN'T THE EQUIPMENT!
DON'T... FIGHT TERRY... DUDE... IT DOESN'T... MATTER.... NOW...
MILTON CANIFF
10-14
Reg. U. S. Pat. Off.; Copyright, 1941, by News Syndicate Co. Inc.

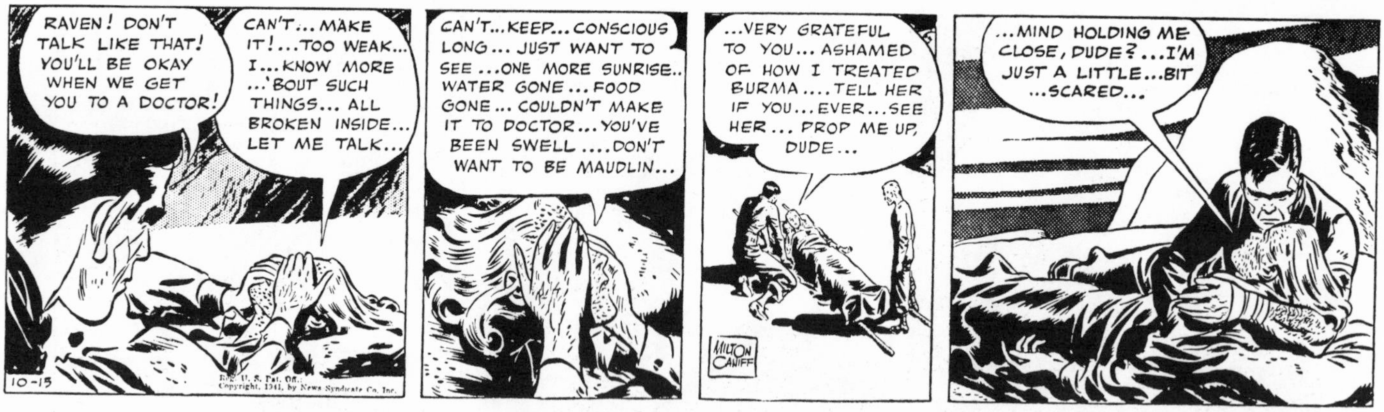
RAVEN! DON'T TALK LIKE THAT! YOU'LL BE OKAY WHEN WE GET YOU TO A DOCTOR!
CAN'T... MAKE IT!... TOO WEAK... I... KNOW MORE ...'BOUT SUCH THINGS... ALL BROKEN INSIDE... LET ME TALK...
CAN'T... KEEP... CONSCIOUS LONG... JUST WANT TO SEE... ONE MORE SUNRISE.. WATER GONE... FOOD GONE... COULDN'T MAKE IT TO DOCTOR... YOU'VE BEEN SWELL.... DON'T WANT TO BE MAUDLIN...
...VERY GRATEFUL TO YOU... ASHAMED OF HOW I TREATED BURMA.... TELL HER IF YOU... EVER... SEE HER... PROP ME UP, DUDE...
...MIND HOLDING ME CLOSE, DUDE?... I'M JUST A LITTLE... BIT ...SCARED...
MILTON CANIFF
10-15
Reg. U. S. Pat. Off.; Copyright, 1941, by News Syndicate Co. Inc.

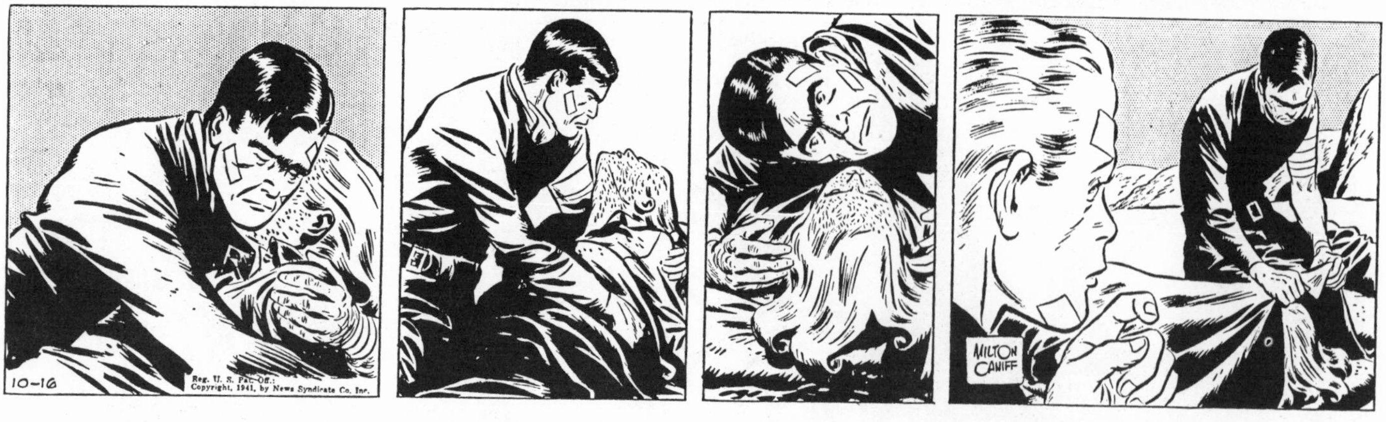
MILTON CANIFF
10-16
Reg. U. S. Pat. Off.; Copyright, 1941, by News Syndicate Co. Inc.

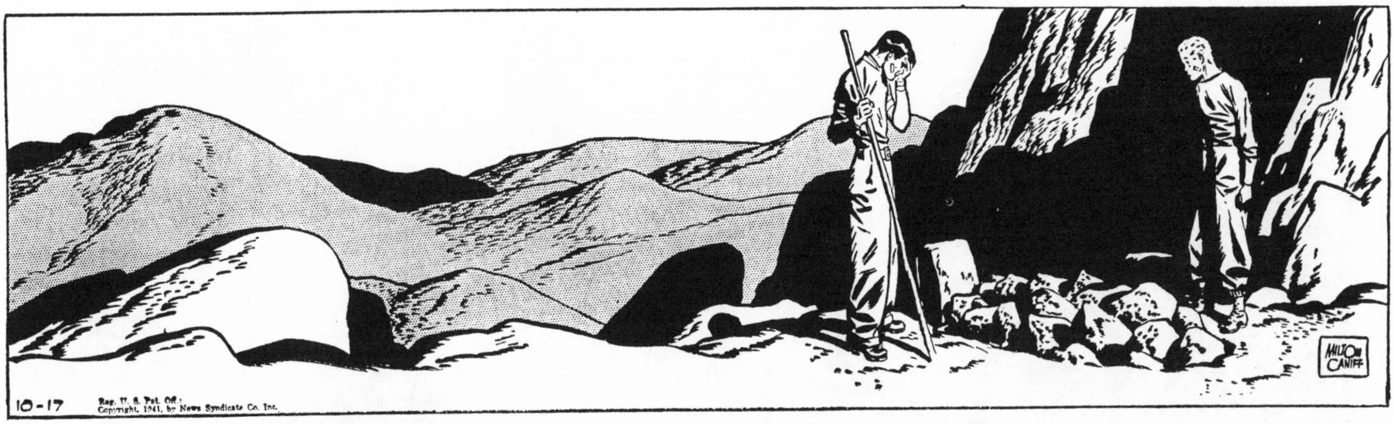
10-17
Reg. U. S. Pat. Off.: Copyright, 1941, by News Syndicate Co. Inc.
MILTON CANIFF

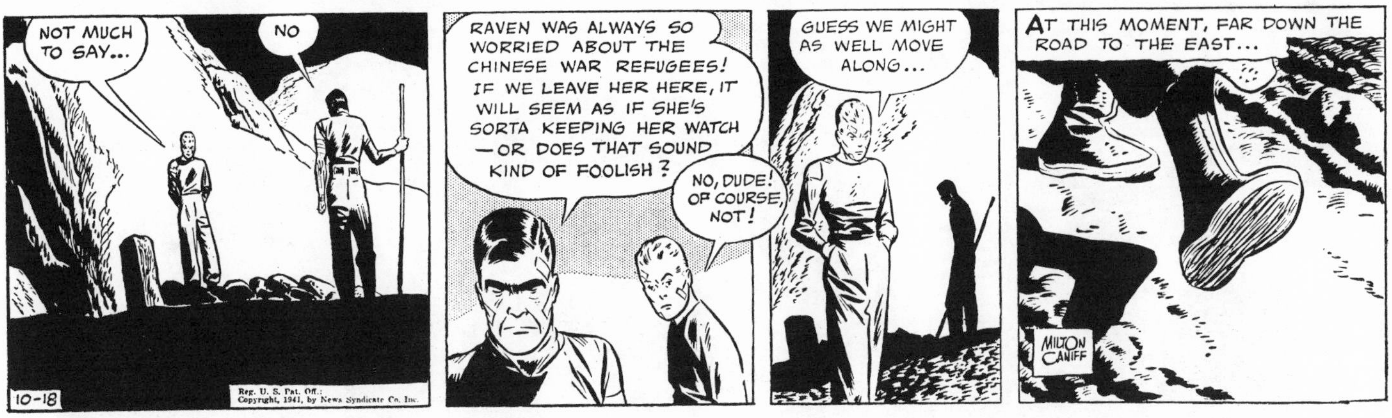
NOT MUCH TO SAY...
NO
10-18
Reg. U. S. Pat. Off.: Copyright, 1941, by News Syndicate Co. Inc.
RAVEN WAS ALWAYS SO WORRIED ABOUT THE CHINESE WAR REFUGEES! IF WE LEAVE HER HERE, IT WILL SEEM AS IF SHE'S SORTA KEEPING HER WATCH —OR DOES THAT SOUND KIND OF FOOLISH?
NO, DUDE! OF COURSE, NOT!
GUESS WE MIGHT AS WELL MOVE ALONG...
AT THIS MOMENT, FAR DOWN THE ROAD TO THE EAST...
MILTON CANIFF

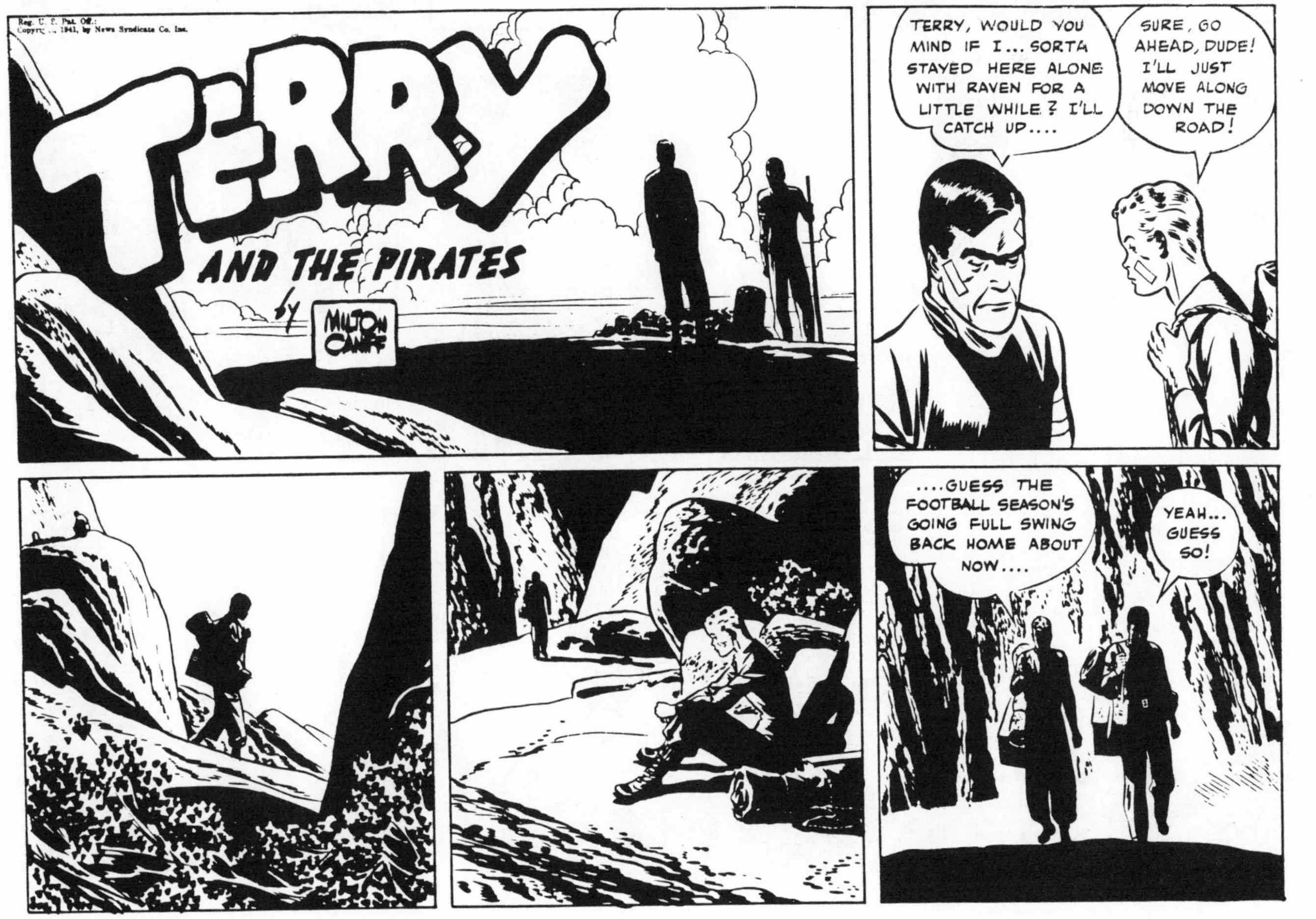
Reg. U. S. Pat. Off.:
1941, by News Syndicate Co. Inc.
TERRY AND THE PIRATES
by MILTON CANIFF
TERRY, WOULD YOU MIND IF I... SORTA STAYED HERE ALONE WITH RAVEN FOR A LITTLE WHILE? I'LL CATCH UP....
SURE, GO AHEAD, DUDE! I'LL JUST MOVE ALONG DOWN THE ROAD!
....GUESS THE FOOTBALL SEASON'S GOING FULL SWING BACK HOME ABOUT NOW....
YEAH... GUESS SO!

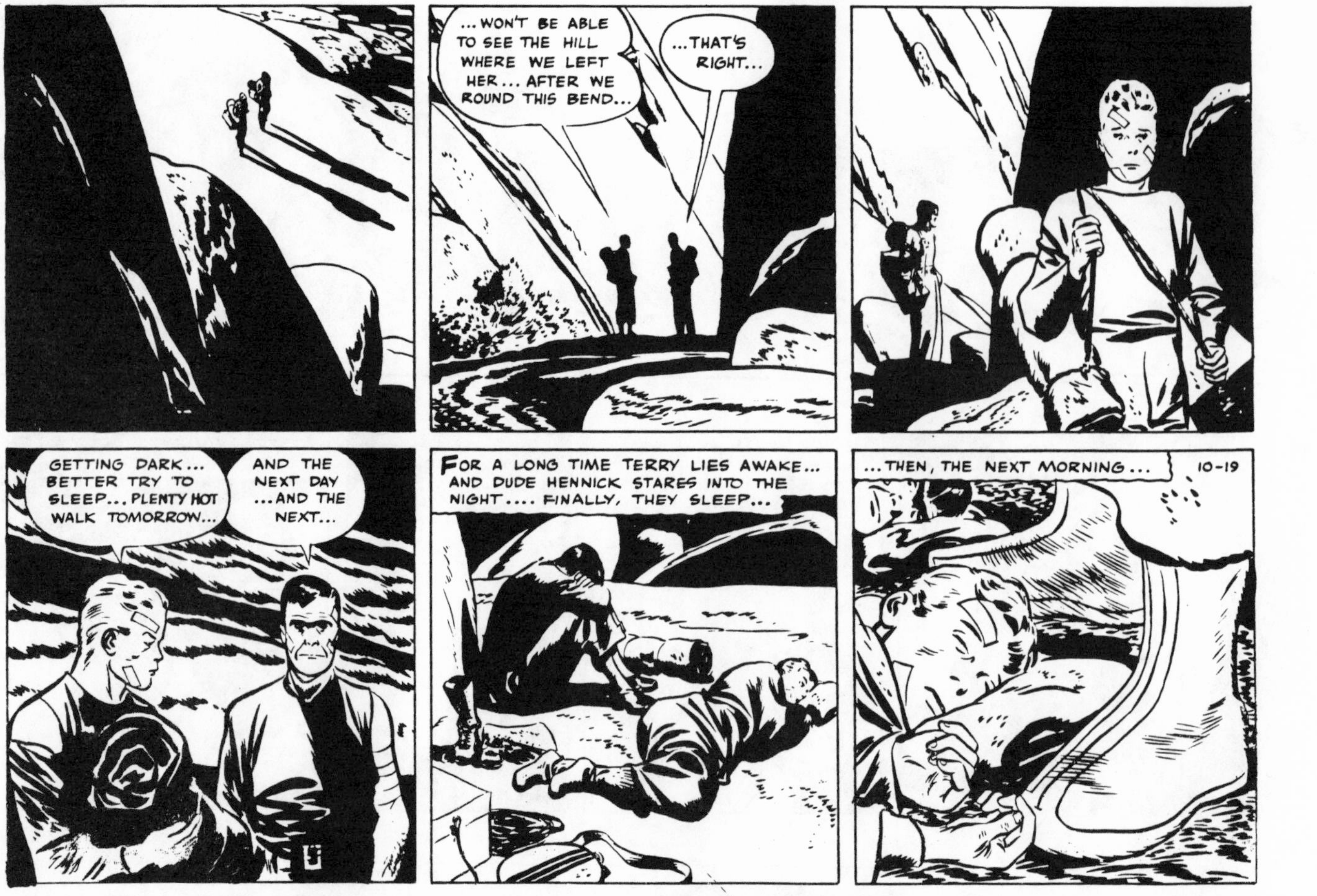
...WON'T BE ABLE TO SEE THE HILL WHERE WE LEFT HER... AFTER WE ROUND THIS BEND...
...THAT'S RIGHT...
GETTING DARK... BETTER TRY TO SLEEP... PLENTY HOT WALK TOMORROW...
AND THE NEXT DAY ...AND THE NEXT...
FOR A LONG TIME TERRY LIES AWAKE... AND DUDE HENNICK STARES INTO THE NIGHT.... FINALLY, THEY SLEEP...
...THEN, THE NEXT MORNING...
10-19

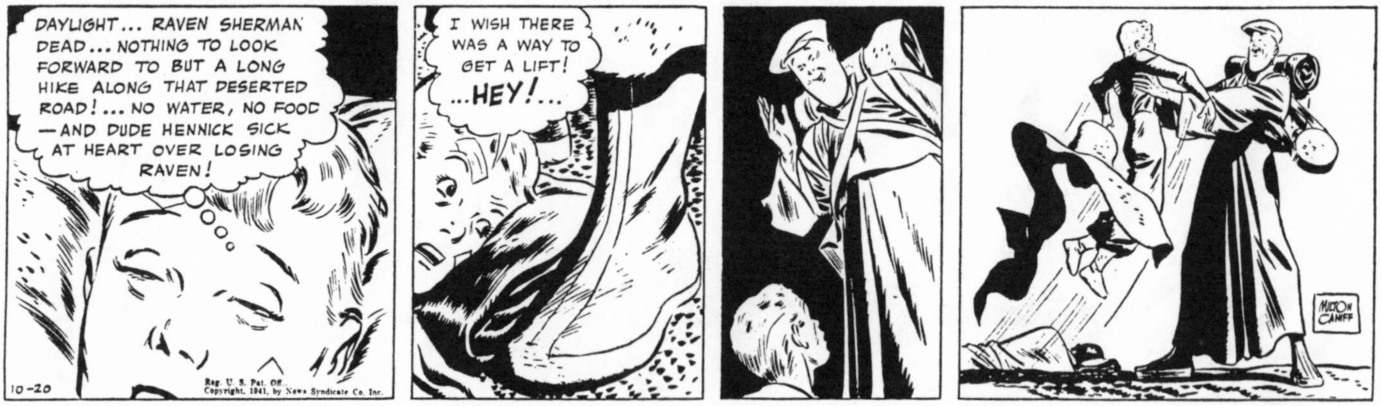
DAYLIGHT... RAVEN SHERMAN DEAD... NOTHING TO LOOK FORWARD TO BUT A LONG HIKE ALONG THAT DESERTED ROAD!... NO WATER, NO FOOD —AND DUDE HENNICK SICK AT HEART OVER LOSING RAVEN!
10-20
Reg. U. S. Pat. Off.
Copyright, 1941, by News Syndicate Co. Inc.
I WISH THERE WAS A WAY TO GET A LIFT!
...HEY!...
MILTON CANIFF

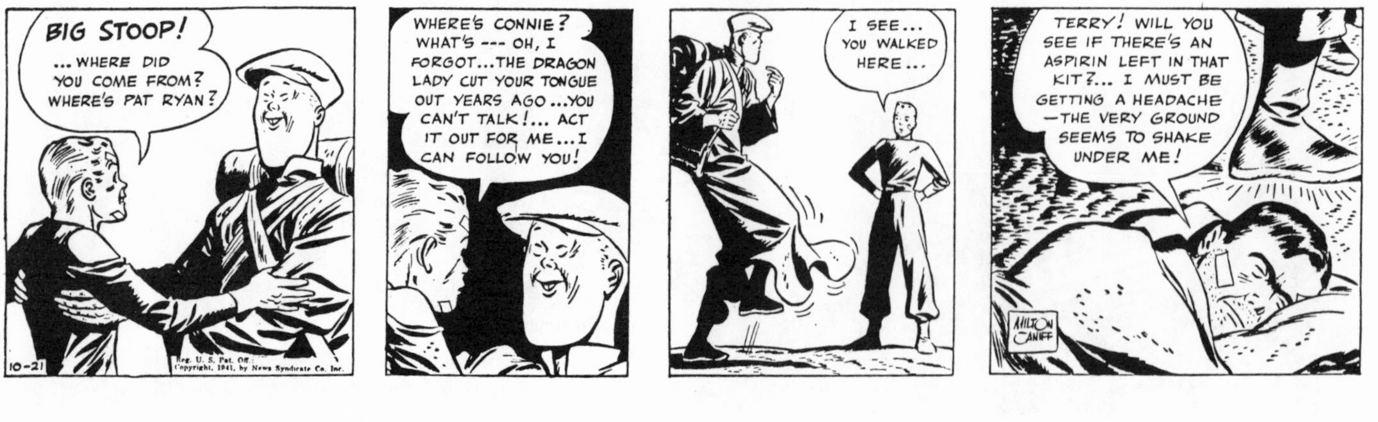
BIG STOOP!
...WHERE DID YOU COME FROM? WHERE'S PAT RYAN?
10-21
Reg. U. S. Pat. Off.
Copyright, 1941, by News Syndicate Co. Inc.
WHERE'S CONNIE? WHAT'S --- OH, I FORGOT...THE DRAGON LADY CUT YOUR TONGUE OUT YEARS AGO...YOU CAN'T TALK!... ACT IT OUT FOR ME...I CAN FOLLOW YOU!
I SEE... YOU WALKED HERE...
MILTON CANIFF
TERRY! WILL YOU SEE IF THERE'S AN ASPIRIN LEFT IN THAT KIT?... I MUST BE GETTING A HEADACHE —THE VERY GROUND SEEMS TO SHAKE UNDER ME!

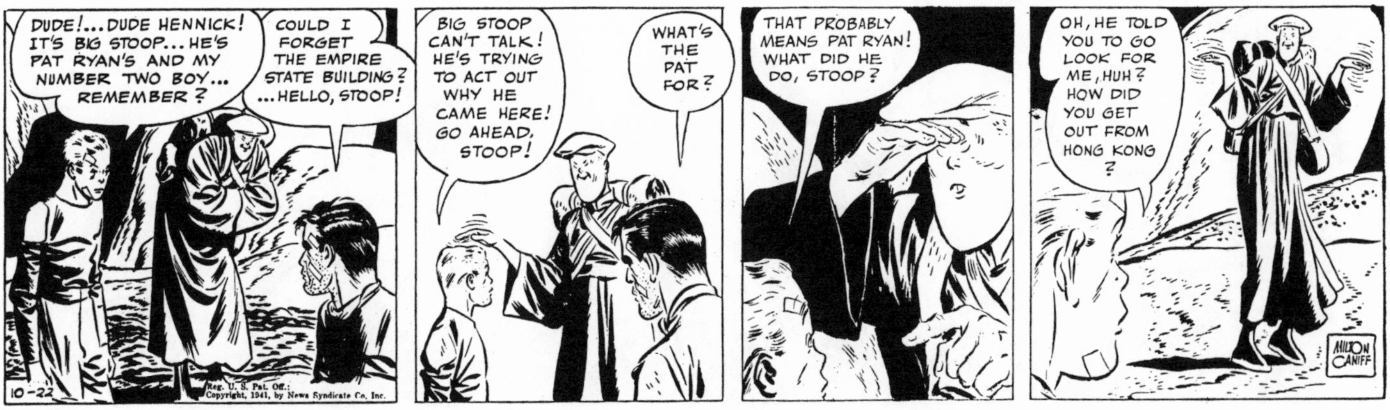
DUDE!... DUDE HENNICK! IT'S BIG STOOP... HE'S PAT RYAN'S AND MY NUMBER TWO BOY... REMEMBER?
COULD I FORGET THE EMPIRE STATE BUILDING? ...HELLO, STOOP!
10-22
Reg. U. S. Pat. Off.; Copyright, 1941, by News Syndicate Co. Inc.
BIG STOOP CAN'T TALK! HE'S TRYING TO ACT OUT WHY HE CAME HERE! GO AHEAD, STOOP!
WHAT'S THE PAT FOR?
THAT PROBABLY MEANS PAT RYAN! WHAT DID HE DO, STOOP?
OH, HE TOLD YOU TO GO LOOK FOR ME, HUH? HOW DID YOU GET OUT FROM HONG KONG?
MILTON CANIFF

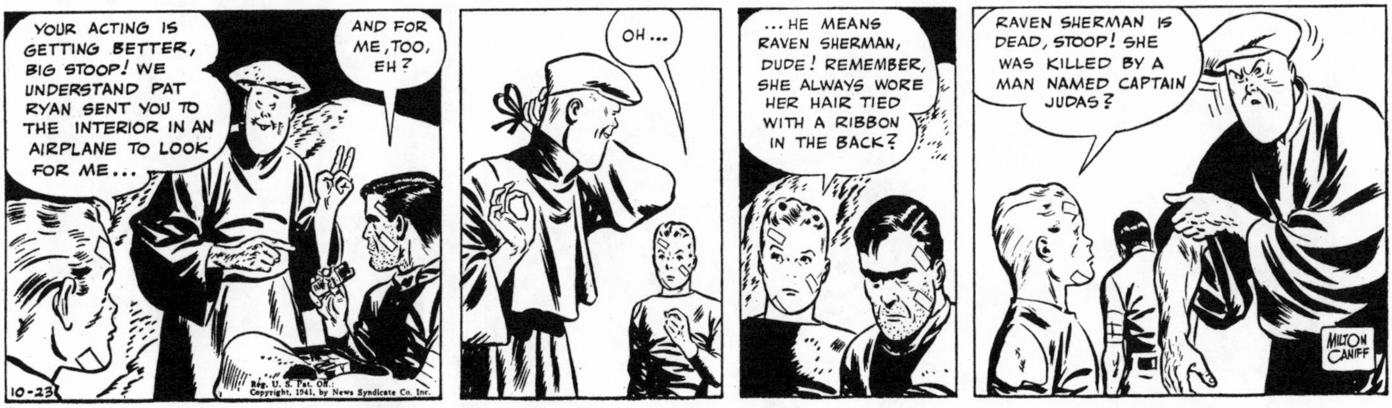
YOUR ACTING IS GETTING BETTER, BIG STOOP! WE UNDERSTAND PAT RYAN SENT YOU TO THE INTERIOR IN AN AIRPLANE TO LOOK FOR ME...
AND FOR ME, TOO, EH?
10-23
Reg. U. S. Pat. Off.; Copyright, 1941, by News Syndicate Co. Inc.
OH...
...HE MEANS RAVEN SHERMAN, DUDE! REMEMBER, SHE ALWAYS WORE HER HAIR TIED WITH A RIBBON IN THE BACK?
RAVEN SHERMAN IS DEAD, STOOP! SHE WAS KILLED BY A MAN NAMED CAPTAIN JUDAS?
MILTON CANIFF

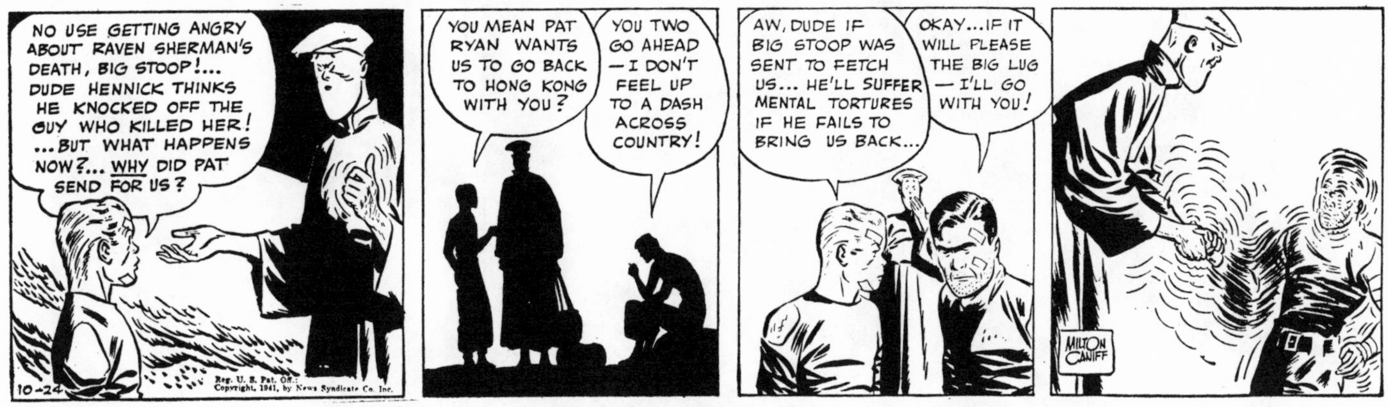
NO USE GETTING ANGRY ABOUT RAVEN SHERMAN'S DEATH, BIG STOOP!... DUDE HENNICK THINKS HE KNOCKED OFF THE GUY WHO KILLED HER! ...BUT WHAT HAPPENS NOW?... WHY DID PAT SEND FOR US?
10-24
Reg. U. S. Pat. Off.; Copyright, 1941, by News Syndicate Co. Inc.
YOU MEAN PAT RYAN WANTS US TO GO BACK TO HONG KONG WITH YOU?
YOU TWO GO AHEAD — I DON'T FEEL UP TO A DASH ACROSS COUNTRY!
AW, DUDE IF BIG STOOP WAS SENT TO FETCH US... HE'LL SUFFER MENTAL TORTURES IF HE FAILS TO BRING US BACK...
OKAY... IF IT WILL PLEASE THE BIG LUG — I'LL GO WITH YOU!
MILTON CANIFF

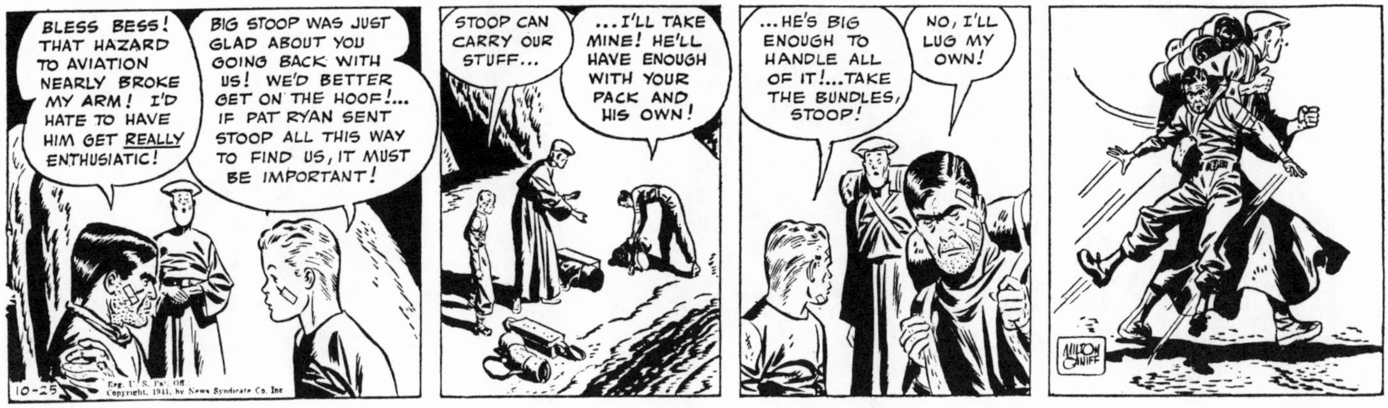
BLESS BESS! THAT HAZARD TO AVIATION NEARLY BROKE MY ARM! I'D HATE TO HAVE HIM GET REALLY ENTHUSIATIC!
BIG STOOP WAS JUST GLAD ABOUT YOU GOING BACK WITH US! WE'D BETTER GET ON THE HOOF!... IF PAT RYAN SENT STOOP ALL THIS WAY TO FIND US, IT MUST BE IMPORTANT!
10-25
Reg. U. S. Pat. Off.; Copyright, 1941, by News Syndicate Co. Inc.
STOOP CAN CARRY OUR STUFF...
...I'LL TAKE MINE! HE'LL HAVE ENOUGH WITH YOUR PACK AND HIS OWN!
...HE'S BIG ENOUGH TO HANDLE ALL OF IT!... TAKE THE BUNDLES, STOOP!
NO, I'LL LUG MY OWN!
MILTON CANIFF

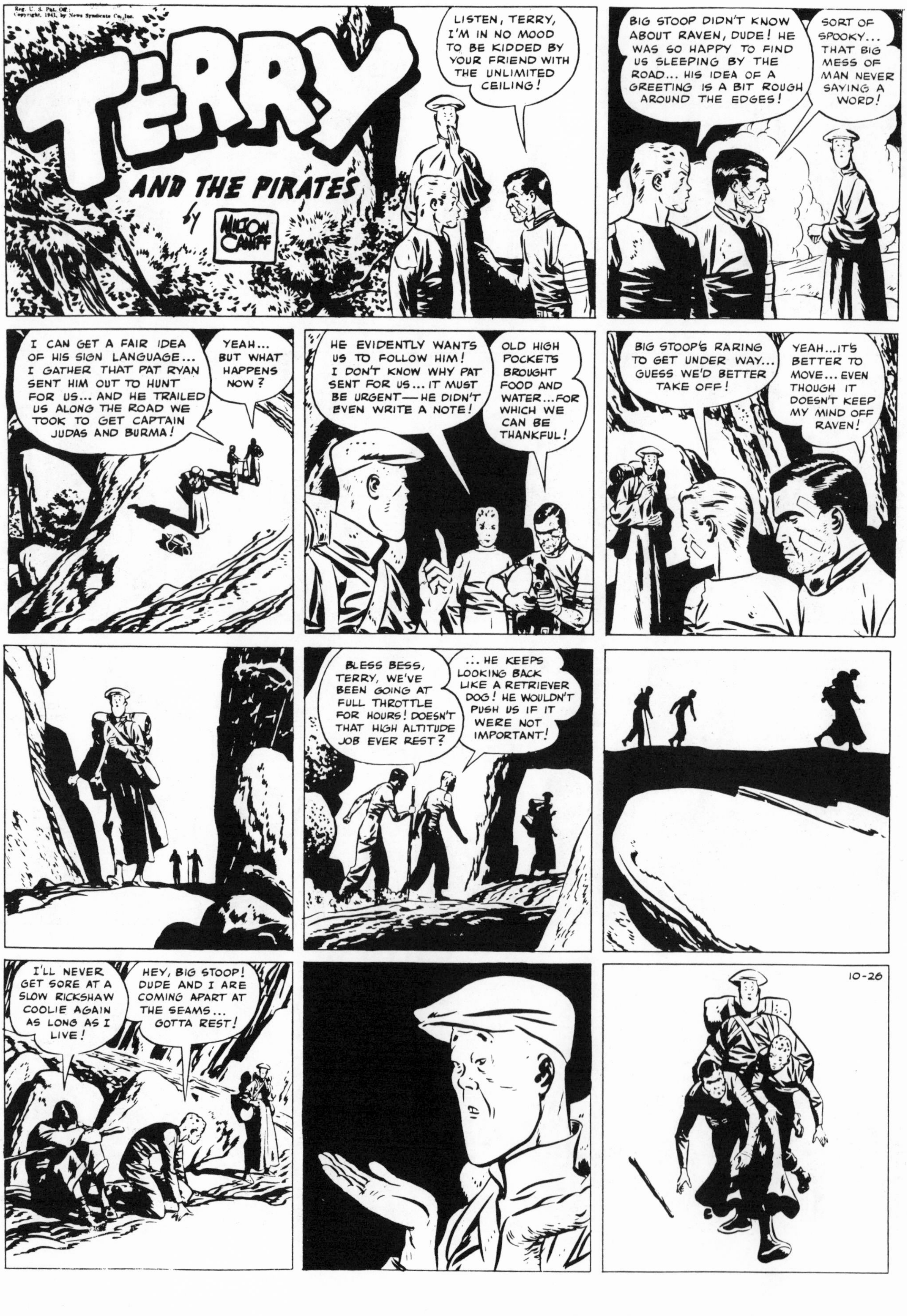

Reg. U. S. Pat. Off.
Copyright, 1941, by News Syndicate Co., Inc.
TERRY AND THE PIRATES
by MILTON CANIFF
LISTEN, TERRY, I'M IN NO MOOD TO BE KIDDED BY YOUR FRIEND WITH THE UNLIMITED CEILING!
BIG STOOP DIDN'T KNOW ABOUT RAVEN, DUDE! HE WAS SO HAPPY TO FIND US SLEEPING BY THE ROAD... HIS IDEA OF A GREETING IS A BIT ROUGH AROUND THE EDGES!
SORT OF SPOOKY... THAT BIG MESS OF MAN NEVER SAYING A WORD!
I CAN GET A FAIR IDEA OF HIS SIGN LANGUAGE... I GATHER THAT PAT RYAN SENT HIM OUT TO HUNT FOR US... AND HE TRAILED US ALONG THE ROAD WE TOOK TO GET CAPTAIN JUDAS AND BURMA!
YEAH... BUT WHAT HAPPENS NOW?
HE EVIDENTLY WANTS US TO FOLLOW HIM! I DON'T KNOW WHY PAT SENT FOR US... IT MUST BE URGENT—HE DIDN'T EVEN WRITE A NOTE!
OLD HIGH POCKETS BROUGHT FOOD AND WATER... FOR WHICH WE CAN BE THANKFUL!
BIG STOOP'S RARING TO GET UNDER WAY... GUESS WE'D BETTER TAKE OFF!
YEAH... IT'S BETTER TO MOVE... EVEN THOUGH IT DOESN'T KEEP MY MIND OFF RAVEN!
BLESS BESS, TERRY, WE'VE BEEN GOING AT FULL THROTTLE FOR HOURS! DOESN'T THAT HIGH ALTITUDE JOB EVER REST?
... HE KEEPS LOOKING BACK LIKE A RETRIEVER DOG! HE WOULDN'T PUSH US IF IT WERE NOT IMPORTANT!
I'LL NEVER GET SORE AT A SLOW RICKSHAW COOLIE AGAIN AS LONG AS I LIVE!
HEY, BIG STOOP! DUDE AND I ARE COMING APART AT THE SEAMS... GOTTA REST!
10-26

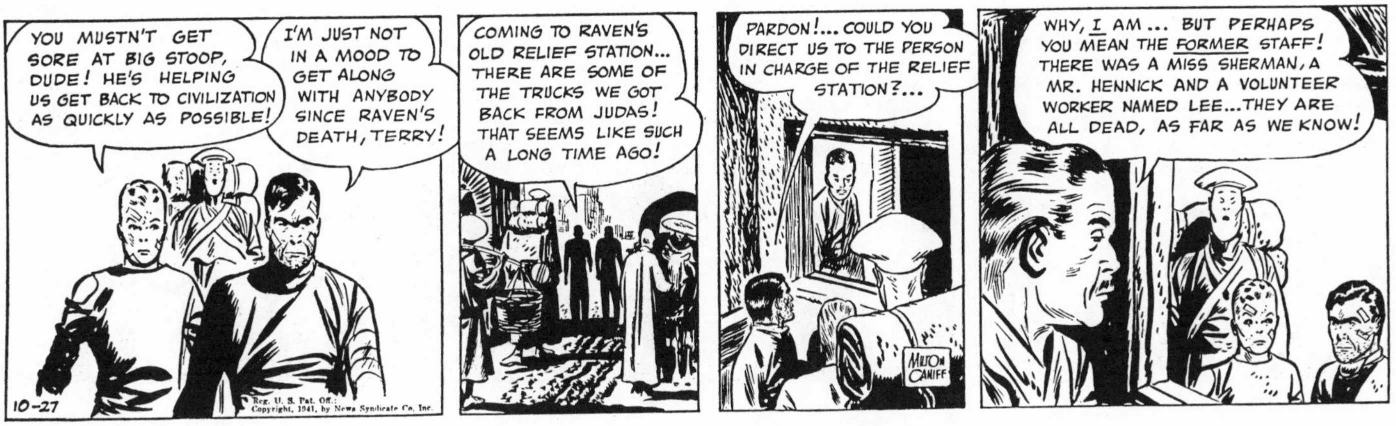
YOU MUSTN'T GET SORE AT BIG STOOP, DUDE! HE'S HELPING US GET BACK TO CIVILIZATION AS QUICKLY AS POSSIBLE!
I'M JUST NOT IN A MOOD TO GET ALONG WITH ANYBODY SINCE RAVEN'S DEATH, TERRY!
10-27
Reg. U. S. Pat. Off.: Copyright, 1941, by News Syndicate Co. Inc.
COMING TO RAVEN'S OLD RELIEF STATION... THERE ARE SOME OF THE TRUCKS WE GOT BACK FROM JUDAS! THAT SEEMS LIKE SUCH A LONG TIME AGO!
PARDON!... COULD YOU DIRECT US TO THE PERSON IN CHARGE OF THE RELIEF STATION?...
MILTON CANIFF
WHY, I AM... BUT PERHAPS YOU MEAN THE FORMER STAFF! THERE WAS A MISS SHERMAN, A MR. HENNICK AND A VOLUNTEER WORKER NAMED LEE... THEY ARE ALL DEAD, AS FAR AS WE KNOW!

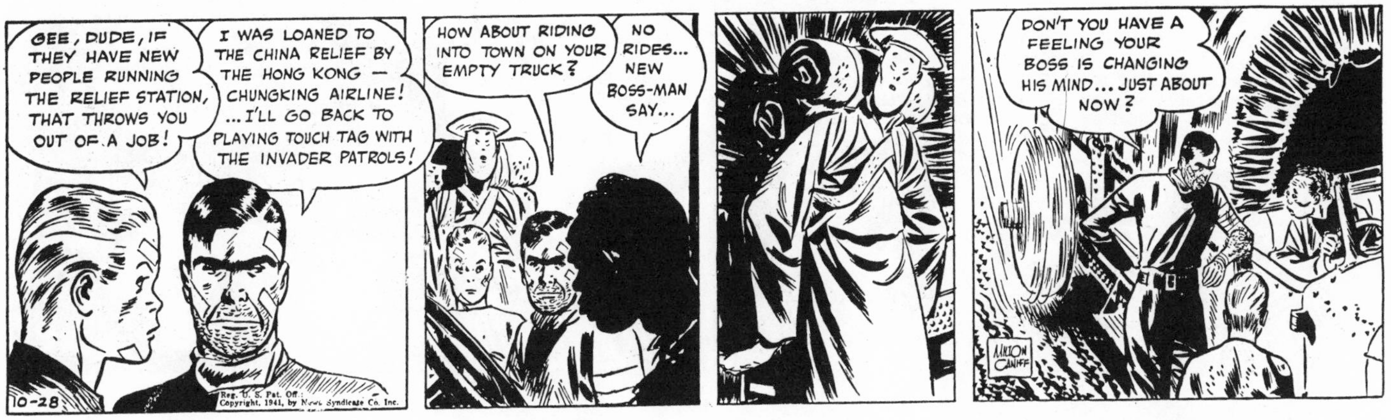
GEE, DUDE, IF THEY HAVE NEW PEOPLE RUNNING THE RELIEF STATION, THAT THROWS YOU OUT OF A JOB!
I WAS LOANED TO THE CHINA RELIEF BY THE HONG KONG — CHUNGKING AIRLINE! ...I'LL GO BACK TO PLAYING TOUCH TAG WITH THE INVADER PATROLS!
10-28
Reg. U. S. Pat. Off.: Copyright, 1941, by News Syndicate Co. Inc.
HOW ABOUT RIDING INTO TOWN ON YOUR EMPTY TRUCK?
NO RIDES... NEW BOSS-MAN SAY...
DON'T YOU HAVE A FEELING YOUR BOSS IS CHANGING HIS MIND... JUST ABOUT NOW?
MILTON CANIFF

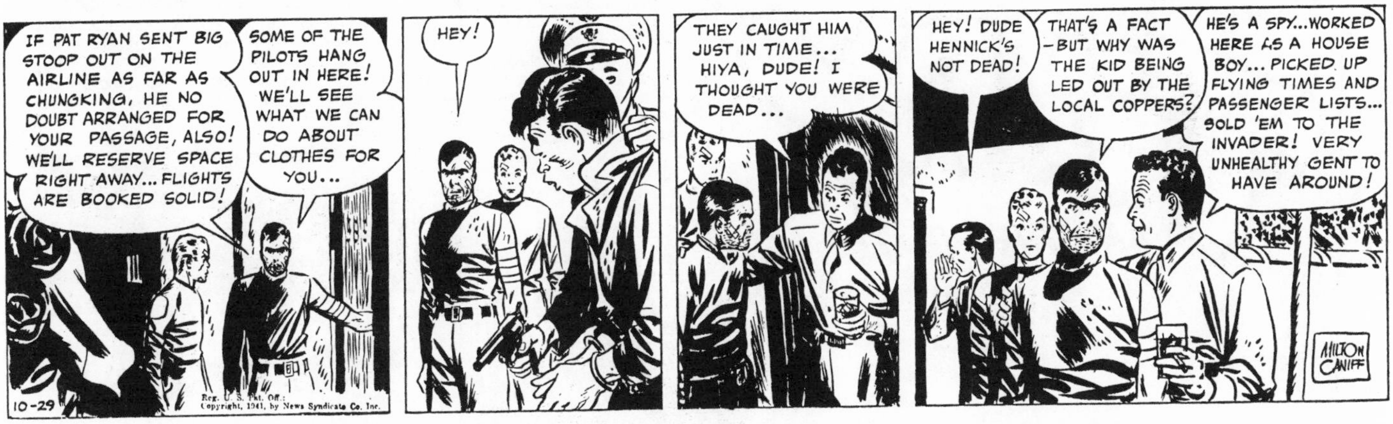
IF PAT RYAN SENT BIG STOOP OUT ON THE AIRLINE AS FAR AS CHUNGKING, HE NO DOUBT ARRANGED FOR YOUR PASSAGE, ALSO! WE'LL RESERVE SPACE RIGHT AWAY... FLIGHTS ARE BOOKED SOLID!
SOME OF THE PILOTS HANG OUT IN HERE! WE'LL SEE WHAT WE CAN DO ABOUT CLOTHES FOR YOU...
10-29
Reg. U. S. Pat. Off.: Copyright, 1941, by News Syndicate Co. Inc.
HEY!
THEY CAUGHT HIM JUST IN TIME... HIYA, DUDE! I THOUGHT YOU WERE DEAD...
HEY! DUDE HENNICK'S NOT DEAD!
THAT'S A FACT — BUT WHY WAS THE KID BEING LED OUT BY THE LOCAL COPPERS?
HE'S A SPY...WORKED HERE AS A HOUSE BOY... PICKED UP FLYING TIMES AND PASSENGER LISTS... SOLD 'EM TO THE INVADER! VERY UNHEALTHY GENT TO HAVE AROUND!
MILTON CANIFF

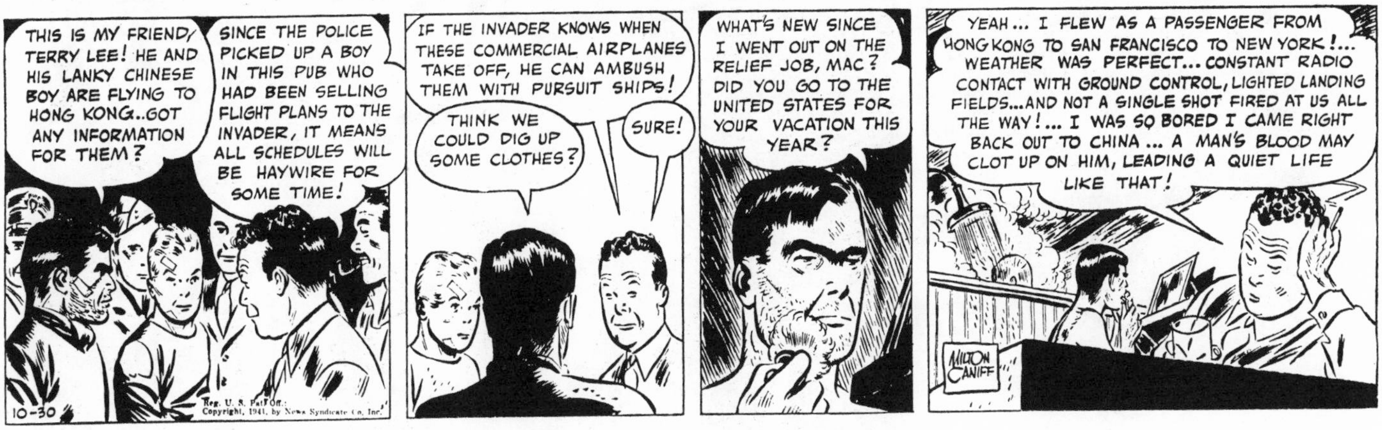
THIS IS MY FRIEND, TERRY LEE! HE AND HIS LANKY CHINESE BOY ARE FLYING TO HONG KONG..GOT ANY INFORMATION FOR THEM?
SINCE THE POLICE PICKED UP A BOY IN THIS PUB WHO HAD BEEN SELLING FLIGHT PLANS TO THE INVADER, IT MEANS ALL SCHEDULES WILL BE HAYWIRE FOR SOME TIME!
10-30
Reg. U. S. Pat. Off.: Copyright, 1941, by News Syndicate Co. Inc.
IF THE INVADER KNOWS WHEN THESE COMMERCIAL AIRPLANES TAKE OFF, HE CAN AMBUSH THEM WITH PURSUIT SHIPS!
THINK WE COULD DIG UP SOME CLOTHES?
SURE!
WHAT'S NEW SINCE I WENT OUT ON THE RELIEF JOB, MAC? DID YOU GO TO THE UNITED STATES FOR YOUR VACATION THIS YEAR?
MILTON CANIFF
YEAH... I FLEW AS A PASSENGER FROM HONG KONG TO SAN FRANCISCO TO NEW YORK!... WEATHER WAS PERFECT... CONSTANT RADIO CONTACT WITH GROUND CONTROL, LIGHTED LANDING FIELDS...AND NOT A SINGLE SHOT FIRED AT US ALL THE WAY!... I WAS SO BORED I CAME RIGHT BACK OUT TO CHINA... A MAN'S BLOOD MAY CLOT UP ON HIM, LEADING A QUIET LIFE LIKE THAT!

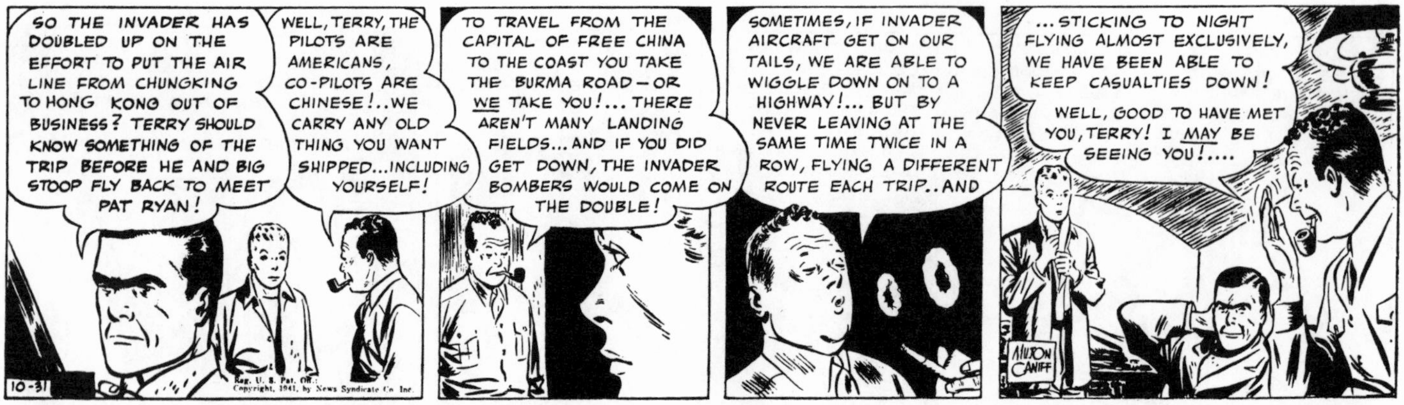
SO THE INVADER HAS DOUBLED UP ON THE EFFORT TO PUT THE AIR LINE FROM CHUNGKING TO HONG KONG OUT OF BUSINESS? TERRY SHOULD KNOW SOMETHING OF THE TRIP BEFORE HE AND BIG STOOP FLY BACK TO MEET PAT RYAN!
WELL, TERRY, THE PILOTS ARE AMERICANS, CO-PILOTS ARE CHINESE!..WE CARRY ANY OLD THING YOU WANT SHIPPED...INCLUDING YOURSELF!
10-31
Reg. U. S. Pat. Off.: Copyright, 1941, by News Syndicate Co. Inc.
TO TRAVEL FROM THE CAPITAL OF FREE CHINA TO THE COAST YOU TAKE THE BURMA ROAD—OR WE TAKE YOU!... THERE AREN'T MANY LANDING FIELDS... AND IF YOU DID GET DOWN, THE INVADER BOMBERS WOULD COME ON THE DOUBLE!
SOMETIMES, IF INVADER AIRCRAFT GET ON OUR TAILS, WE ARE ABLE TO WIGGLE DOWN ON TO A HIGHWAY!... BUT BY NEVER LEAVING AT THE SAME TIME TWICE IN A ROW, FLYING A DIFFERENT ROUTE EACH TRIP..AND
...STICKING TO NIGHT FLYING ALMOST EXCLUSIVELY, WE HAVE BEEN ABLE TO KEEP CASUALTIES DOWN!
WELL, GOOD TO HAVE MET YOU, TERRY! I MAY BE SEEING YOU!....
MILTON CANIFF

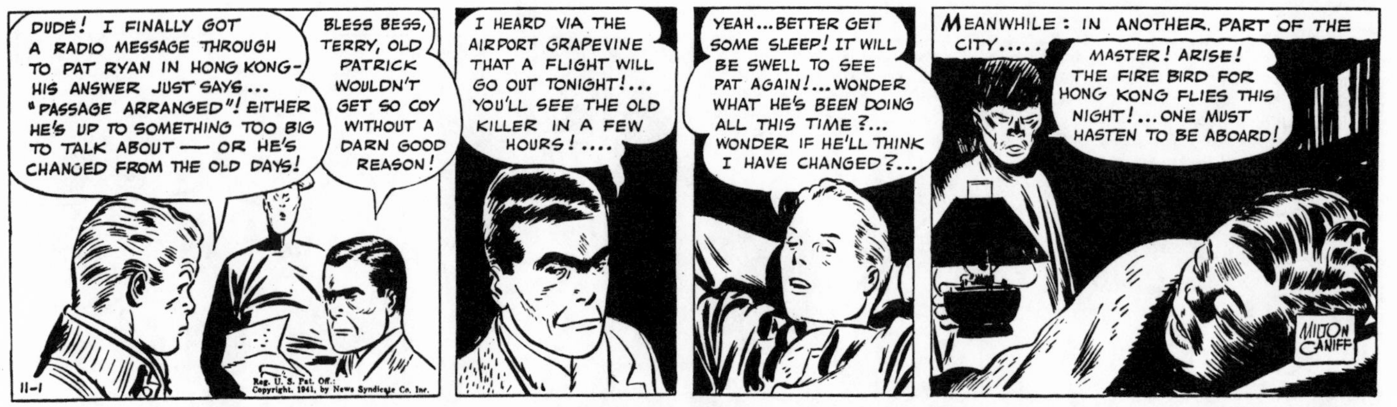
DUDE! I FINALLY GOT A RADIO MESSAGE THROUGH TO PAT RYAN IN HONG KONG - HIS ANSWER JUST SAYS... "PASSAGE ARRANGED"! EITHER HE'S UP TO SOMETHING TOO BIG TO TALK ABOUT — OR HE'S CHANGED FROM THE OLD DAYS!
BLESS BESS, TERRY, OLD PATRICK WOULDN'T GET SO COY WITHOUT A DARN GOOD REASON!
11-1
Reg. U. S. Pat. Off.: Copyright, 1941, by News Syndicate Co. Inc.
I HEARD VIA THE AIRPORT GRAPEVINE THAT A FLIGHT WILL GO OUT TONIGHT!... YOU'LL SEE THE OLD KILLER IN A FEW HOURS!....
YEAH...BETTER GET SOME SLEEP! IT WILL BE SWELL TO SEE PAT AGAIN!...WONDER WHAT HE'S BEEN DOING ALL THIS TIME?... WONDER IF HE'LL THINK I HAVE CHANGED?...
MEANWHILE: IN ANOTHER PART OF THE CITY.....
MASTER! ARISE! THE FIRE BIRD FOR HONG KONG FLIES THIS NIGHT!...ONE MUST HASTEN TO BE ABOARD!
MILTON CANIFF

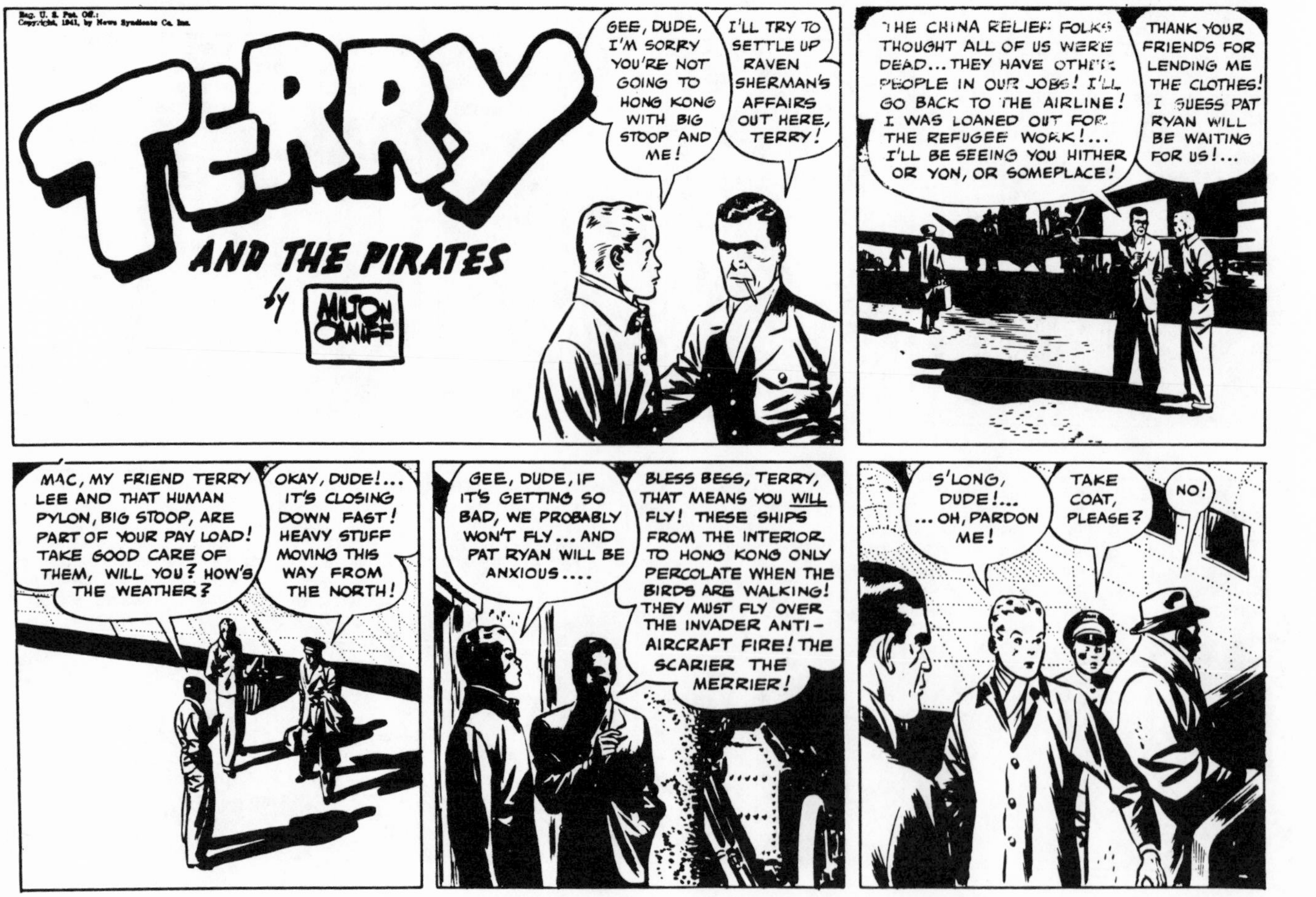
Reg. U. S. Pat. Off.: Copyright, 1941, by News Syndicate Co. Inc.
TERRY AND THE PIRATES by MILTON CANIFF
GEE, DUDE, I'M SORRY YOU'RE NOT GOING TO HONG KONG WITH BIG STOOP AND ME!
I'LL TRY TO SETTLE UP RAVEN SHERMAN'S AFFAIRS OUT HERE, TERRY!
THE CHINA RELIEF FOLKS THOUGHT ALL OF US WERE DEAD... THEY HAVE OTHER PEOPLE IN OUR JOBS! I'LL GO BACK TO THE AIRLINE! I WAS LOANED OUT FOR THE REFUGEE WORK!... I'LL BE SEEING YOU HITHER OR YON, OR SOMEPLACE!
THANK YOUR FRIENDS FOR LENDING ME THE CLOTHES! I GUESS PAT RYAN WILL BE WAITING FOR US!...
MAC, MY FRIEND TERRY LEE AND THAT HUMAN PYLON, BIG STOOP, ARE PART OF YOUR PAY LOAD! TAKE GOOD CARE OF THEM, WILL YOU? HOW'S THE WEATHER?
OKAY, DUDE!... IT'S CLOSING DOWN FAST! HEAVY STUFF MOVING THIS WAY FROM THE NORTH!
GEE, DUDE, IF IT'S GETTING SO BAD, WE PROBABLY WON'T FLY... AND PAT RYAN WILL BE ANXIOUS....
BLESS BESS, TERRY, THAT MEANS YOU WILL FLY! THESE SHIPS FROM THE INTERIOR TO HONG KONG ONLY PERCOLATE WHEN THE BIRDS ARE WALKING! THEY MUST FLY OVER THE INVADER ANTI-AIRCRAFT FIRE! THE SCARIER THE MERRIER!
S'LONG, DUDE!... ...OH, PARDON ME!
TAKE COAT, PLEASE?
NO!

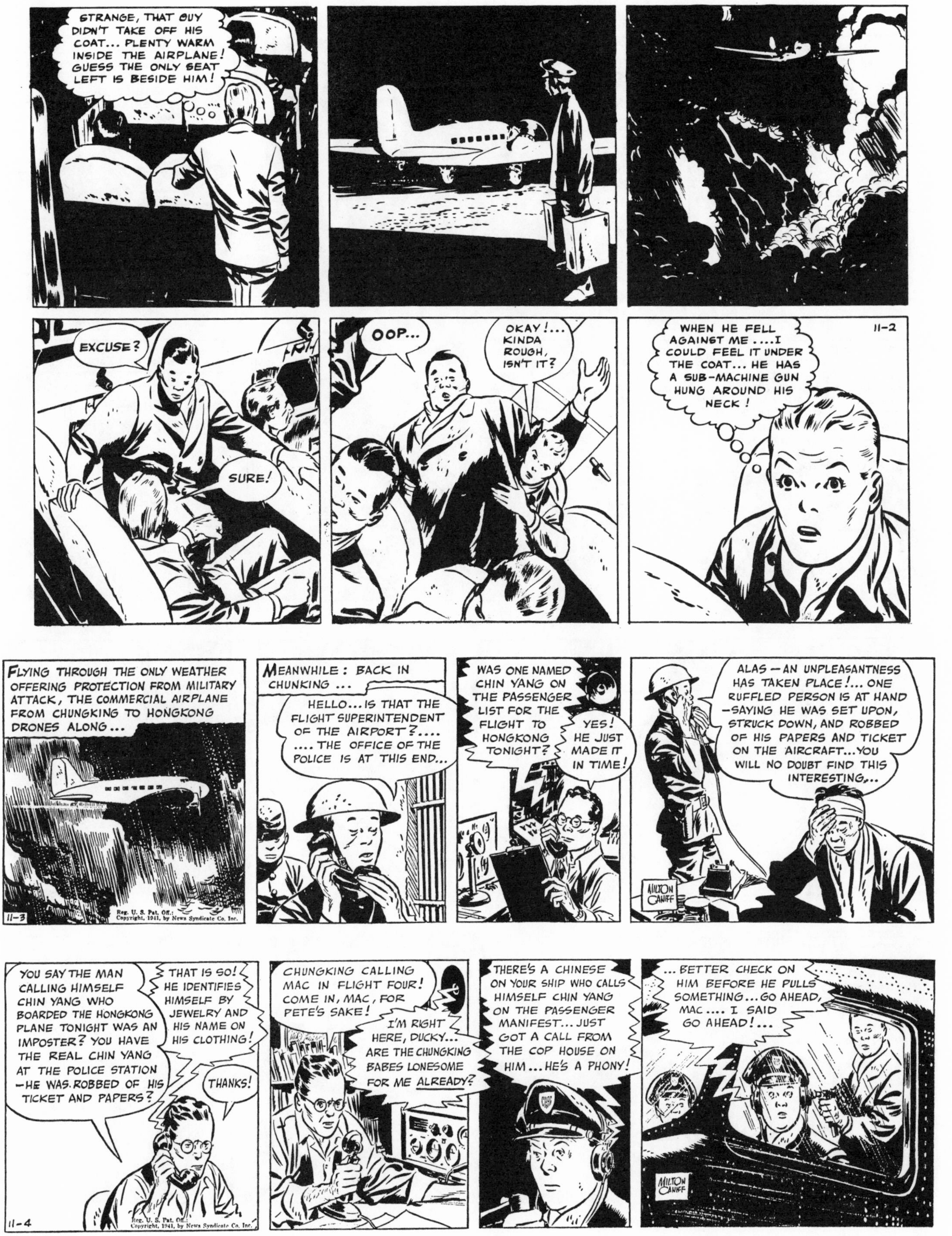

STRANGE, THAT GUY DIDN'T TAKE OFF HIS COAT... PLENTY WARM INSIDE THE AIRPLANE! GUESS THE ONLY SEAT LEFT IS BESIDE HIM!
EXCUSE?
SURE!
OOP...
OKAY!... KINDA ROUGH, ISN'T IT?
11-2
WHEN HE FELL AGAINST ME....I COULD FEEL IT UNDER THE COAT... HE HAS A SUB-MACHINE GUN HUNG AROUND HIS NECK!
FLYING THROUGH THE ONLY WEATHER OFFERING PROTECTION FROM MILITARY ATTACK, THE COMMERCIAL AIRPLANE FROM CHUNGKING TO HONGKONG DRONES ALONG...
11-3
Reg. U. S. Pat. Off.: Copyright, 1941, by News Syndicate Co. Inc.
MEANWHILE: BACK IN CHUNKING...
HELLO... IS THAT THE FLIGHT SUPERINTENDENT OF THE AIRPORT?.... .... THE OFFICE OF THE POLICE IS AT THIS END...
WAS ONE NAMED CHIN YANG ON THE PASSENGER LIST FOR THE FLIGHT TO HONGKONG TONIGHT?
YES! HE JUST MADE IT IN TIME!
ALAS — AN UNPLEASANTNESS HAS TAKEN PLACE!... ONE RUFFLED PERSON IS AT HAND —SAYING HE WAS SET UPON, STRUCK DOWN, AND ROBBED OF HIS PAPERS AND TICKET ON THE AIRCRAFT... YOU WILL NO DOUBT FIND THIS INTERESTING,...
MILTON CANIFF
YOU SAY THE MAN CALLING HIMSELF CHIN YANG WHO BOARDED THE HONGKONG PLANE TONIGHT WAS AN IMPOSTER? YOU HAVE THE REAL CHIN YANG AT THE POLICE STATION —HE WAS ROBBED OF HIS TICKET AND PAPERS?
THAT IS SO! HE IDENTIFIES HIMSELF BY JEWELRY AND HIS NAME ON HIS CLOTHING!
THANKS!
11-4
Reg. U. S. Pat. Off.: Copyright, 1941, by News Syndicate Co. Inc.
CHUNGKING CALLING MAC IN FLIGHT FOUR! COME IN, MAC, FOR PETE'S SAKE!
I'M RIGHT HERE, DUCKY... ARE THE CHUNGKING BABES LONESOME FOR ME ALREADY?
THERE'S A CHINESE ON YOUR SHIP WHO CALLS HIMSELF CHIN YANG ON THE PASSENGER MANIFEST... JUST GOT A CALL FROM THE COP HOUSE ON HIM... HE'S A PHONY!
... BETTER CHECK ON HIM BEFORE HE PULLS SOMETHING... GO AHEAD, MAC.... I SAID GO AHEAD!...
MILTON CANIFF

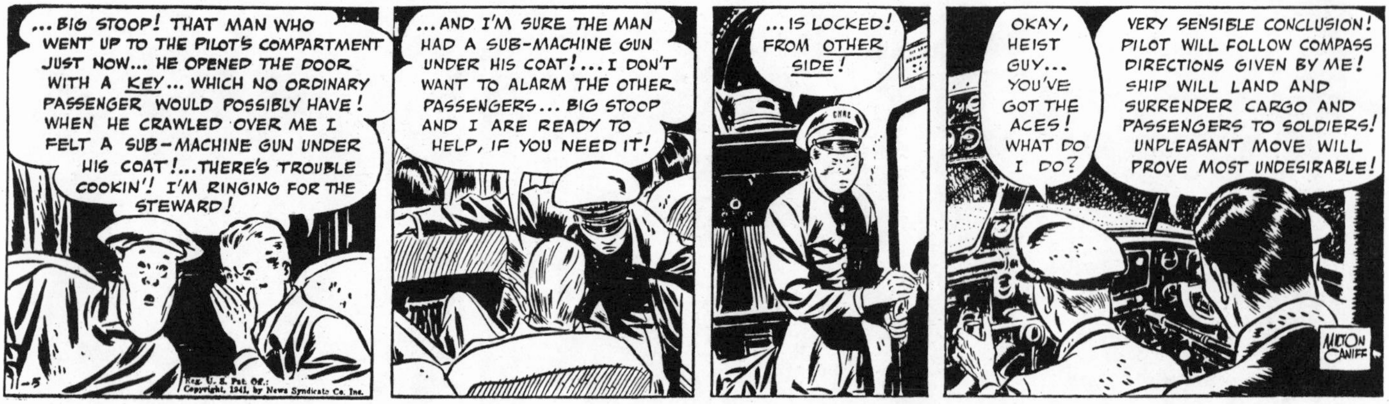
...BIG STOOP! THAT MAN WHO WENT UP TO THE PILOT'S COMPARTMENT JUST NOW... HE OPENED THE DOOR WITH A KEY... WHICH NO ORDINARY PASSENGER WOULD POSSIBLY HAVE! WHEN HE CRAWLED OVER ME I FELT A SUB-MACHINE GUN UNDER HIS COAT!...THERE'S TROUBLE COOKIN'! I'M RINGING FOR THE STEWARD!
...AND I'M SURE THE MAN HAD A SUB-MACHINE GUN UNDER HIS COAT!...I DON'T WANT TO ALARM THE OTHER PASSENGERS... BIG STOOP AND I ARE READY TO HELP, IF YOU NEED IT!
...IS LOCKED! FROM OTHER SIDE!
OKAY, HEIST GUY... YOU'VE GOT THE ACES! WHAT DO I DO?
VERY SENSIBLE CONCLUSION! PILOT WILL FOLLOW COMPASS DIRECTIONS GIVEN BY ME! SHIP WILL LAND AND SURRENDER CARGO AND PASSENGERS TO SOLDIERS! UNPLEASANT MOVE WILL PROVE MOST UNDESIRABLE!
11-5
Reg. U. S. Pat. Off.: Copyright, 1941, by News Syndicate Co. Inc.
MILTON CANIFF

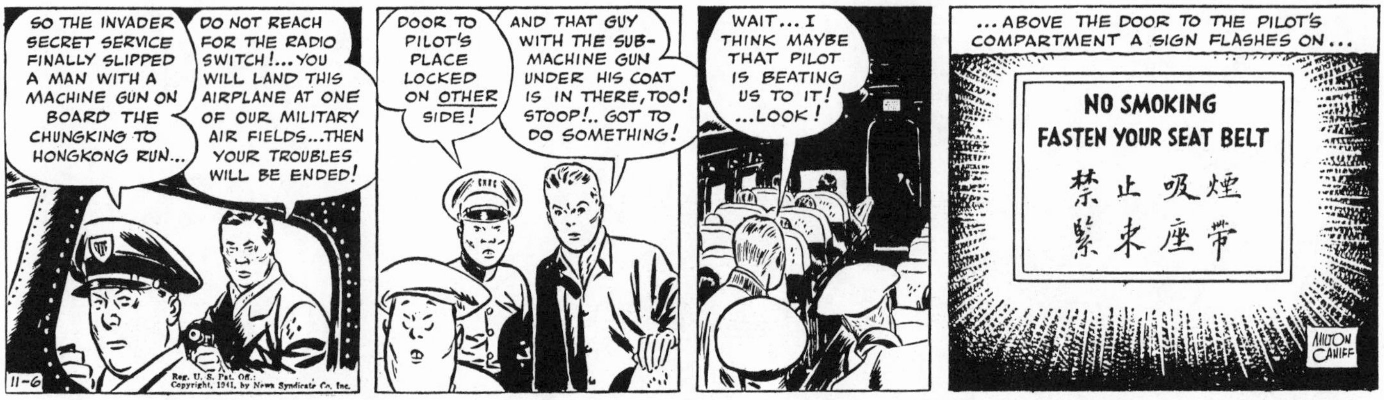
SO THE INVADER SECRET SERVICE FINALLY SLIPPED A MAN WITH A MACHINE GUN ON BOARD THE CHUNGKING TO HONGKONG RUN...
DO NOT REACH FOR THE RADIO SWITCH!...YOU WILL LAND THIS AIRPLANE AT ONE OF OUR MILITARY AIR FIELDS...THEN YOUR TROUBLES WILL BE ENDED!
DOOR TO PILOT'S PLACE LOCKED ON OTHER SIDE!
AND THAT GUY WITH THE SUB-MACHINE GUN UNDER HIS COAT IS IN THERE, TOO! STOOP!.. GOT TO DO SOMETHING!
WAIT...I THINK MAYBE THAT PILOT IS BEATING US TO IT! ...LOOK!
...ABOVE THE DOOR TO THE PILOT'S COMPARTMENT A SIGN FLASHES ON...
NO SMOKING
FASTEN YOUR SEAT BELT
禁止吸煙
繫束座帶
11-6
Reg. U. S. Pat. Off.: Copyright, 1941, by News Syndicate Co. Inc.
MILTON CANIFF

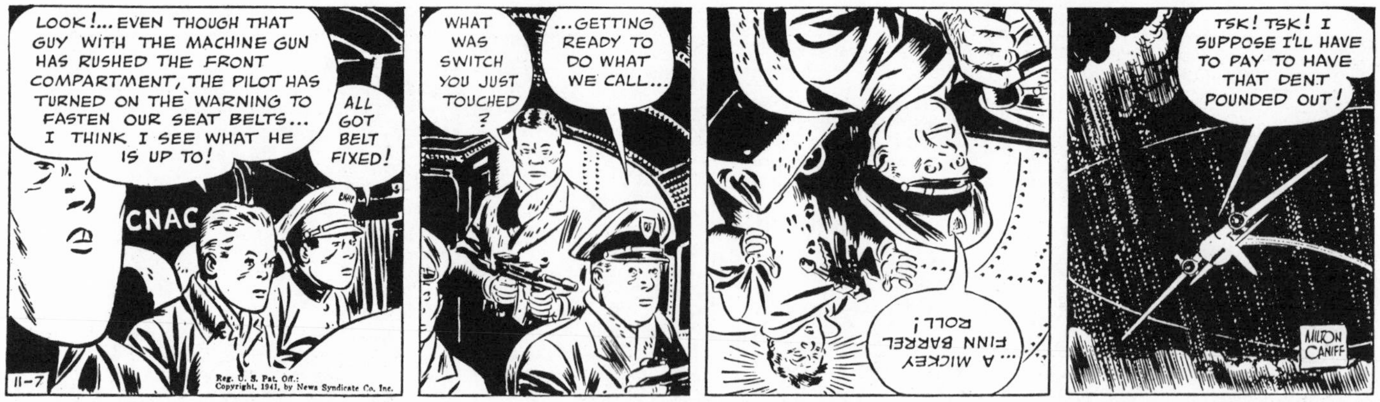
LOOK!...EVEN THOUGH THAT GUY WITH THE MACHINE GUN HAS RUSHED THE FRONT COMPARTMENT, THE PILOT HAS TURNED ON THE WARNING TO FASTEN OUR SEAT BELTS... I THINK I SEE WHAT HE IS UP TO!
ALL GOT BELT FIXED!
CNAC
WHAT WAS SWITCH YOU JUST TOUCHED?
...GETTING READY TO DO WHAT WE CALL...
...A MICKEY FINN BARREL ROLL!
TSK! TSK! I SUPPOSE I'LL HAVE TO PAY TO HAVE THAT DENT POUNDED OUT!
11-7
Reg. U. S. Pat. Off.: Copyright, 1941, by News Syndicate Co. Inc.
MILTON CANIFF

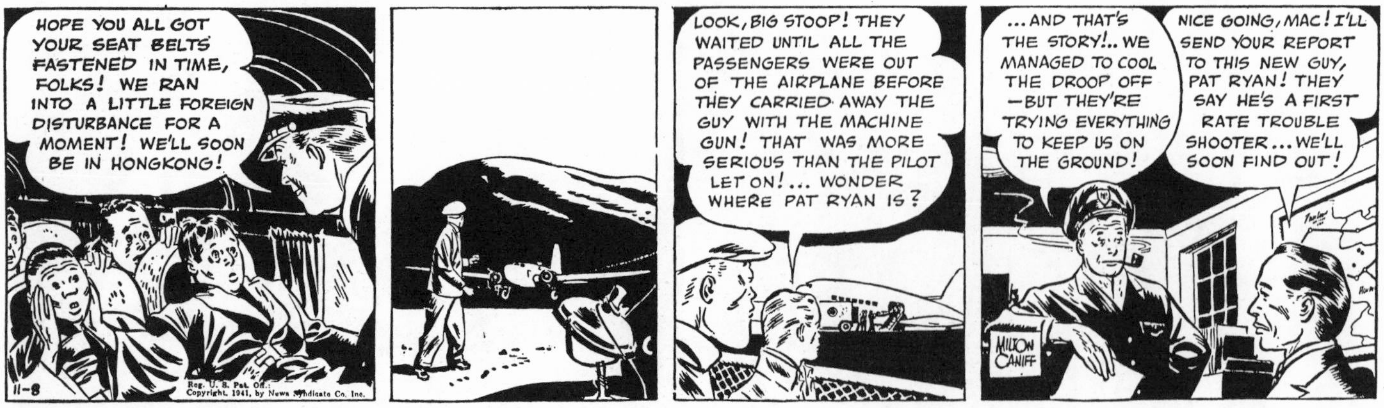
HOPE YOU ALL GOT YOUR SEAT BELTS FASTENED IN TIME, FOLKS! WE RAN INTO A LITTLE FOREIGN DISTURBANCE FOR A MOMENT! WE'LL SOON BE IN HONGKONG!
LOOK, BIG STOOP! THEY WAITED UNTIL ALL THE PASSENGERS WERE OUT OF THE AIRPLANE BEFORE THEY CARRIED AWAY THE GUY WITH THE MACHINE GUN! THAT WAS MORE SERIOUS THAN THE PILOT LET ON!... WONDER WHERE PAT RYAN IS?
...AND THAT'S THE STORY!.. WE MANAGED TO COOL THE DROOP OFF —BUT THEY'RE TRYING EVERYTHING TO KEEP US ON THE GROUND!
NICE GOING, MAC! I'LL SEND YOUR REPORT TO THIS NEW GUY, PAT RYAN! THEY SAY HE'S A FIRST RATE TROUBLE SHOOTER...WE'LL SOON FIND OUT!
11-8
Reg. U. S. Pat. Off.: Copyright, 1941, by News Syndicate Co. Inc.
MILTON CANIFF

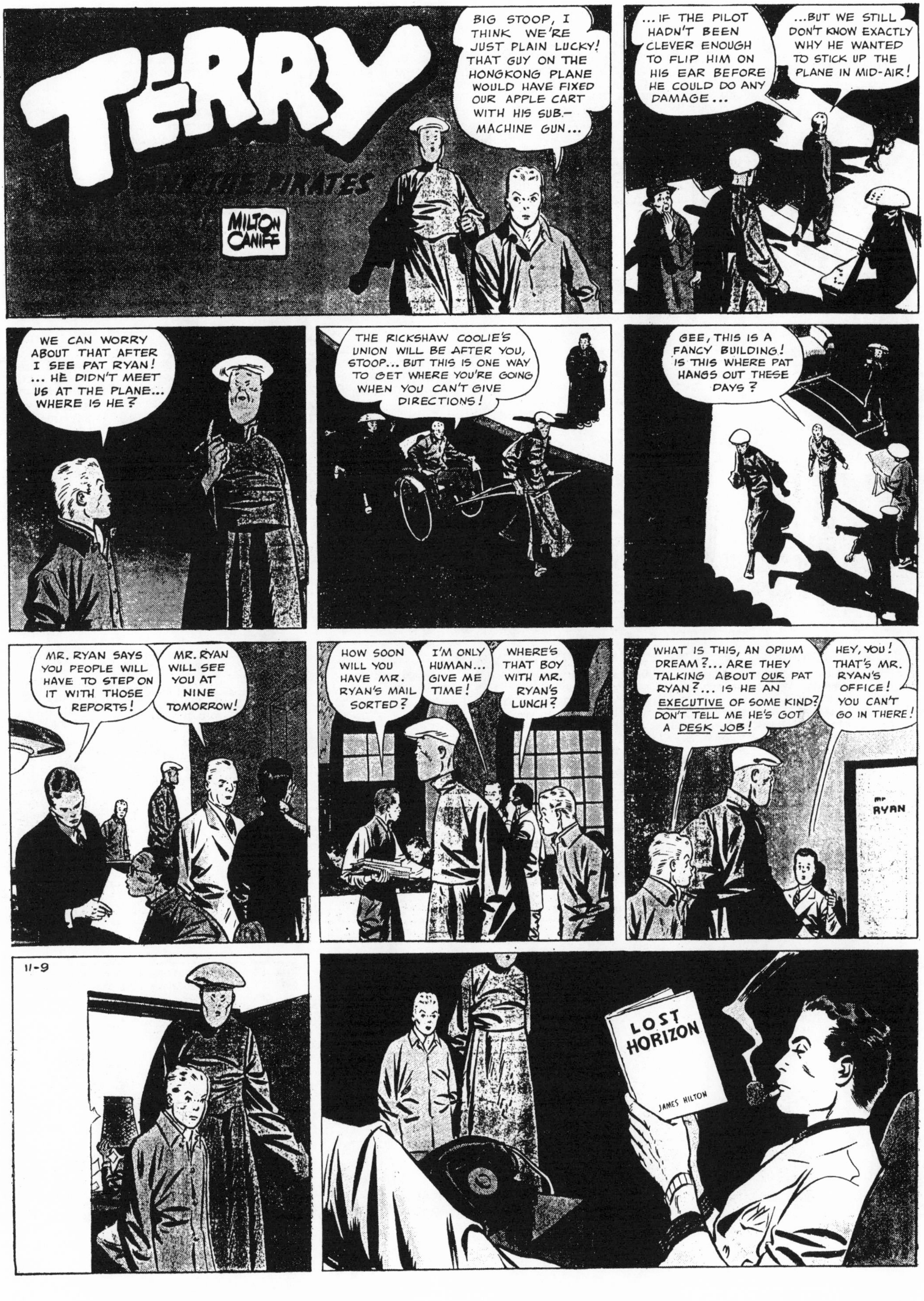
TERRY AND THE PIRATES
MILTON CANIFF
BIG STOOP, I THINK WE'RE JUST PLAIN LUCKY! THAT GUY ON THE HONGKONG PLANE WOULD HAVE FIXED OUR APPLE CART WITH HIS SUB-MACHINE GUN...
...IF THE PILOT HADN'T BEEN CLEVER ENOUGH TO FLIP HIM ON HIS EAR BEFORE HE COULD DO ANY DAMAGE...
...BUT WE STILL DON'T KNOW EXACTLY WHY HE WANTED TO STICK UP THE PLANE IN MID-AIR!
WE CAN WORRY ABOUT THAT AFTER I SEE PAT RYAN! ... HE DIDN'T MEET US AT THE PLANE... WHERE IS HE?
THE RICKSHAW COOLIE'S UNION WILL BE AFTER YOU, STOOP... BUT THIS IS ONE WAY TO GET WHERE YOU'RE GOING WHEN YOU CAN'T GIVE DIRECTIONS!
GEE, THIS IS A FANCY BUILDING! IS THIS WHERE PAT HANGS OUT THESE DAYS?
MR. RYAN SAYS YOU PEOPLE WILL HAVE TO STEP ON IT WITH THOSE REPORTS!
MR. RYAN WILL SEE YOU AT NINE TOMORROW!
HOW SOON WILL YOU HAVE MR. RYAN'S MAIL SORTED?
I'M ONLY HUMAN... GIVE ME TIME!
WHERE'S THAT BOY WITH MR. RYAN'S LUNCH?
WHAT IS THIS, AN OPIUM DREAM?... ARE THEY TALKING ABOUT OUR PAT RYAN?... IS HE AN EXECUTIVE OF SOME KIND? DON'T TELL ME HE'S GOT A DESK JOB!
HEY, YOU! THAT'S MR. RYAN'S OFFICE! YOU CAN'T GO IN THERE!
MR RYAN
11-9
LOST HORIZON
JAMES HILTON

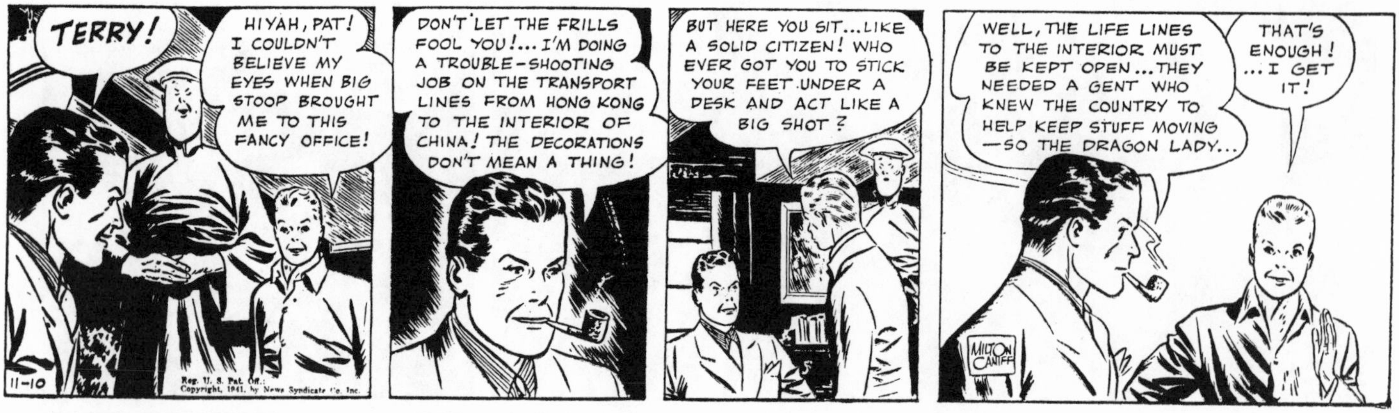
TERRY!
HIYAH, PAT! I COULDN'T BELIEVE MY EYES WHEN BIG STOOP BROUGHT ME TO THIS FANCY OFFICE!
DON'T LET THE FRILLS FOOL YOU!... I'M DOING A TROUBLE-SHOOTING JOB ON THE TRANSPORT LINES FROM HONG KONG TO THE INTERIOR OF CHINA! THE DECORATIONS DON'T MEAN A THING!
BUT HERE YOU SIT... LIKE A SOLID CITIZEN! WHO EVER GOT YOU TO STICK YOUR FEET UNDER A DESK AND ACT LIKE A BIG SHOT?
WELL, THE LIFE LINES TO THE INTERIOR MUST BE KEPT OPEN... THEY NEEDED A GENT WHO KNEW THE COUNTRY TO HELP KEEP STUFF MOVING —SO THE DRAGON LADY...
THAT'S ENOUGH! ...I GET IT!
11-10
Reg. U. S. Pat. Off.: Copyright, 1941, by News Syndicate Co. Inc.
MILTON CANIFF

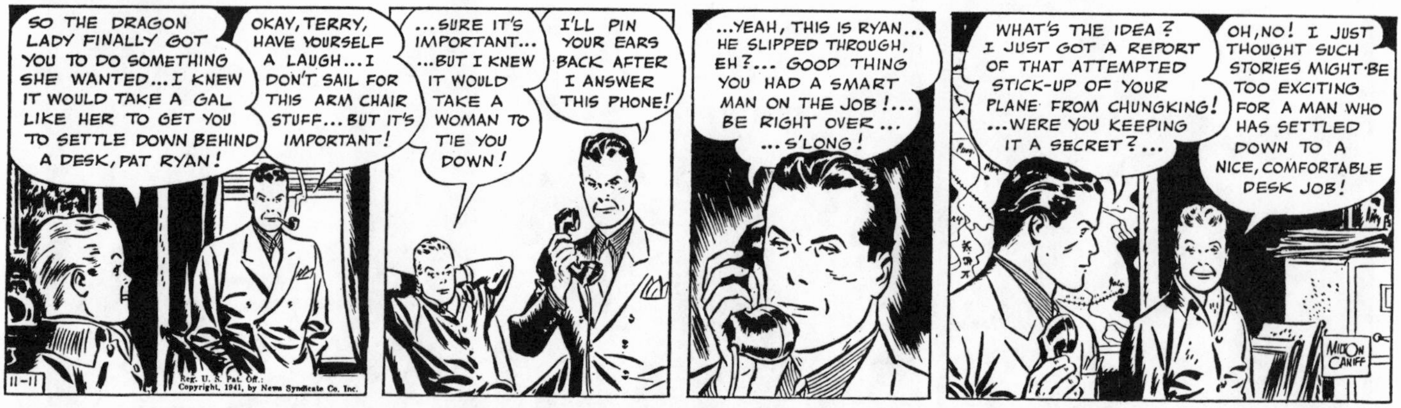
SO THE DRAGON LADY FINALLY GOT YOU TO DO SOMETHING SHE WANTED... I KNEW IT WOULD TAKE A GAL LIKE HER TO GET YOU TO SETTLE DOWN BEHIND A DESK, PAT RYAN!
OKAY, TERRY, HAVE YOURSELF A LAUGH... I DON'T SAIL FOR THIS ARM CHAIR STUFF... BUT IT'S IMPORTANT!
...SURE IT'S IMPORTANT... ...BUT I KNEW IT WOULD TAKE A WOMAN TO TIE YOU DOWN!
I'LL PIN YOUR EARS BACK AFTER I ANSWER THIS PHONE!
...YEAH, THIS IS RYAN... HE SLIPPED THROUGH, EH?... GOOD THING YOU HAD A SMART MAN ON THE JOB!... BE RIGHT OVER... ...S'LONG!
WHAT'S THE IDEA? I JUST GOT A REPORT OF THAT ATTEMPTED STICK-UP OF YOUR PLANE FROM CHUNGKING! ...WERE YOU KEEPING IT A SECRET?...
OH, NO! I JUST THOUGHT SUCH STORIES MIGHT BE TOO EXCITING FOR A MAN WHO HAS SETTLED DOWN TO A NICE, COMFORTABLE DESK JOB!
11-11
Reg. U. S. Pat. Off.: Copyright, 1941, by News Syndicate Co. Inc.
MILTON CANIFF

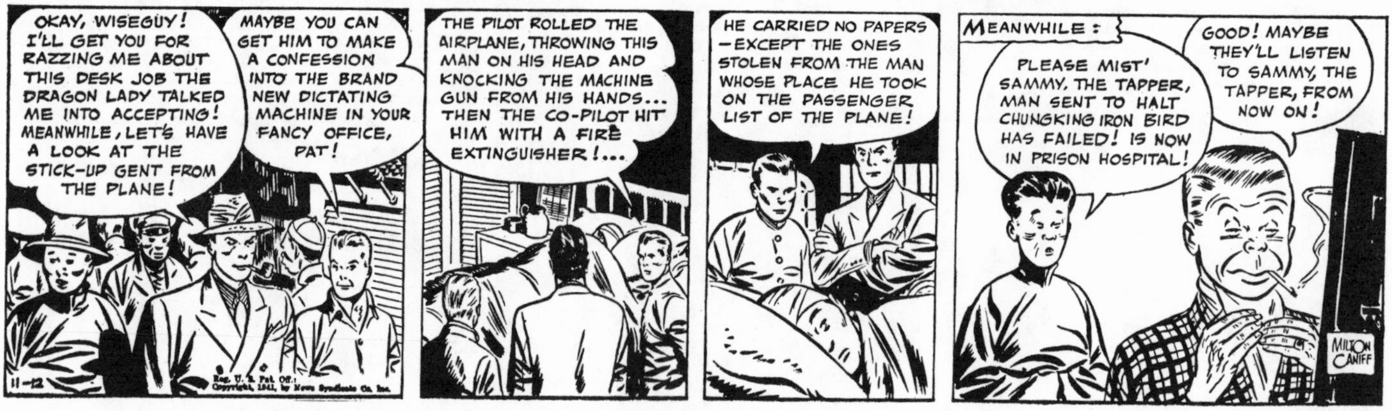
OKAY, WISEGUY! I'LL GET YOU FOR RAZZING ME ABOUT THIS DESK JOB THE DRAGON LADY TALKED ME INTO ACCEPTING! MEANWHILE, LET'S HAVE A LOOK AT THE STICK-UP GENT FROM THE PLANE!
MAYBE YOU CAN GET HIM TO MAKE A CONFESSION INTO THE BRAND NEW DICTATING MACHINE IN YOUR FANCY OFFICE, PAT!
THE PILOT ROLLED THE AIRPLANE, THROWING THIS MAN ON HIS HEAD AND KNOCKING THE MACHINE GUN FROM HIS HANDS... THEN THE CO-PILOT HIT HIM WITH A FIRE EXTINGUISHER!...
HE CARRIED NO PAPERS —EXCEPT THE ONES STOLEN FROM THE MAN WHOSE PLACE HE TOOK ON THE PASSENGER LIST OF THE PLANE!
MEANWHILE:
PLEASE MIST' SAMMY, THE TAPPER, MAN SENT TO HALT CHUNGKING IRON BIRD HAS FAILED! IS NOW IN PRISON HOSPITAL!
GOOD! MAYBE THEY'LL LISTEN TO SAMMY, THE TAPPER, FROM NOW ON!
11-12
Reg. U. S. Pat. Off.: Copyright, 1941, by News Syndicate Co. Inc.
MILTON CANIFF

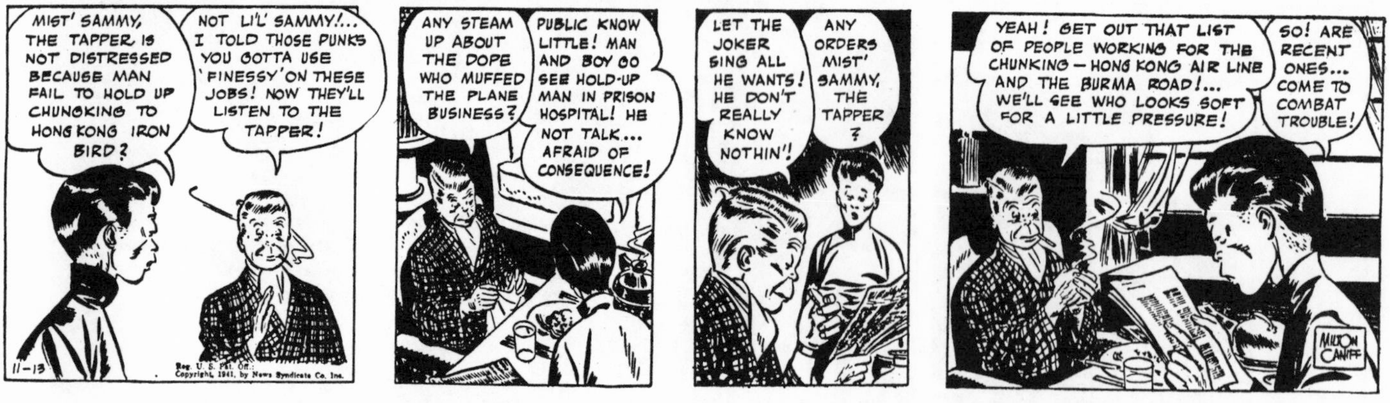
MIST' SAMMY, THE TAPPER IS NOT DISTRESSED BECAUSE MAN FAIL TO HOLD UP CHUNGKING TO HONG KONG IRON BIRD?
NOT LI'L' SAMMY!... I TOLD THOSE PUNKS YOU GOTTA USE 'FINESSY' ON THESE JOBS! NOW THEY'LL LISTEN TO THE TAPPER!
ANY STEAM UP ABOUT THE DOPE WHO MUFFED THE PLANE BUSINESS?
PUBLIC KNOW LITTLE! MAN AND BOY GO SEE HOLD-UP MAN IN PRISON HOSPITAL! HE NOT TALK... AFRAID OF CONSEQUENCE!
LET THE JOKER SING ALL HE WANTS! HE DON'T REALLY KNOW NOTHIN'!
ANY ORDERS MIST' SAMMY, THE TAPPER?
YEAH! GET OUT THAT LIST OF PEOPLE WORKING FOR THE CHUNKING — HONG KONG AIR LINE AND THE BURMA ROAD!... WE'LL SEE WHO LOOKS SOFT FOR A LITTLE PRESSURE!
SO! ARE RECENT ONES... COME TO COMBAT TROUBLE!
11-13
Reg. U. S. Pat. Off.: Copyright, 1941, by News Syndicate Co. Inc.
MILTON CANIFF

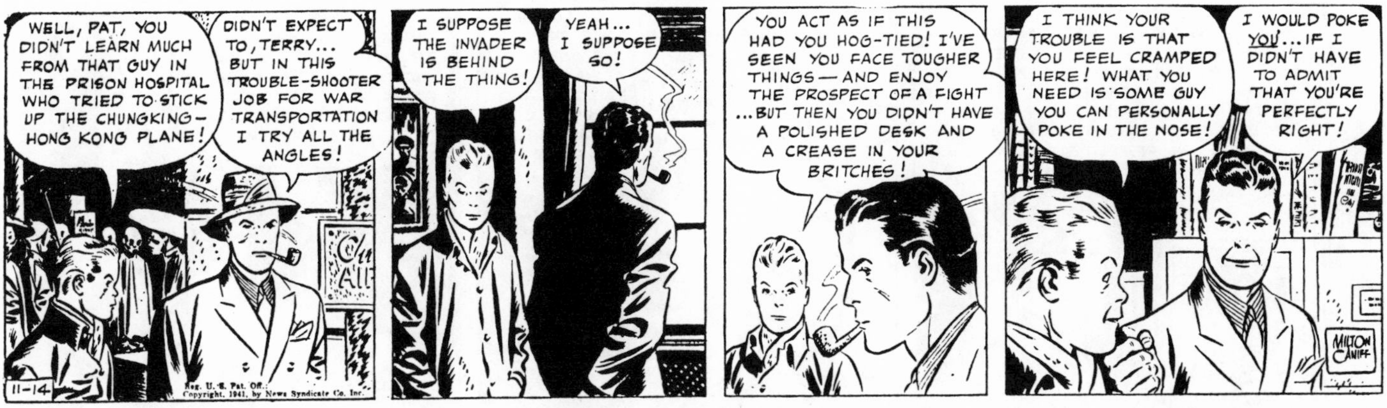
WELL, PAT, YOU DIDN'T LEARN MUCH FROM THAT GUY IN THE PRISON HOSPITAL WHO TRIED TO STICK UP THE CHUNGKING-HONG KONG PLANE!
DIDN'T EXPECT TO, TERRY... BUT IN THIS TROUBLE-SHOOTER JOB FOR WAR TRANSPORTATION I TRY ALL THE ANGLES!
11-14
Reg. U. S. Pat. Off.: Copyright, 1941, by News Syndicate Co. Inc.
I SUPPOSE THE INVADER IS BEHIND THE THING!
YEAH... I SUPPOSE SO!
YOU ACT AS IF THIS HAD YOU HOG-TIED! I'VE SEEN YOU FACE TOUGHER THINGS — AND ENJOY THE PROSPECT OF A FIGHT ...BUT THEN YOU DIDN'T HAVE A POLISHED DESK AND A CREASE IN YOUR BRITCHES!
I THINK YOUR TROUBLE IS THAT YOU FEEL CRAMPED HERE! WHAT YOU NEED IS SOME GUY YOU CAN PERSONALLY POKE IN THE NOSE!
I WOULD POKE YOU... IF I DIDN'T HAVE TO ADMIT THAT YOU'RE PERFECTLY RIGHT!
MILTON CANIFF

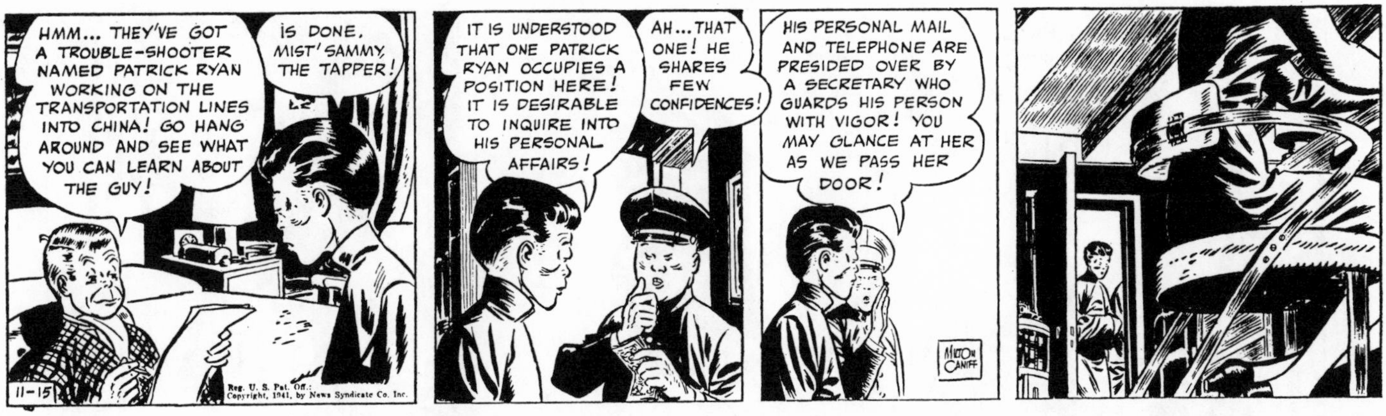
HMM... THEY'VE GOT A TROUBLE-SHOOTER NAMED PATRICK RYAN WORKING ON THE TRANSPORTATION LINES INTO CHINA! GO HANG AROUND AND SEE WHAT YOU CAN LEARN ABOUT THE GUY!
IS DONE, MIST' SAMMY, THE TAPPER!
11-15
Reg. U. S. Pat. Off.: Copyright, 1941, by News Syndicate Co. Inc.
IT IS UNDERSTOOD THAT ONE PATRICK RYAN OCCUPIES A POSITION HERE! IT IS DESIRABLE TO INQUIRE INTO HIS PERSONAL AFFAIRS!
AH... THAT ONE! HE SHARES FEW CONFIDENCES!
HIS PERSONAL MAIL AND TELEPHONE ARE PRESIDED OVER BY A SECRETARY WHO GUARDS HIS PERSON WITH VIGOR! YOU MAY GLANCE AT HER AS WE PASS HER DOOR!
MILTON CANIFF

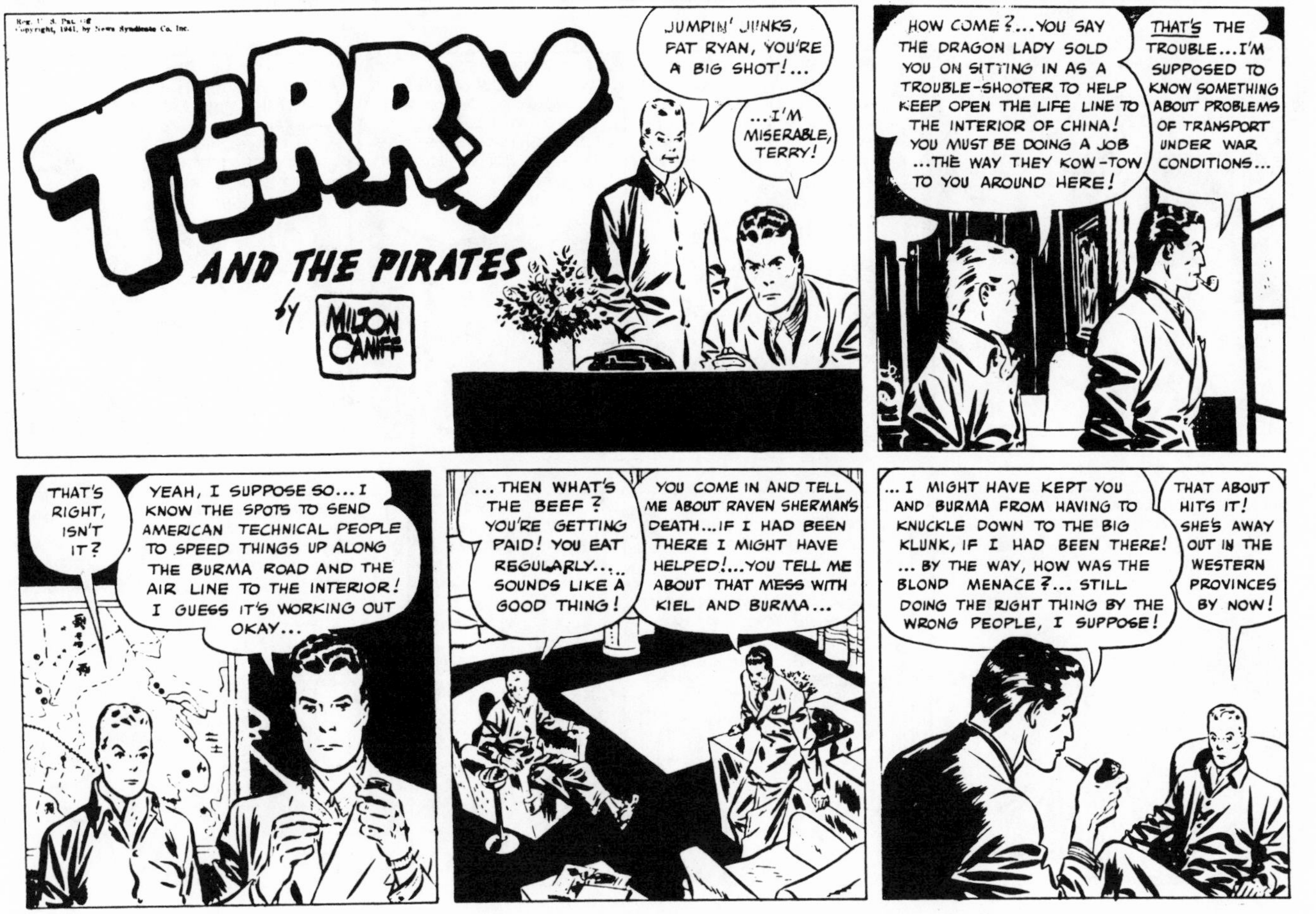
Reg. U. S. Pat. Off.: Copyright, 1941, by News Syndicate Co. Inc.
TERRY
AND THE PIRATES
by MILTON CANIFF
JUMPIN' JUNKS, PAT RYAN, YOU'RE A BIG SHOT!...
...I'M MISERABLE, TERRY!
HOW COME?... YOU SAY THE DRAGON LADY SOLD YOU ON SITTING IN AS A TROUBLE-SHOOTER TO HELP KEEP OPEN THE LIFE LINE TO THE INTERIOR OF CHINA! YOU MUST BE DOING A JOB ...THE WAY THEY KOW-TOW TO YOU AROUND HERE!
THAT'S THE TROUBLE... I'M SUPPOSED TO KNOW SOMETHING ABOUT PROBLEMS OF TRANSPORT UNDER WAR CONDITIONS...
THAT'S RIGHT, ISN'T IT?
YEAH, I SUPPOSE SO... I KNOW THE SPOTS TO SEND AMERICAN TECHNICAL PEOPLE TO SPEED THINGS UP ALONG THE BURMA ROAD AND THE AIR LINE TO THE INTERIOR! I GUESS IT'S WORKING OUT OKAY...
... THEN WHAT'S THE BEEF? YOU'RE GETTING PAID! YOU EAT REGULARLY... SOUNDS LIKE A GOOD THING!
YOU COME IN AND TELL ME ABOUT RAVEN SHERMAN'S DEATH... IF I HAD BEEN THERE I MIGHT HAVE HELPED!... YOU TELL ME ABOUT THAT MESS WITH KIEL AND BURMA...
... I MIGHT HAVE KEPT YOU AND BURMA FROM HAVING TO KNUCKLE DOWN TO THE BIG KLUNK, IF I HAD BEEN THERE! ... BY THE WAY, HOW WAS THE BLOND MENACE?... STILL DOING THE RIGHT THING BY THE WRONG PEOPLE, I SUPPOSE!
THAT ABOUT HITS IT! SHE'S AWAY OUT IN THE WESTERN PROVINCES BY NOW!

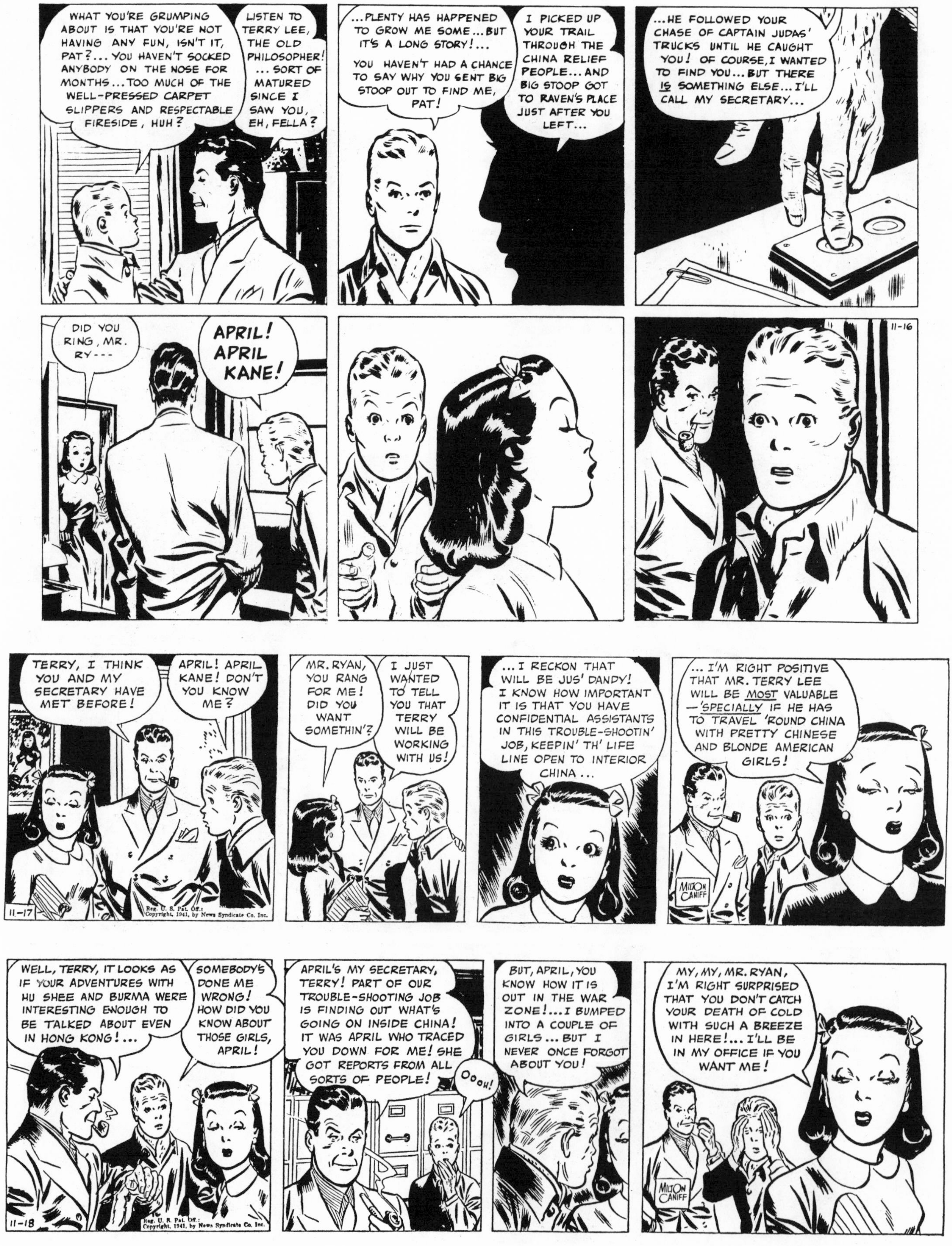

WHAT YOU'RE GRUMPING ABOUT IS THAT YOU'RE NOT HAVING ANY FUN, ISN'T IT, PAT?... YOU HAVEN'T SOCKED ANYBODY ON THE NOSE FOR MONTHS... TOO MUCH OF THE WELL-PRESSED CARPET SLIPPERS AND RESPECTABLE FIRESIDE, HUH?
LISTEN TO TERRY LEE, THE OLD PHILOSOPHER! ... SORT OF MATURED SINCE I SAW YOU, EH, FELLA?
...PLENTY HAS HAPPENED TO GROW ME SOME... BUT IT'S A LONG STORY!...
YOU HAVEN'T HAD A CHANCE TO SAY WHY YOU SENT BIG STOOP OUT TO FIND ME, PAT!
I PICKED UP YOUR TRAIL THROUGH THE CHINA RELIEF PEOPLE... AND BIG STOOP GOT TO RAVEN'S PLACE JUST AFTER YOU LEFT...
...HE FOLLOWED YOUR CHASE OF CAPTAIN JUDAS' TRUCKS UNTIL HE CAUGHT YOU! OF COURSE, I WANTED TO FIND YOU... BUT THERE IS SOMETHING ELSE... I'LL CALL MY SECRETARY...
DID YOU RING, MR. RY---
APRIL! APRIL KANE!
11-16
TERRY, I THINK YOU AND MY SECRETARY HAVE MET BEFORE!
APRIL! APRIL KANE! DON'T YOU KNOW ME?
11-17
Reg. U. S. Pat. Off.: Copyright, 1941, by News Syndicate Co. Inc.
MR. RYAN, YOU RANG FOR ME! DID YOU WANT SOMETHIN'?
I JUST WANTED TO TELL YOU THAT TERRY WILL BE WORKING WITH US!
...I RECKON THAT WILL BE JUS' DANDY! I KNOW HOW IMPORTANT IT IS THAT YOU HAVE CONFIDENTIAL ASSISTANTS IN THIS TROUBLE-SHOOTIN' JOB, KEEPIN' TH' LIFE LINE OPEN TO INTERIOR CHINA...
...I'M RIGHT POSITIVE THAT MR. TERRY LEE WILL BE MOST VALUABLE —'SPECIALLY IF HE HAS TO TRAVEL 'ROUND CHINA WITH PRETTY CHINESE AND BLONDE AMERICAN GIRLS!
MILTON CANIFF
WELL, TERRY, IT LOOKS AS IF YOUR ADVENTURES WITH HU SHEE AND BURMA WERE INTERESTING ENOUGH TO BE TALKED ABOUT EVEN IN HONG KONG!...
SOMEBODY'S DONE ME WRONG! HOW DID YOU KNOW ABOUT THOSE GIRLS, APRIL!
11-18
Reg. U. S. Pat. Off.: Copyright, 1941, by News Syndicate Co. Inc.
APRIL'S MY SECRETARY, TERRY! PART OF OUR TROUBLE-SHOOTING JOB IS FINDING OUT WHAT'S GOING ON INSIDE CHINA! IT WAS APRIL WHO TRACED YOU DOWN FOR ME! SHE GOT REPORTS FROM ALL SORTS OF PEOPLE!
OOOH!
BUT, APRIL, YOU KNOW HOW IT IS OUT IN THE WAR ZONE!... I BUMPED INTO A COUPLE OF GIRLS... BUT I NEVER ONCE FORGOT ABOUT YOU!
MY, MY, MR. RYAN, I'M RIGHT SURPRISED THAT YOU DON'T CATCH YOUR DEATH OF COLD WITH SUCH A BREEZE IN HERE!... I'LL BE IN MY OFFICE IF YOU WANT ME!
MILTON CANIFF

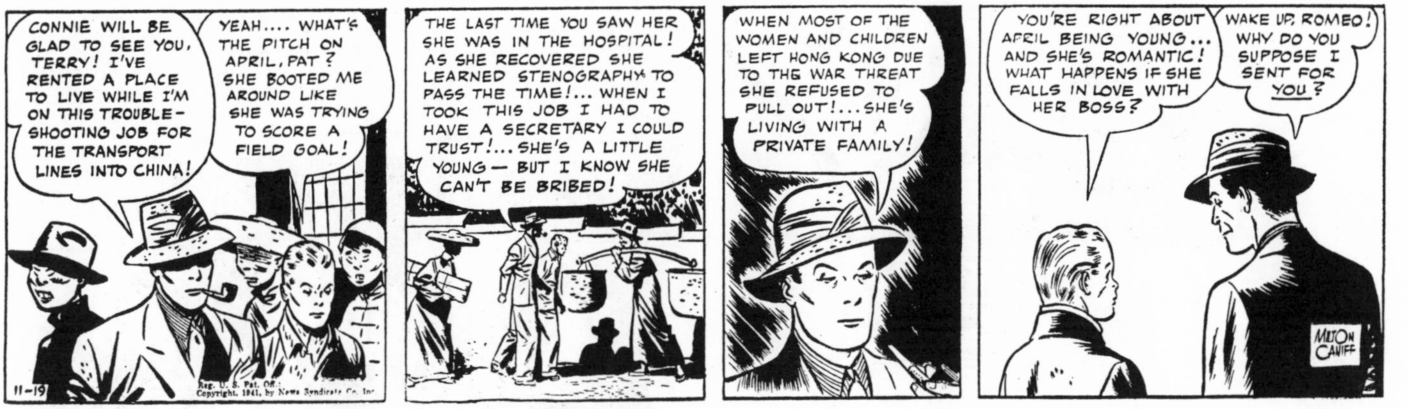
CONNIE WILL BE GLAD TO SEE YOU, TERRY! I'VE RENTED A PLACE TO LIVE WHILE I'M ON THIS TROUBLE-SHOOTING JOB FOR THE TRANSPORT LINES INTO CHINA!
YEAH.... WHAT'S THE PITCH ON APRIL, PAT? SHE BOOTED ME AROUND LIKE SHE WAS TRYING TO SCORE A FIELD GOAL!
11-19
Reg. U. S. Pat. Off.: Copyright, 1941, by News Syndicate Co. Inc.
THE LAST TIME YOU SAW HER SHE WAS IN THE HOSPITAL! AS SHE RECOVERED SHE LEARNED STENOGRAPHY TO PASS THE TIME!... WHEN I TOOK THIS JOB I HAD TO HAVE A SECRETARY I COULD TRUST!... SHE'S A LITTLE YOUNG — BUT I KNOW SHE CAN'T BE BRIBED!
WHEN MOST OF THE WOMEN AND CHILDREN LEFT HONG KONG DUE TO THE WAR THREAT SHE REFUSED TO PULL OUT!... SHE'S LIVING WITH A PRIVATE FAMILY!
YOU'RE RIGHT ABOUT APRIL BEING YOUNG... AND SHE'S ROMANTIC! WHAT HAPPENS IF SHE FALLS IN LOVE WITH HER BOSS?
WAKE UP, ROMEO! WHY DO YOU SUPPOSE I SENT FOR YOU?
MILTON CANIFF

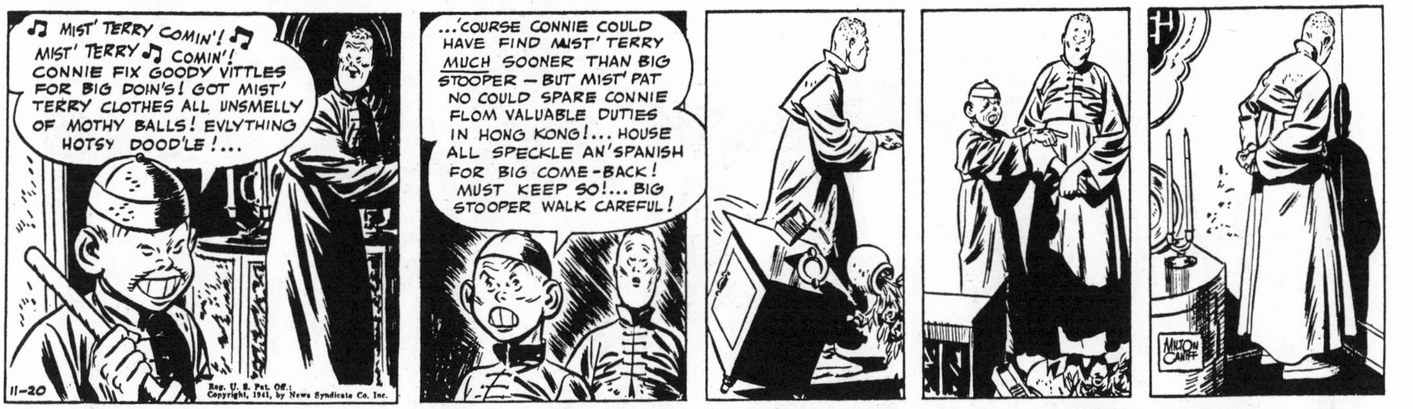
♫ MIST' TERRY COMIN'! ♫ MIST' TERRY ♫ COMIN'! CONNIE FIX GOODY VITTLES FOR BIG DOIN'S! GOT MIST' TERRY CLOTHES ALL UNSMELLY OF MOTHY BALLS! EVLYTHING HOTSY DOOD'LE!...
11-20
Reg. U. S. Pat. Off.: Copyright, 1941, by News Syndicate Co. Inc.
...'COURSE CONNIE COULD HAVE FIND MIST' TERRY MUCH SOONER THAN BIG STOOPER — BUT MIST' PAT NO COULD SPARE CONNIE FLOM VALUABLE DUTIES IN HONG KONG!... HOUSE ALL SPECKLE AN' SPANISH FOR BIG COME-BACK! MUST KEEP SO!... BIG STOOPER WALK CAREFUL!
MILTON CANIFF

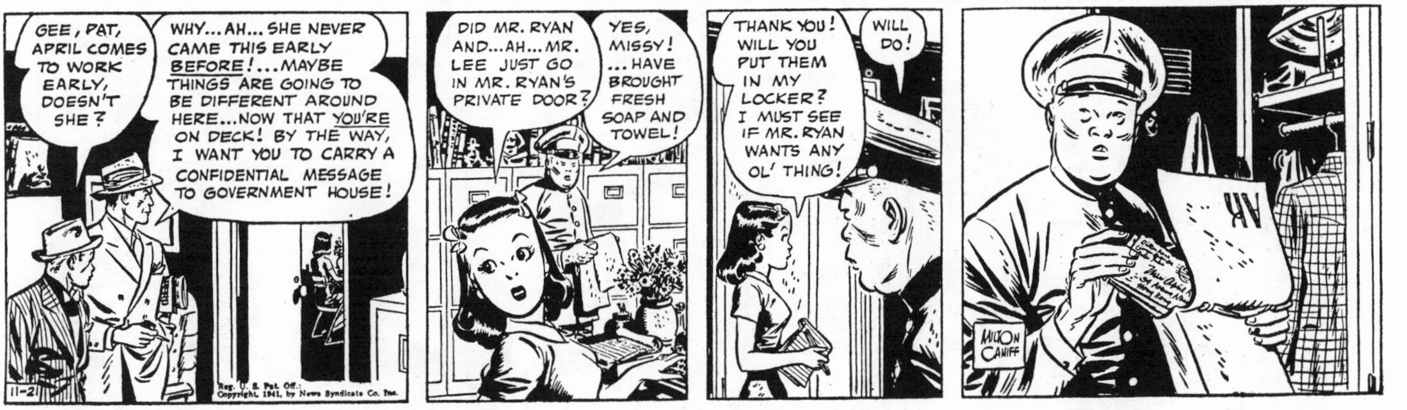
GEE, PAT, APRIL COMES TO WORK EARLY, DOESN'T SHE?
WHY... AH... SHE NEVER CAME THIS EARLY BEFORE!... MAYBE THINGS ARE GOING TO BE DIFFERENT AROUND HERE... NOW THAT YOU'RE ON DECK! BY THE WAY, I WANT YOU TO CARRY A CONFIDENTIAL MESSAGE TO GOVERNMENT HOUSE!
11-21
Reg. U. S. Pat. Off.: Copyright, 1941, by News Syndicate Co. Inc.
DID MR. RYAN AND... AH... MR. LEE JUST GO IN MR. RYAN'S PRIVATE DOOR?
YES, MISSY! ... HAVE BROUGHT FRESH SOAP AND TOWEL!
THANK YOU! WILL YOU PUT THEM IN MY LOCKER? I MUST SEE IF MR. RYAN WANTS ANY OL' THING!
WILL DO!
MILTON CANIFF
AK

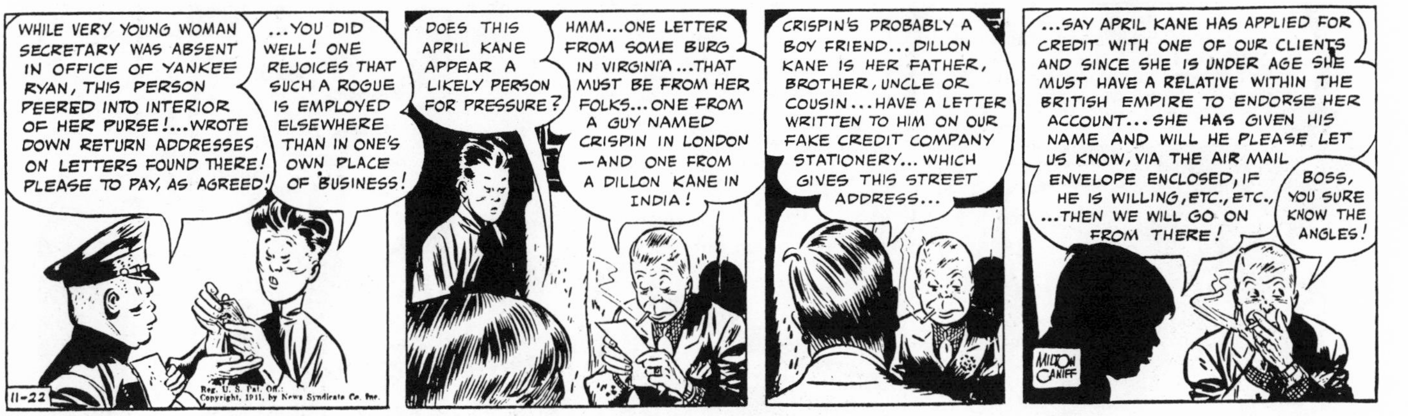
WHILE VERY YOUNG WOMAN SECRETARY WAS ABSENT IN OFFICE OF YANKEE RYAN, THIS PERSON PEERED INTO INTERIOR OF HER PURSE!... WROTE DOWN RETURN ADDRESSES ON LETTERS FOUND THERE! PLEASE TO PAY, AS AGREED!
...YOU DID WELL! ONE REJOICES THAT SUCH A ROGUE IS EMPLOYED ELSEWHERE THAN IN ONE'S OWN PLACE OF BUSINESS!
11-22
Reg. U. S. Pat. Off.: Copyright, 1941, by News Syndicate Co. Inc.
DOES THIS APRIL KANE APPEAR A LIKELY PERSON FOR PRESSURE?
HMM... ONE LETTER FROM SOME BURG IN VIRGINIA... THAT MUST BE FROM HER FOLKS... ONE FROM A GUY NAMED CRISPIN IN LONDON — AND ONE FROM A DILLON KANE IN INDIA!
CRISPIN'S PROBABLY A BOY FRIEND... DILLON KANE IS HER FATHER, BROTHER, UNCLE OR COUSIN... HAVE A LETTER WRITTEN TO HIM ON OUR FAKE CREDIT COMPANY STATIONERY... WHICH GIVES THIS STREET ADDRESS...
...SAY APRIL KANE HAS APPLIED FOR CREDIT WITH ONE OF OUR CLIENTS AND SINCE SHE IS UNDER AGE SHE MUST HAVE A RELATIVE WITHIN THE BRITISH EMPIRE TO ENDORSE HER ACCOUNT... SHE HAS GIVEN HIS NAME AND WILL HE PLEASE LET US KNOW, VIA THE AIR MAIL ENVELOPE ENCLOSED, IF HE IS WILLING, ETC., ETC., ...THEN WE WILL GO ON FROM THERE!
BOSS, YOU SURE KNOW THE ANGLES!
MILTON CANIFF

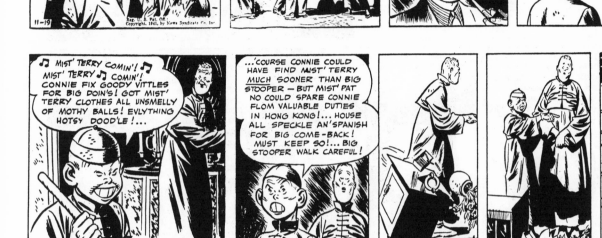

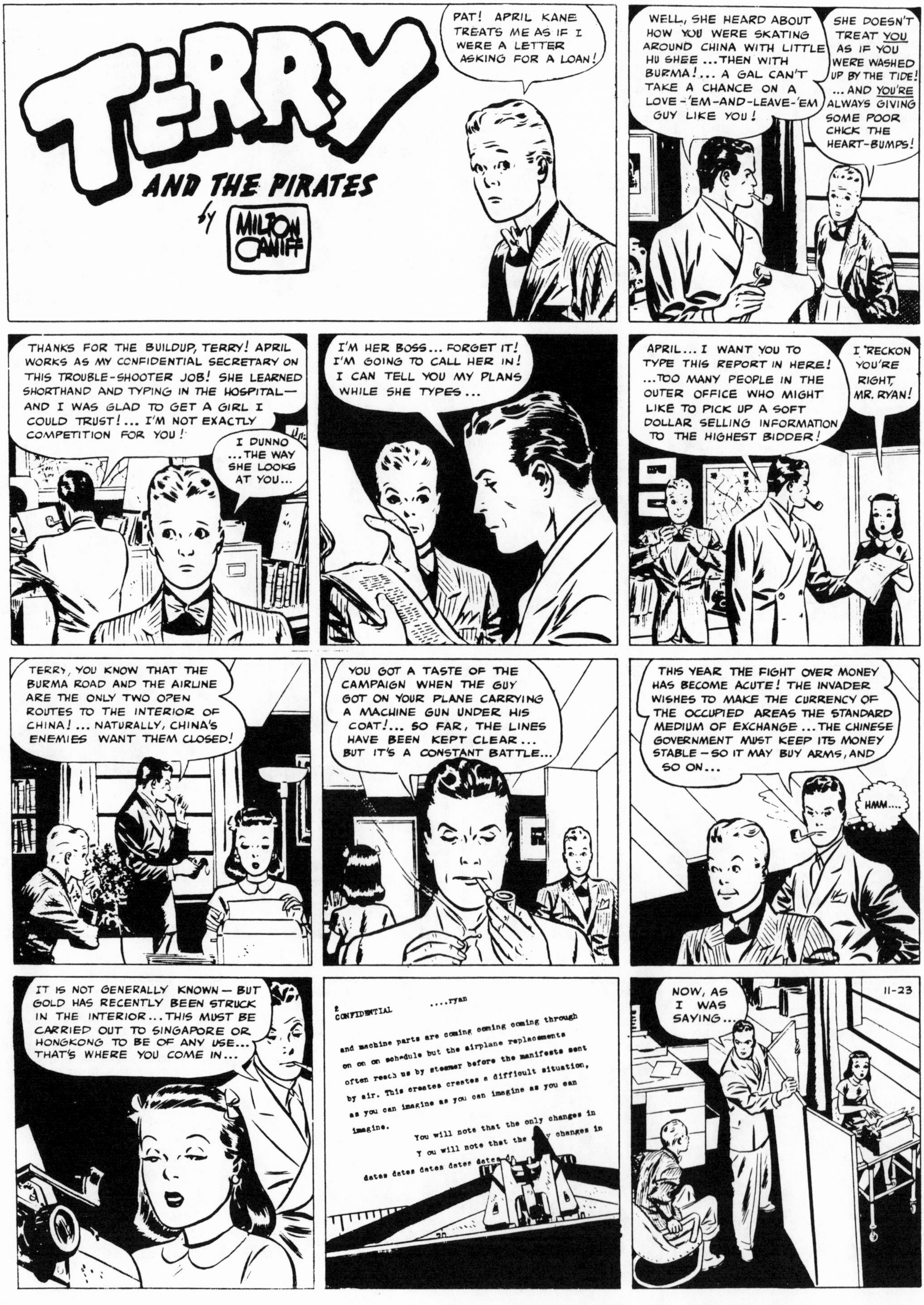
TERRY AND THE PIRATES
by MILTON CANIFF
PAT! APRIL KANE TREATS ME AS IF I WERE A LETTER ASKING FOR A LOAN!
WELL, SHE HEARD ABOUT HOW YOU WERE SKATING AROUND CHINA WITH LITTLE HU SHEE ... THEN WITH BURMA! ... A GAL CAN'T TAKE A CHANCE ON A LOVE-'EM-AND-LEAVE-'EM GUY LIKE YOU!
SHE DOESN'T TREAT YOU AS IF YOU WERE WASHED UP BY THE TIDE! ... AND YOU'RE ALWAYS GIVING SOME POOR CHICK THE HEART-BUMPS!
THANKS FOR THE BUILDUP, TERRY! APRIL WORKS AS MY CONFIDENTIAL SECRETARY ON THIS TROUBLE-SHOOTER JOB! SHE LEARNED SHORTHAND AND TYPING IN THE HOSPITAL— AND I WAS GLAD TO GET A GIRL I COULD TRUST! ... I'M NOT EXACTLY COMPETITION FOR YOU!
I DUNNO ... THE WAY SHE LOOKS AT YOU ...
I'M HER BOSS ... FORGET IT! I'M GOING TO CALL HER IN! I CAN TELL YOU MY PLANS WHILE SHE TYPES ...
APRIL ... I WANT YOU TO TYPE THIS REPORT IN HERE! ... TOO MANY PEOPLE IN THE OUTER OFFICE WHO MIGHT LIKE TO PICK UP A SOFT DOLLAR SELLING INFORMATION TO THE HIGHEST BIDDER!
I RECKON YOU'RE RIGHT, MR. RYAN!
TERRY, YOU KNOW THAT THE BURMA ROAD AND THE AIRLINE ARE THE ONLY TWO OPEN ROUTES TO THE INTERIOR OF CHINA! ... NATURALLY, CHINA'S ENEMIES WANT THEM CLOSED!
YOU GOT A TASTE OF THE CAMPAIGN WHEN THE GUY GOT ON YOUR PLANE CARRYING A MACHINE GUN UNDER HIS COAT! ... SO FAR, THE LINES HAVE BEEN KEPT CLEAR ... BUT IT'S A CONSTANT BATTLE ...
THIS YEAR THE FIGHT OVER MONEY HAS BECOME ACUTE! THE INVADER WISHES TO MAKE THE CURRENCY OF THE OCCUPIED AREAS THE STANDARD MEDIUM OF EXCHANGE ... THE CHINESE GOVERNMENT MUST KEEP ITS MONEY STABLE — SO IT MAY BUY ARMS, AND SO ON ...
HMM....
IT IS NOT GENERALLY KNOWN — BUT GOLD HAS RECENTLY BEEN STRUCK IN THE INTERIOR ... THIS MUST BE CARRIED OUT TO SINGAPORE OR HONGKONG TO BE OF ANY USE ... THAT'S WHERE YOU COME IN ...
2
CONFIDENTIAL ....ryan
and machine parts are coming coming coming through
on on on sch-dule but the airplane replacements
often reach us by steamer before the manifests sent
by air. This creates creates a difficult situation,
as you can imagine as you can imagine as you can
imagine.
You will note that the only changes in
Y ou will note that the
dates dates dates dates dates d
NOW, AS I WAS SAYING ...
11-23

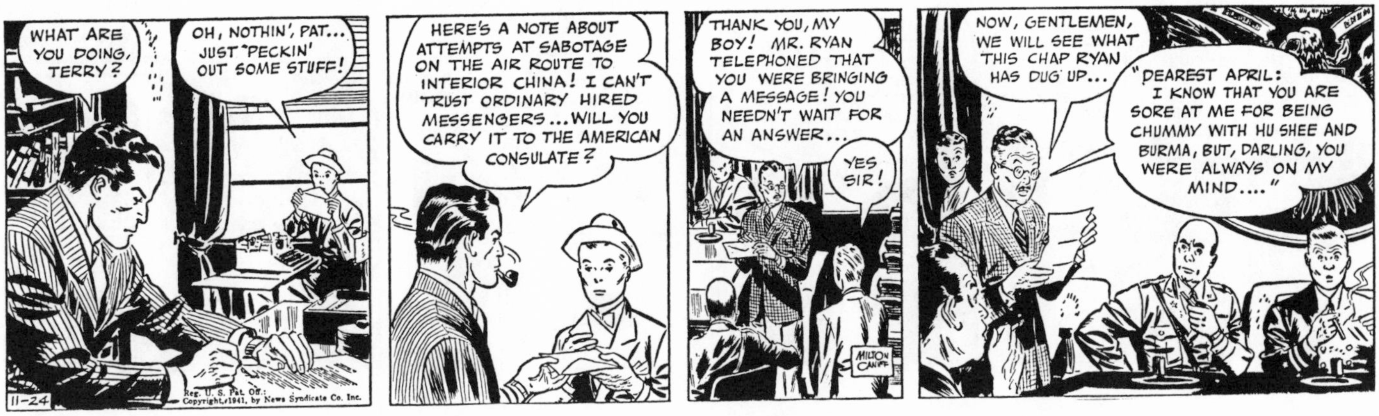
WHAT ARE YOU DOING, TERRY?
OH, NOTHIN', PAT... JUST "PECKIN' OUT SOME STUFF!
11-24
Reg. U. S. Pat. Off.: Copyright, 1941, by News Syndicate Co. Inc.
HERE'S A NOTE ABOUT ATTEMPTS AT SABOTAGE ON THE AIR ROUTE TO INTERIOR CHINA! I CAN'T TRUST ORDINARY HIRED MESSENGERS ... WILL YOU CARRY IT TO THE AMERICAN CONSULATE?
THANK YOU, MY BOY! MR. RYAN TELEPHONED THAT YOU WERE BRINGING A MESSAGE! YOU NEEDN'T WAIT FOR AN ANSWER...
YES SIR!
MILTON CANIFF
NOW, GENTLEMEN, WE WILL SEE WHAT THIS CHAP RYAN HAS DUG UP...
"DEAREST APRIL: I KNOW THAT YOU ARE SORE AT ME FOR BEING CHUMMY WITH HU SHEE AND BURMA, BUT, DARLING, YOU WERE ALWAYS ON MY MIND...."

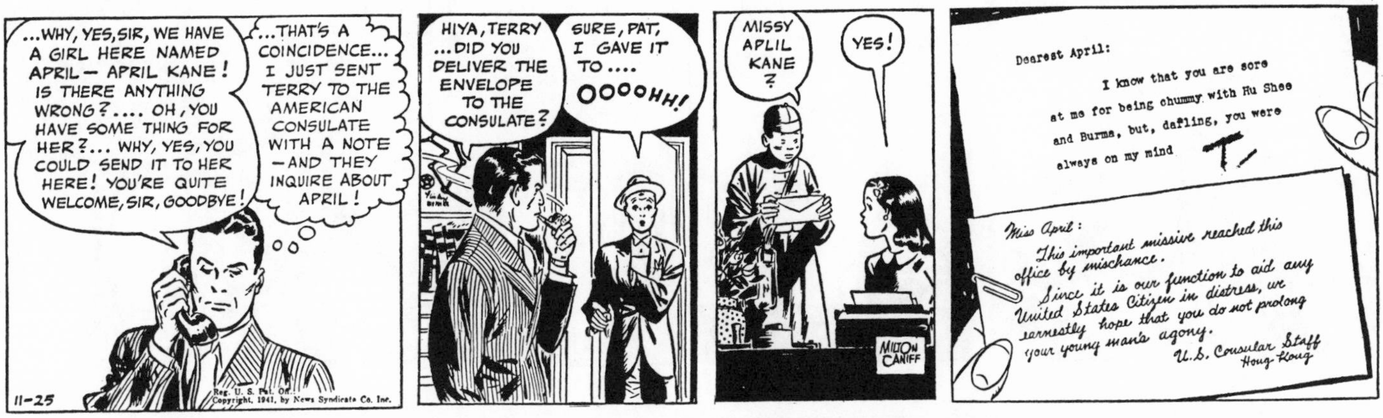
...WHY, YES, SIR, WE HAVE A GIRL HERE NAMED APRIL — APRIL KANE! IS THERE ANYTHING WRONG?.... OH, YOU HAVE SOME THING FOR HER?... WHY, YES, YOU COULD SEND IT TO HER HERE! YOU'RE QUITE WELCOME, SIR, GOODBYE!
...THAT'S A COINCIDENCE... I JUST SENT TERRY TO THE AMERICAN CONSULATE WITH A NOTE — AND THEY INQUIRE ABOUT APRIL!
11-25
Reg. U. S. Pat. Off.: Copyright, 1941, by News Syndicate Co. Inc.
HIYA, TERRY ...DID YOU DELIVER THE ENVELOPE TO THE CONSULATE?
SURE, PAT, I GAVE IT TO ....
OOOOHH!
MISSY APLIL KANE?
YES!
MILTON CANIFF
Dearest April:
I know that you are sore at me for being chummy with Hu Shee and Burma, but, darling, you were always on my mind
T
Miss April:
This important missive reached this office by mischance.
Since it is our function to aid any United States Citizen in distress, we earnestly hope that you do not prolong your young man's agony.
U. S. Consular Staff
Hong Kong

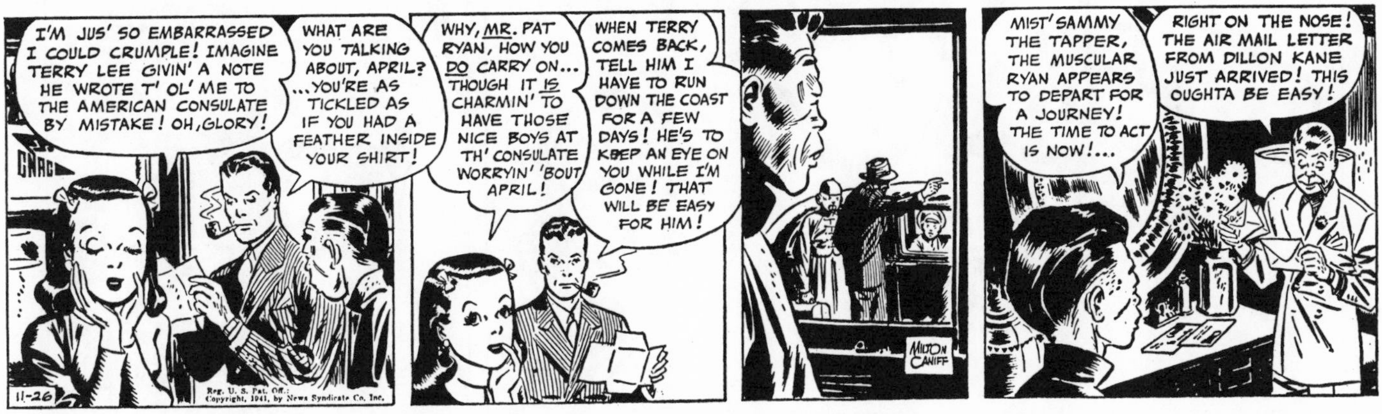
I'M JUS' SO EMBARRASSED I COULD CRUMPLE! IMAGINE TERRY LEE GIVIN' A NOTE HE WROTE T' OL' ME TO THE AMERICAN CONSULATE BY MISTAKE! OH, GLORY!
WHAT ARE YOU TALKING ABOUT, APRIL? ...YOU'RE AS TICKLED AS IF YOU HAD A FEATHER INSIDE YOUR SHIRT!
CNAC
11-26
Reg. U. S. Pat. Off.: Copyright, 1941, by News Syndicate Co. Inc.
WHY, MR. PAT RYAN, HOW YOU DO CARRY ON... THOUGH IT IS CHARMIN' TO HAVE THOSE NICE BOYS AT TH' CONSULATE WORRYIN' 'BOUT APRIL!
WHEN TERRY COMES BACK, TELL HIM I HAVE TO RUN DOWN THE COAST FOR A FEW DAYS! HE'S TO KEEP AN EYE ON YOU WHILE I'M GONE! THAT WILL BE EASY FOR HIM!
MILTON CANIFF
MIST' SAMMY THE TAPPER, THE MUSCULAR RYAN APPEARS TO DEPART FOR A JOURNEY! THE TIME TO ACT IS NOW!...
RIGHT ON THE NOSE! THE AIR MAIL LETTER FROM DILLON KANE JUST ARRIVED! THIS OUGHTA BE EASY!

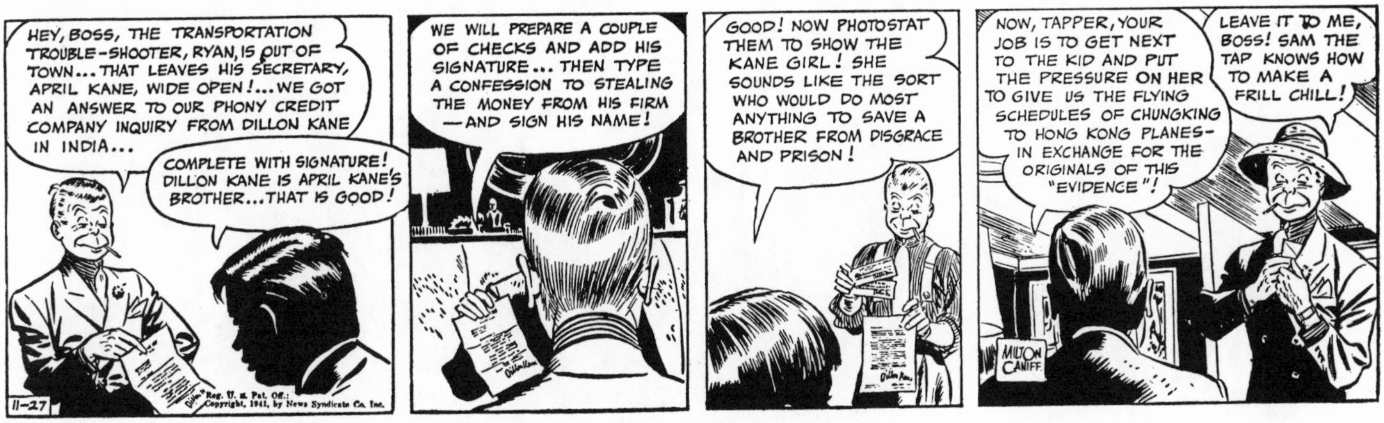
HEY, BOSS, THE TRANSPORTATION TROUBLE-SHOOTER, RYAN, IS OUT OF TOWN... THAT LEAVES HIS SECRETARY, APRIL KANE, WIDE OPEN!... WE GOT AN ANSWER TO OUR PHONY CREDIT COMPANY INQUIRY FROM DILLON KANE IN INDIA...
COMPLETE WITH SIGNATURE! DILLON KANE IS APRIL KANE'S BROTHER... THAT IS GOOD!
11-27
Reg. U. S. Pat. Off.: Copyright, 1941, by News Syndicate Co. Inc.
WE WILL PREPARE A COUPLE OF CHECKS AND ADD HIS SIGNATURE... THEN TYPE A CONFESSION TO STEALING THE MONEY FROM HIS FIRM — AND SIGN HIS NAME!
GOOD! NOW PHOTOSTAT THEM TO SHOW THE KANE GIRL! SHE SOUNDS LIKE THE SORT WHO WOULD DO MOST ANYTHING TO SAVE A BROTHER FROM DISGRACE AND PRISON!
NOW, TAPPER, YOUR JOB IS TO GET NEXT TO THE KID AND PUT THE PRESSURE ON HER TO GIVE US THE FLYING SCHEDULES OF CHUNGKING TO HONG KONG PLANES — IN EXCHANGE FOR THE ORIGINALS OF THIS "EVIDENCE"!
LEAVE IT TO ME, BOSS! SAM THE TAP KNOWS HOW TO MAKE A FRILL CHILL!
MILTON CANIFF

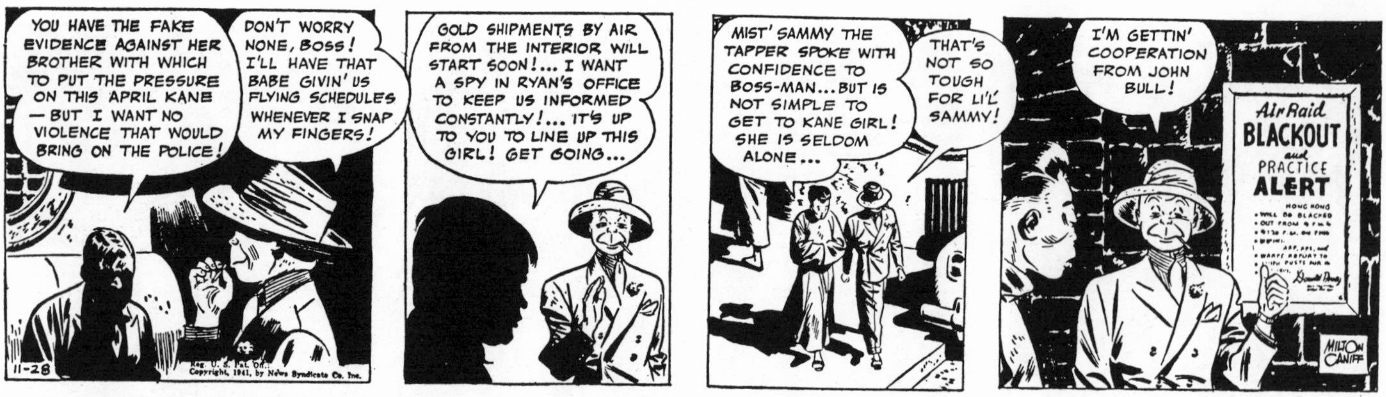
YOU HAVE THE FAKE EVIDENCE AGAINST HER BROTHER WITH WHICH TO PUT THE PRESSURE ON THIS APRIL KANE — BUT I WANT NO VIOLENCE THAT WOULD BRING ON THE POLICE!
DON'T WORRY NONE, BOSS! I'LL HAVE THAT BABE GIVIN' US FLYING SCHEDULES WHENEVER I SNAP MY FINGERS!
11-28
Reg. U. S. Pat. Off.: Copyright, 1941, by News Syndicate Co. Inc.
GOLD SHIPMENTS BY AIR FROM THE INTERIOR WILL START SOON!... I WANT A SPY IN RYAN'S OFFICE TO KEEP US INFORMED CONSTANTLY!... IT'S UP TO YOU TO LINE UP THIS GIRL! GET GOING...
MIST' SAMMY THE TAPPER SPOKE WITH CONFIDENCE TO BOSS-MAN... BUT IS NOT SIMPLE TO GET TO KANE GIRL! SHE IS SELDOM ALONE...
THAT'S NOT SO TOUGH FOR LI'L SAMMY!
I'M GETTIN' COOPERATION FROM JOHN BULL!
Air Raid BLACKOUT and PRACTICE ALERT
MILTON CANIFF

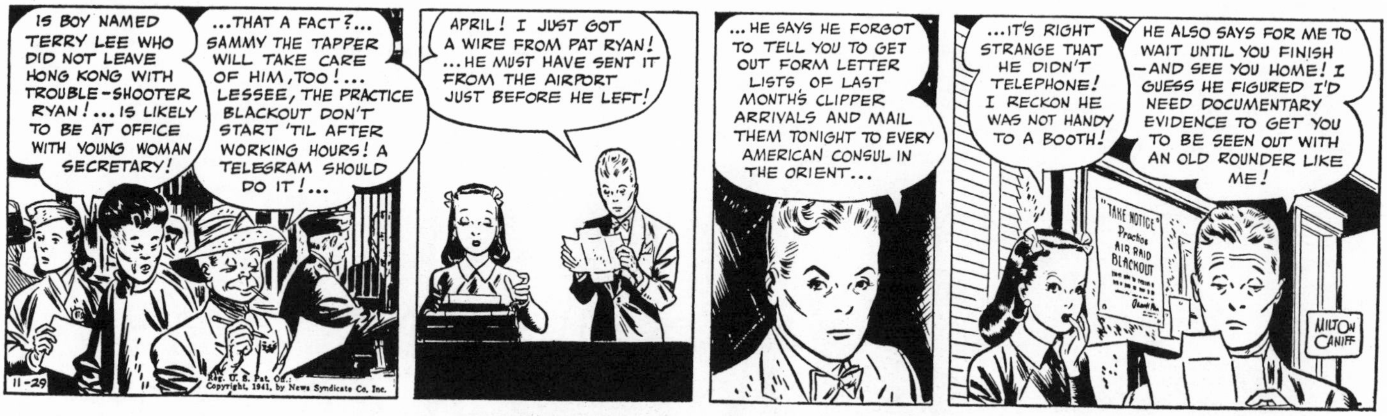
IS BOY NAMED TERRY LEE WHO DID NOT LEAVE HONG KONG WITH TROUBLE-SHOOTER RYAN!... IS LIKELY TO BE AT OFFICE WITH YOUNG WOMAN SECRETARY!
...THAT A FACT?... SAMMY THE TAPPER WILL TAKE CARE OF HIM, TOO!... LESSEE, THE PRACTICE BLACKOUT DON'T START 'TIL AFTER WORKING HOURS! A TELEGRAM SHOULD DO IT!...
11-29
Reg. U. S. Pat. Off.: Copyright, 1941, by News Syndicate Co. Inc.
APRIL! I JUST GOT A WIRE FROM PAT RYAN! ...HE MUST HAVE SENT IT FROM THE AIRPORT JUST BEFORE HE LEFT!
...HE SAYS HE FORGOT TO TELL YOU TO GET OUT FORM LETTER LISTS OF LAST MONTH'S CLIPPER ARRIVALS AND MAIL THEM TONIGHT TO EVERY AMERICAN CONSUL IN THE ORIENT...
...IT'S RIGHT STRANGE THAT HE DIDN'T TELEPHONE! I RECKON HE WAS NOT HANDY TO A BOOTH!
HE ALSO SAYS FOR ME TO WAIT UNTIL YOU FINISH — AND SEE YOU HOME! I GUESS HE FIGURED I'D NEED DOCUMENTARY EVIDENCE TO GET YOU TO BE SEEN OUT WITH AN OLD ROUNDER LIKE ME!
"TAKE NOTICE" Practice AIR RAID BLACKOUT
MILTON CANIFF

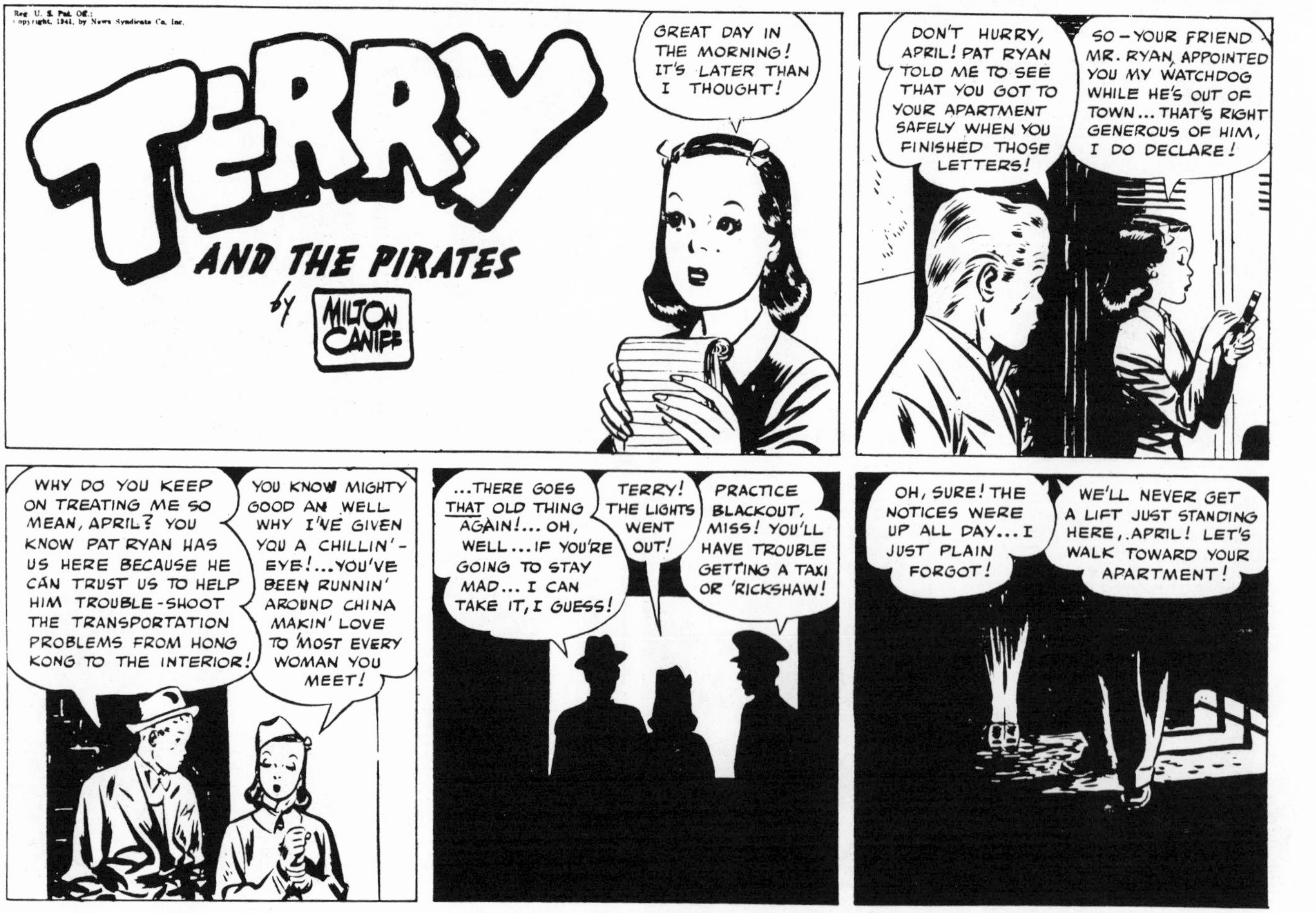
Reg. U. S. Pat. Off.: Copyright, 1941, by News Syndicate Co. Inc.
TERRY AND THE PIRATES
by MILTON CANIFF
GREAT DAY IN THE MORNING! IT'S LATER THAN I THOUGHT!
DON'T HURRY, APRIL! PAT RYAN TOLD ME TO SEE THAT YOU GOT TO YOUR APARTMENT SAFELY WHEN YOU FINISHED THOSE LETTERS!
SO — YOUR FRIEND MR. RYAN, APPOINTED YOU MY WATCHDOG WHILE HE'S OUT OF TOWN... THAT'S RIGHT GENEROUS OF HIM, I DO DECLARE!
WHY DO YOU KEEP ON TREATING ME SO MEAN, APRIL? YOU KNOW PAT RYAN HAS US HERE BECAUSE HE CAN TRUST US TO HELP HIM TROUBLE-SHOOT THE TRANSPORTATION PROBLEMS FROM HONG KONG TO THE INTERIOR!
YOU KNOW MIGHTY GOOD AN' WELL WHY I'VE GIVEN YOU A CHILLIN'-EYE!...YOU'VE BEEN RUNNIN' AROUND CHINA MAKIN' LOVE TO 'MOST EVERY WOMAN YOU MEET!
...THERE GOES THAT OLD THING AGAIN!... OH, WELL... IF YOU'RE GOING TO STAY MAD... I CAN TAKE IT, I GUESS!
TERRY! THE LIGHTS WENT OUT!
PRACTICE BLACKOUT, MISS! YOU'LL HAVE TROUBLE GETTING A TAXI OR 'RICKSHAW!
OH, SURE! THE NOTICES WERE UP ALL DAY... I JUST PLAIN FORGOT!
WE'LL NEVER GET A LIFT JUST STANDING HERE, APRIL! LET'S WALK TOWARD YOUR APARTMENT!

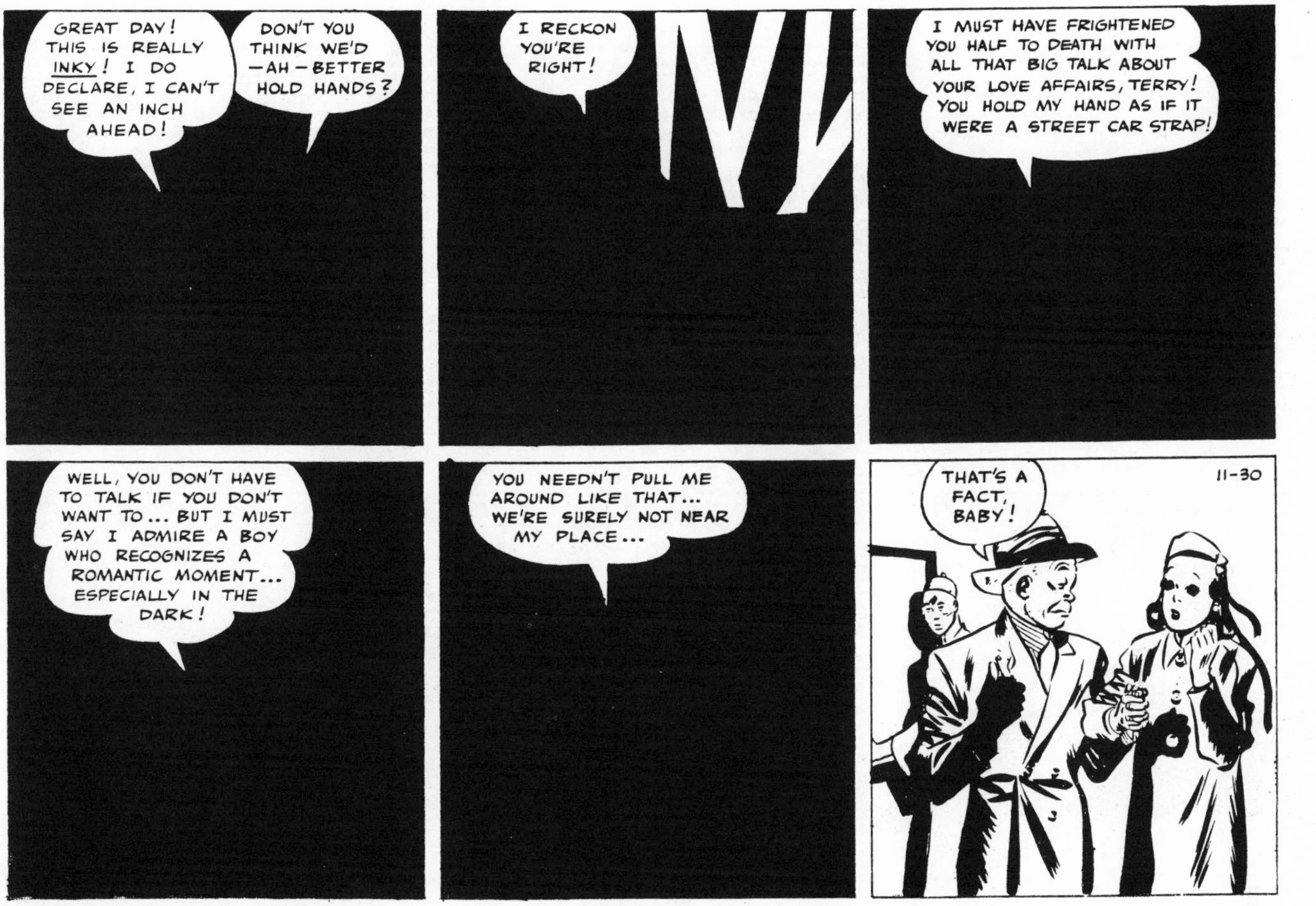
GREAT DAY! THIS IS REALLY INKY! I DO DECLARE, I CAN'T SEE AN INCH AHEAD!
DON'T YOU THINK WE'D —AH— BETTER HOLD HANDS?
I RECKON YOU'RE RIGHT!
I MUST HAVE FRIGHTENED YOU HALF TO DEATH WITH ALL THAT BIG TALK ABOUT YOUR LOVE AFFAIRS, TERRY! YOU HOLD MY HAND AS IF IT WERE A STREET CAR STRAP!
WELL, YOU DON'T HAVE TO TALK IF YOU DON'T WANT TO... BUT I MUST SAY I ADMIRE A BOY WHO RECOGNIZES A ROMANTIC MOMENT... ESPECIALLY IN THE DARK!
YOU NEEDN'T PULL ME AROUND LIKE THAT... WE'RE SURELY NOT NEAR MY PLACE...
THAT'S A FACT, BABY!
11-30

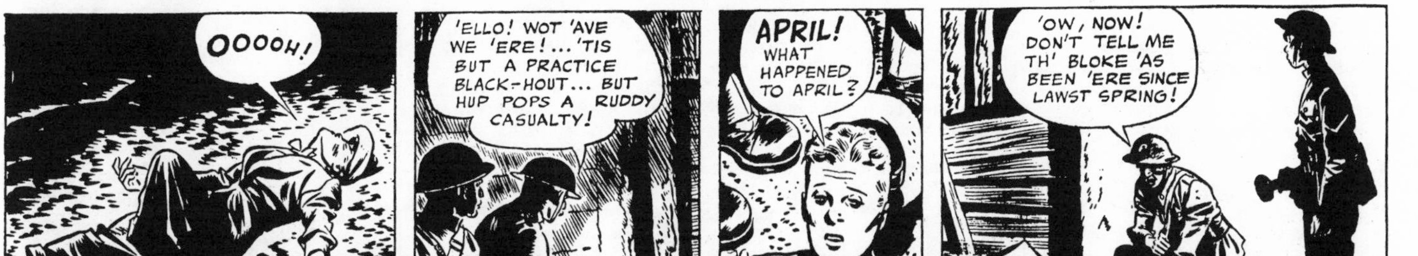
OOOOH!
12-1
Reg. U. S. Pat. Off.: Copyright, 1941, by News Syndicate Co. Inc.
'ELLO! WOT 'AVE WE 'ERE!... 'TIS BUT A PRACTICE BLACK-HOUT... BUT HUP POPS A RUDDY CASUALTY!
APRIL! WHAT HAPPENED TO APRIL?
'OW, NOW! DON'T TELL ME TH' BLOKE 'AS BEEN 'ERE SINCE LAWST SPRING!
MILTON CANIFF

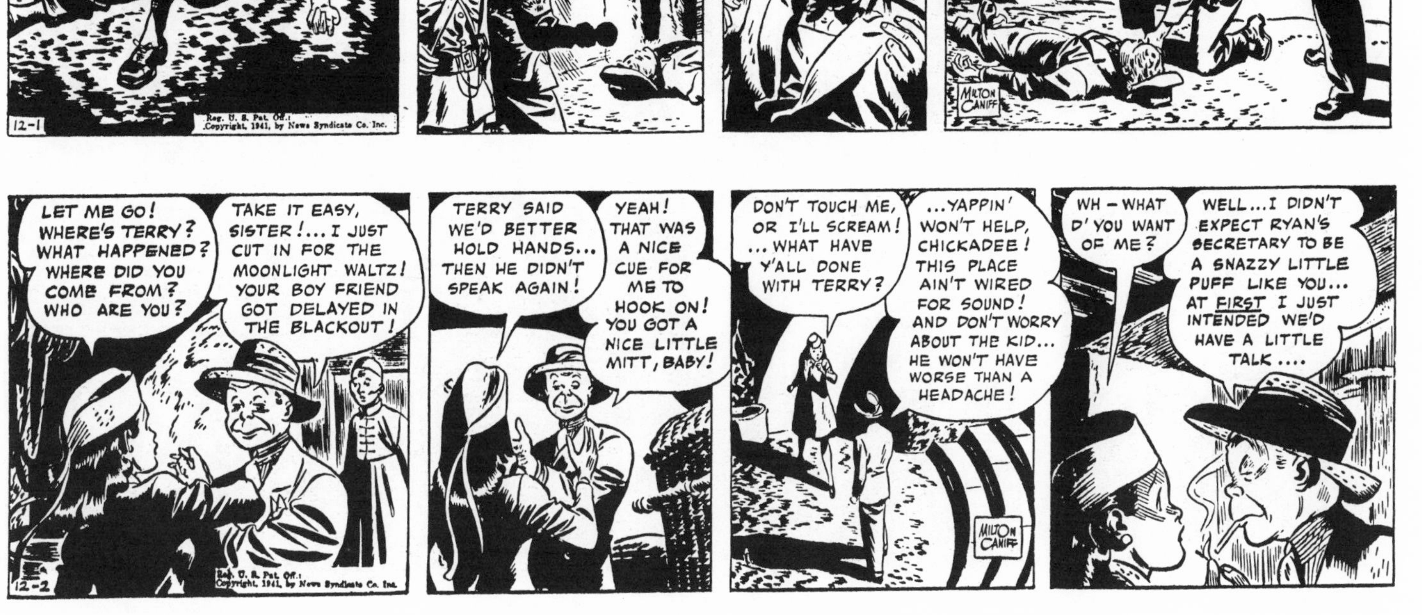
LET ME GO! WHERE'S TERRY? WHAT HAPPENED? WHERE DID YOU COME FROM? WHO ARE YOU?
TAKE IT EASY, SISTER!... I JUST CUT IN FOR THE MOONLIGHT WALTZ! YOUR BOY FRIEND GOT DELAYED IN THE BLACKOUT!
12-2
Reg. U. S. Pat. Off.: Copyright, 1941, by News Syndicate Co. Inc.
TERRY SAID WE'D BETTER HOLD HANDS... THEN HE DIDN'T SPEAK AGAIN!
YEAH! THAT WAS A NICE CUE FOR ME TO HOOK ON! YOU GOT A NICE LITTLE MITT, BABY!
DON'T TOUCH ME, OR I'LL SCREAM! ... WHAT HAVE Y'ALL DONE WITH TERRY?
...YAPPIN' WON'T HELP, CHICKADEE! THIS PLACE AIN'T WIRED FOR SOUND! AND DON'T WORRY ABOUT THE KID... HE WON'T HAVE WORSE THAN A HEADACHE!
MILTON CANIFF
WH-WHAT D' YOU WANT OF ME?
WELL... I DIDN'T EXPECT RYAN'S SECRETARY TO BE A SNAZZY LITTLE PUFF LIKE YOU... AT FIRST I JUST INTENDED WE'D HAVE A LITTLE TALK....

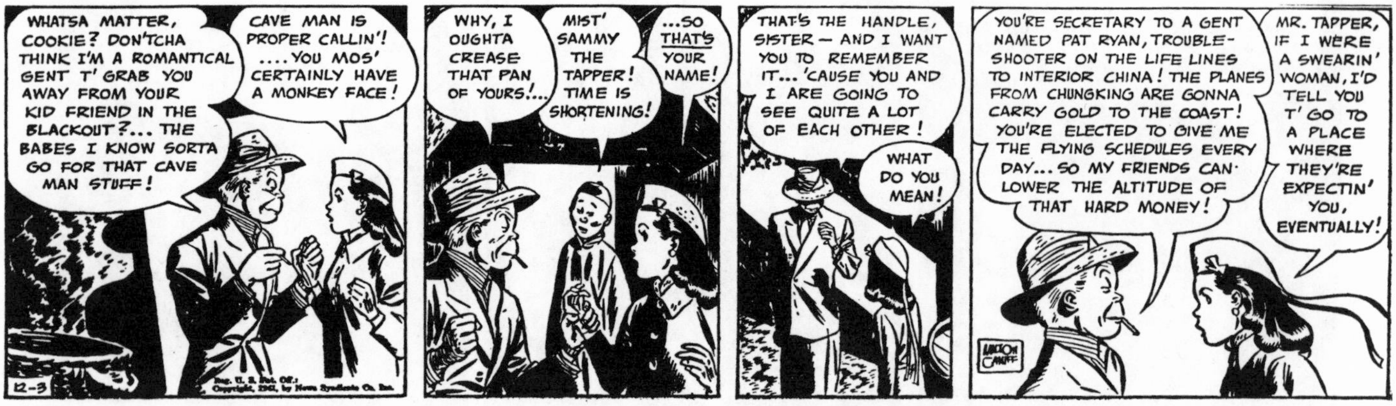
WHATSA MATTER, COOKIE? DON'TCHA THINK I'M A ROMANTICAL GENT T' GRAB YOU AWAY FROM YOUR KID FRIEND IN THE BLACKOUT?... THE BABES I KNOW SORTA GO FOR THAT CAVE MAN STUFF!
CAVE MAN IS PROPER CALLIN'! ....YOU MOS' CERTAINLY HAVE A MONKEY FACE!
WHY, I OUGHTA CREASE THAT PAN OF YOURS!...
MIST' SAMMY THE TAPPER! TIME IS SHORTENING!
...SO THAT'S YOUR NAME!
THAT'S THE HANDLE, SISTER — AND I WANT YOU TO REMEMBER IT...'CAUSE YOU AND I ARE GOING TO SEE QUITE A LOT OF EACH OTHER!
WHAT DO YOU MEAN!
YOU'RE SECRETARY TO A GENT NAMED PAT RYAN, TROUBLE-SHOOTER ON THE LIFE LINES TO INTERIOR CHINA! THE PLANES FROM CHUNGKING ARE GONNA CARRY GOLD TO THE COAST! YOU'RE ELECTED TO GIVE ME THE FLYING SCHEDULES EVERY DAY... SO MY FRIENDS CAN LOWER THE ALTITUDE OF THAT HARD MONEY!
MR. TAPPER, IF I WERE A SWEARIN' WOMAN, I'D TELL YOU T' GO TO A PLACE WHERE THEY'RE EXPECTIN' YOU, EVENTUALLY!
12-3
Reg. U. S. Pat. Off.: Copyright, 1941, by News Syndicate Co. Inc.
MILTON CANIFF

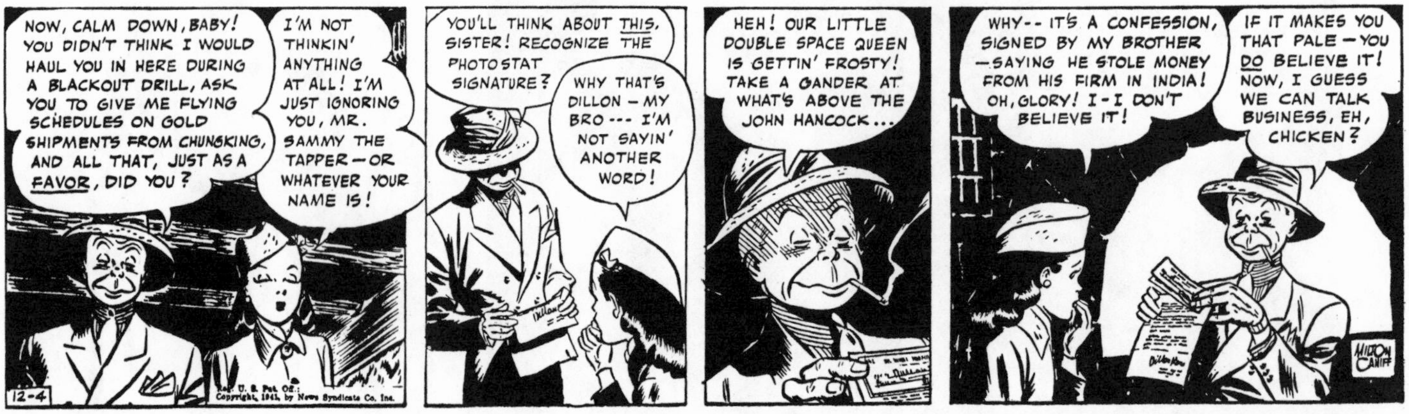
NOW, CALM DOWN, BABY! YOU DIDN'T THINK I WOULD HAUL YOU IN HERE DURING A BLACKOUT DRILL, ASK YOU TO GIVE ME FLYING SCHEDULES ON GOLD SHIPMENTS FROM CHUNGKING, AND ALL THAT, JUST AS A FAVOR, DID YOU?
I'M NOT THINKIN' ANYTHING AT ALL! I'M JUST IGNORING YOU, MR. SAMMY THE TAPPER — OR WHATEVER YOUR NAME IS!
YOU'LL THINK ABOUT THIS, SISTER! RECOGNIZE THE PHOTOSTAT SIGNATURE?
WHY THAT'S DILLON — MY BRO --- I'M NOT SAYIN' ANOTHER WORD!
HEH! OUR LITTLE DOUBLE SPACE QUEEN IS GETTIN' FROSTY! TAKE A GANDER AT WHAT'S ABOVE THE JOHN HANCOCK...
WHY-- IT'S A CONFESSION, SIGNED BY MY BROTHER —SAYING HE STOLE MONEY FROM HIS FIRM IN INDIA! OH, GLORY! I-I DON'T BELIEVE IT!
IF IT MAKES YOU THAT PALE — YOU DO BELIEVE IT! NOW, I GUESS WE CAN TALK BUSINESS, EH, CHICKEN?
12-4
Reg. U. S. Pat. Off.: Copyright, 1941, by News Syndicate Co. Inc.
MILTON CANIFF

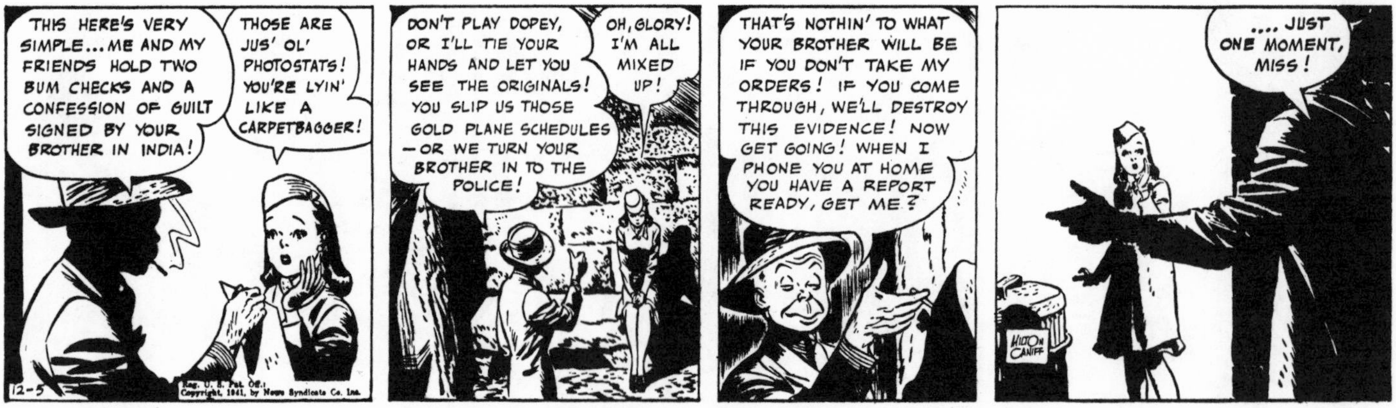
THIS HERE'S VERY SIMPLE... ME AND MY FRIENDS HOLD TWO BUM CHECKS AND A CONFESSION OF GUILT SIGNED BY YOUR BROTHER IN INDIA!
THOSE ARE JUS' OL' PHOTOSTATS! YOU'RE LYIN' LIKE A CARPETBAGGER!
DON'T PLAY DOPEY, OR I'LL TIE YOUR HANDS AND LET YOU SEE THE ORIGINALS! YOU SLIP US THOSE GOLD PLANE SCHEDULES —OR WE TURN YOUR BROTHER IN TO THE POLICE!
OH, GLORY! I'M ALL MIXED UP!
THAT'S NOTHIN' TO WHAT YOUR BROTHER WILL BE IF YOU DON'T TAKE MY ORDERS! IF YOU COME THROUGH, WE'LL DESTROY THIS EVIDENCE! NOW GET GOING! WHEN I PHONE YOU AT HOME YOU HAVE A REPORT READY, GET ME?
.... JUST ONE MOMENT, MISS!
12-5
Reg. U. S. Pat. Off.: Copyright, 1941, by News Syndicate Co. Inc.
MILTON CANIFF

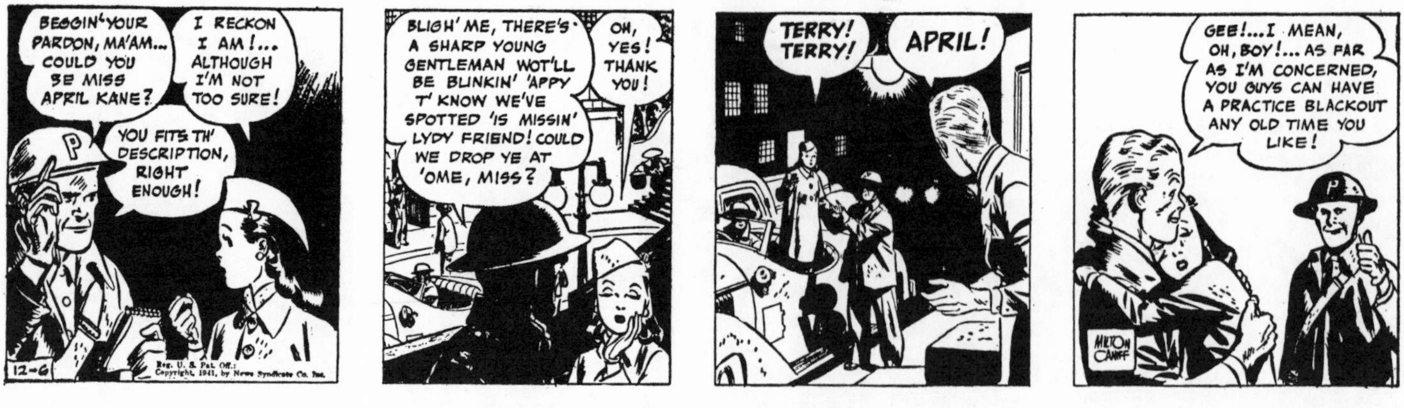
BEGGIN' YOUR PARDON, MA'AM... COULD YOU BE MISS APRIL KANE?
I RECKON I AM!... ALTHOUGH I'M NOT TOO SURE!
YOU FITS TH' DESCRIPTION, RIGHT ENOUGH!
BLIGH' ME, THERE'S A SHARP YOUNG GENTLEMAN WOT'LL BE BLINKIN' 'APPY T' KNOW WE'VE SPOTTED 'IS MISSIN' LYDY FRIEND! COULD WE DROP YE AT 'OME, MISS?
OH, YES! THANK YOU!
TERRY! TERRY!
APRIL!
GEE!...I MEAN, OH, BOY!... AS FAR AS I'M CONCERNED, YOU GUYS CAN HAVE A PRACTICE BLACKOUT ANY OLD TIME YOU LIKE!
12-6
Reg. U. S. Pat. Off.: Copyright, 1941, by News Syndicate Co. Inc.
MILTON CANIFF

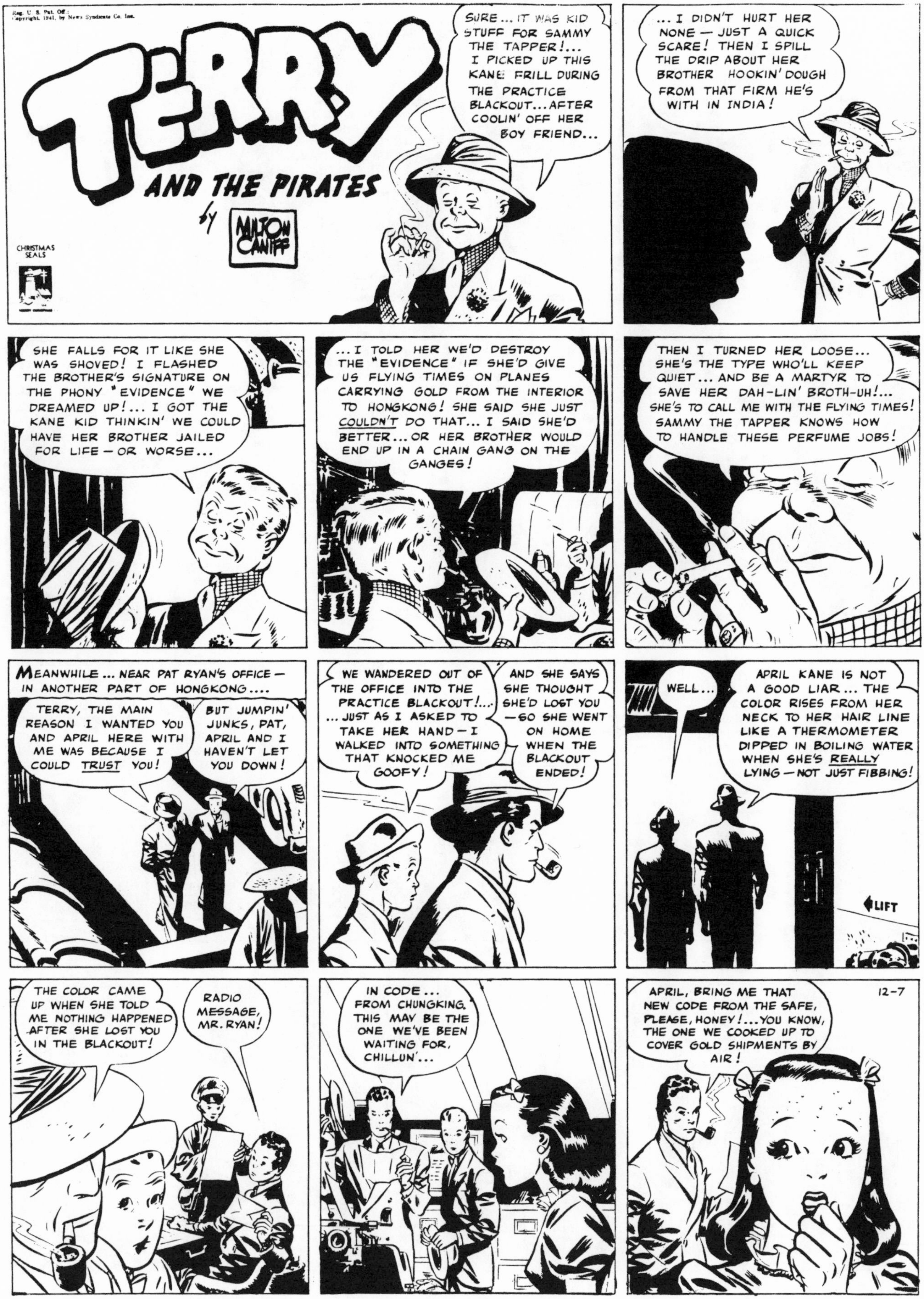

Reg. U. S. Pat. Off.:
Copyright, 1941, by News Syndicate Co. Inc.
TERRY AND THE PIRATES
by MILTON CANIFF
CHRISTMAS SEALS
SURE... IT WAS KID STUFF FOR SAMMY THE TAPPER!... I PICKED UP THIS KANE FRILL DURING THE PRACTICE BLACKOUT... AFTER COOLIN' OFF HER BOY FRIEND...
... I DIDN'T HURT HER NONE — JUST A QUICK SCARE! THEN I SPILL THE DRIP ABOUT HER BROTHER HOOKIN' DOUGH FROM THAT FIRM HE'S WITH IN INDIA!
SHE FALLS FOR IT LIKE SHE WAS SHOVED! I FLASHED THE BROTHER'S SIGNATURE ON THE PHONY "EVIDENCE" WE DREAMED UP!... I GOT THE KANE KID THINKIN' WE COULD HAVE HER BROTHER JAILED FOR LIFE — OR WORSE...
... I TOLD HER WE'D DESTROY THE "EVIDENCE" IF SHE'D GIVE US FLYING TIMES ON PLANES CARRYING GOLD FROM THE INTERIOR TO HONGKONG! SHE SAID SHE JUST COULDN'T DO THAT... I SAID SHE'D BETTER... OR HER BROTHER WOULD END UP IN A CHAIN GANG ON THE GANGES!
THEN I TURNED HER LOOSE... SHE'S THE TYPE WHO'LL KEEP QUIET... AND BE A MARTYR TO SAVE HER DAH-LIN' BROTH-UH!... SHE'S TO CALL ME WITH THE FLYING TIMES! SAMMY THE TAPPER KNOWS HOW TO HANDLE THESE PERFUME JOBS!
MEANWHILE... NEAR PAT RYAN'S OFFICE — IN ANOTHER PART OF HONGKONG....
TERRY, THE MAIN REASON I WANTED YOU AND APRIL HERE WITH ME WAS BECAUSE I COULD TRUST YOU!
BUT JUMPIN' JUNKS, PAT, APRIL AND I HAVEN'T LET YOU DOWN!
WE WANDERED OUT OF THE OFFICE INTO THE PRACTICE BLACKOUT!... ... JUST AS I ASKED TO TAKE HER HAND — I WALKED INTO SOMETHING THAT KNOCKED ME GOOFY!
AND SHE SAYS SHE THOUGHT SHE'D LOST YOU — SO SHE WENT ON HOME WHEN THE BLACKOUT ENDED!
WELL...
APRIL KANE IS NOT A GOOD LIAR... THE COLOR RISES FROM HER NECK TO HER HAIR LINE LIKE A THERMOMETER DIPPED IN BOILING WATER WHEN SHE'S REALLY LYING — NOT JUST FIBBING!
LIFT
THE COLOR CAME UP WHEN SHE TOLD ME NOTHING HAPPENED AFTER SHE LOST YOU IN THE BLACKOUT!
RADIO MESSAGE, MR. RYAN!
IN CODE... FROM CHUNGKING. THIS MAY BE THE ONE WE'VE BEEN WAITING FOR, CHILLUN'...
APRIL, BRING ME THAT NEW CODE FROM THE SAFE, PLEASE, HONEY!... YOU KNOW, THE ONE WE COOKED UP TO COVER GOLD SHIPMENTS BY AIR!
12-7

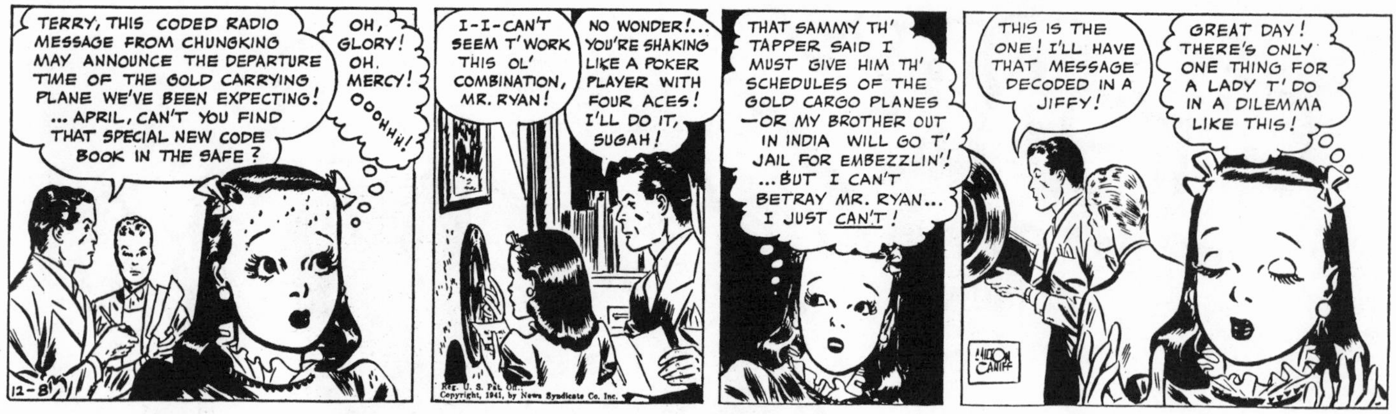
12-8
TERRY, THIS CODED RADIO MESSAGE FROM CHUNGKING MAY ANNOUNCE THE DEPARTURE TIME OF THE GOLD CARRYING PLANE WE'VE BEEN EXPECTING! ... APRIL, CAN'T YOU FIND THAT SPECIAL NEW CODE BOOK IN THE SAFE?
OH, GLORY! OH, MERCY! OOOHHH!
I-I-CAN'T SEEM T' WORK THIS OL' COMBINATION, MR. RYAN!
NO WONDER!... YOU'RE SHAKING LIKE A POKER PLAYER WITH FOUR ACES! I'LL DO IT, SUGAH!
Reg. U. S. Pat. Off. Copyright, 1941, by News Syndicate Co. Inc.
THAT SAMMY TH' TAPPER SAID I MUST GIVE HIM TH' SCHEDULES OF THE GOLD CARGO PLANES —OR MY BROTHER OUT IN INDIA WILL GO T' JAIL FOR EMBEZZLIN'! ... BUT I CAN'T BETRAY MR. RYAN... I JUST CAN'T!
MILTON CANIFF
THIS IS THE ONE! I'LL HAVE THAT MESSAGE DECODED IN A JIFFY!
GREAT DAY! THERE'S ONLY ONE THING FOR A LADY T' DO IN A DILEMMA LIKE THIS!

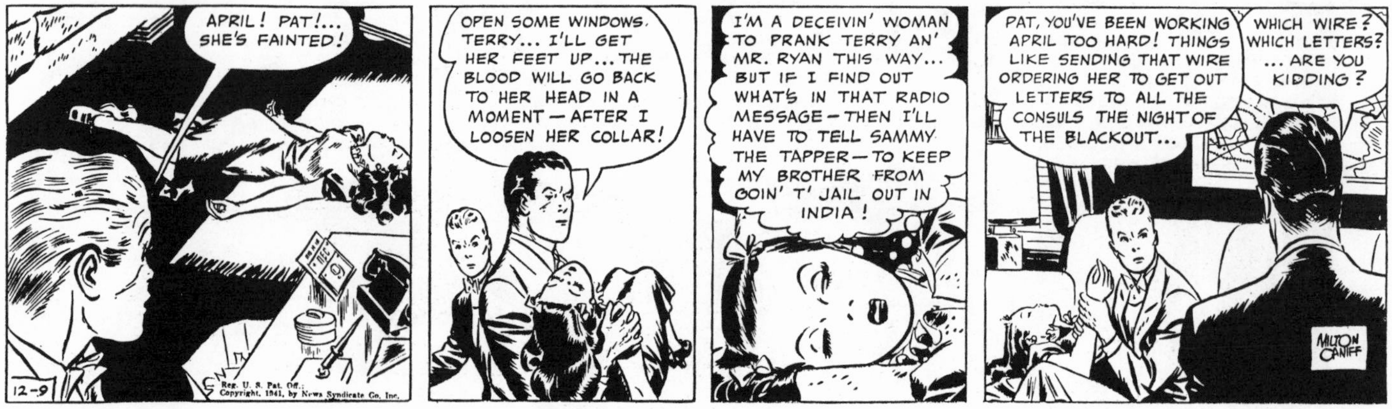
12-9
APRIL! PAT!... SHE'S FAINTED!
Reg. U. S. Pat. Off.: Copyright, 1941, by News Syndicate Co. Inc.
OPEN SOME WINDOWS, TERRY... I'LL GET HER FEET UP... THE BLOOD WILL GO BACK TO HER HEAD IN A MOMENT — AFTER I LOOSEN HER COLLAR!
I'M A DECEIVIN' WOMAN TO PRANK TERRY AN' MR. RYAN THIS WAY... BUT IF I FIND OUT WHAT'S IN THAT RADIO MESSAGE — THEN I'LL HAVE TO TELL SAMMY THE TAPPER — TO KEEP MY BROTHER FROM GOIN' T' JAIL OUT IN INDIA!
PAT, YOU'VE BEEN WORKING APRIL TOO HARD! THINGS LIKE SENDING THAT WIRE ORDERING HER TO GET OUT LETTERS TO ALL THE CONSULS THE NIGHT OF THE BLACKOUT...
WHICH WIRE? WHICH LETTERS? ... ARE YOU KIDDING?
MILTON CANIFF

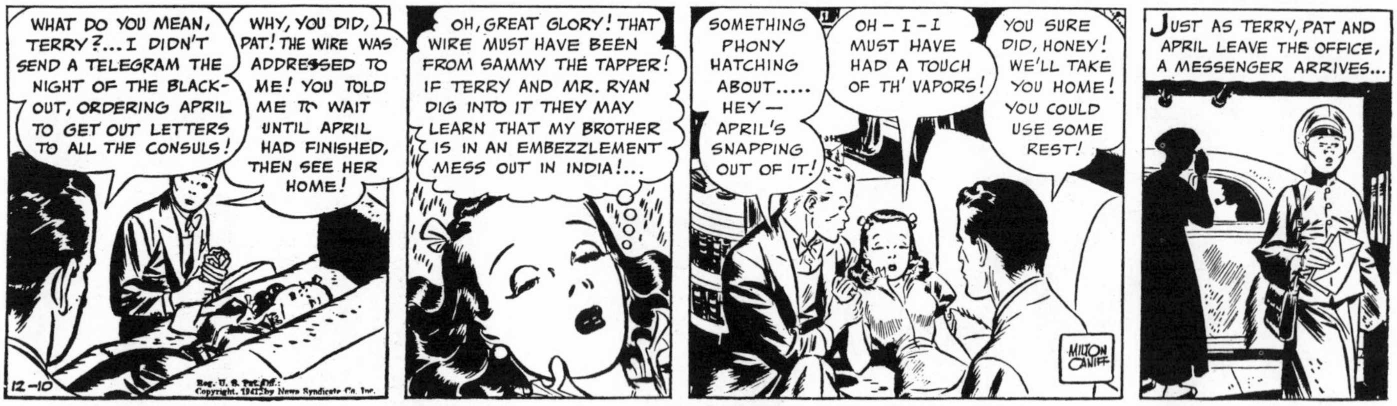
12-10
WHAT DO YOU MEAN, TERRY?... I DIDN'T SEND A TELEGRAM THE NIGHT OF THE BLACK-OUT, ORDERING APRIL TO GET OUT LETTERS TO ALL THE CONSULS!
WHY, YOU DID, PAT! THE WIRE WAS ADDRESSED TO ME! YOU TOLD ME TO WAIT UNTIL APRIL HAD FINISHED, THEN SEE HER HOME!
Reg. U. S. Pat. Off.: Copyright, 1941, by News Syndicate Co. Inc.
OH, GREAT GLORY! THAT WIRE MUST HAVE BEEN FROM SAMMY THE TAPPER! IF TERRY AND MR. RYAN DIG INTO IT THEY MAY LEARN THAT MY BROTHER IS IN AN EMBEZZLEMENT MESS OUT IN INDIA!...
SOMETHING PHONY HATCHING ABOUT..... HEY — APRIL'S SNAPPING OUT OF IT!
OH — I — I MUST HAVE HAD A TOUCH OF TH' VAPORS!
YOU SURE DID, HONEY! WE'LL TAKE YOU HOME! YOU COULD USE SOME REST!
MILTON CANIFF
JUST AS TERRY, PAT AND APRIL LEAVE THE OFFICE, A MESSENGER ARRIVES...

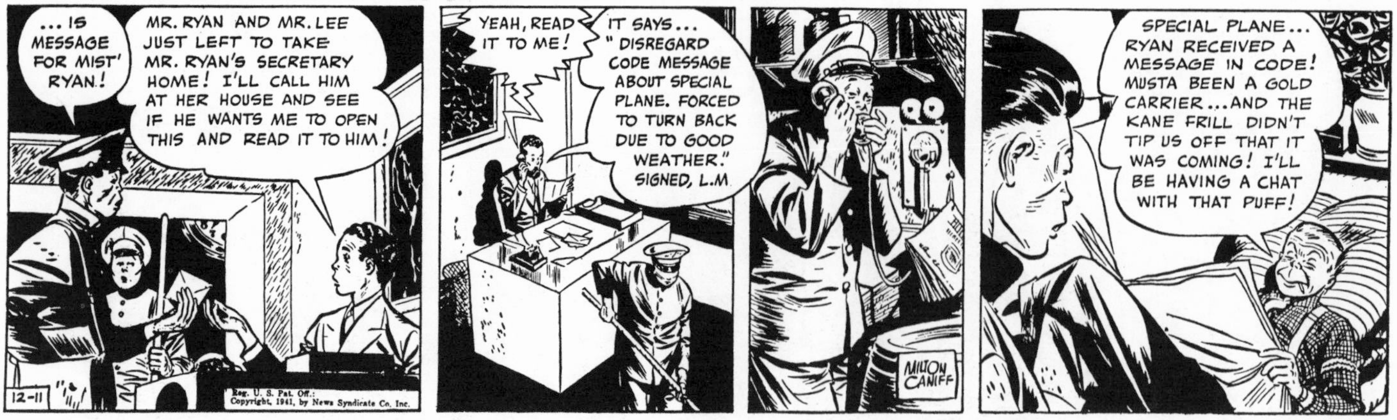
12-11
... IS MESSAGE FOR MIST' RYAN!
MR. RYAN AND MR. LEE JUST LEFT TO TAKE MR. RYAN'S SECRETARY HOME! I'LL CALL HIM AT HER HOUSE AND SEE IF HE WANTS ME TO OPEN THIS AND READ IT TO HIM!
Reg. U. S. Pat. Off.: Copyright, 1941, by News Syndicate Co. Inc.
YEAH, READ IT TO ME!
IT SAYS... "DISREGARD CODE MESSAGE ABOUT SPECIAL PLANE. FORCED TO TURN BACK DUE TO GOOD WEATHER." SIGNED, L.M
MILTON CANIFF
SPECIAL PLANE... RYAN RECEIVED A MESSAGE IN CODE! MUSTA BEEN A GOLD CARRIER... AND THE KANE FRILL DIDN'T TIP US OFF THAT IT WAS COMING! I'LL BE HAVING A CHAT WITH THAT PUFF!

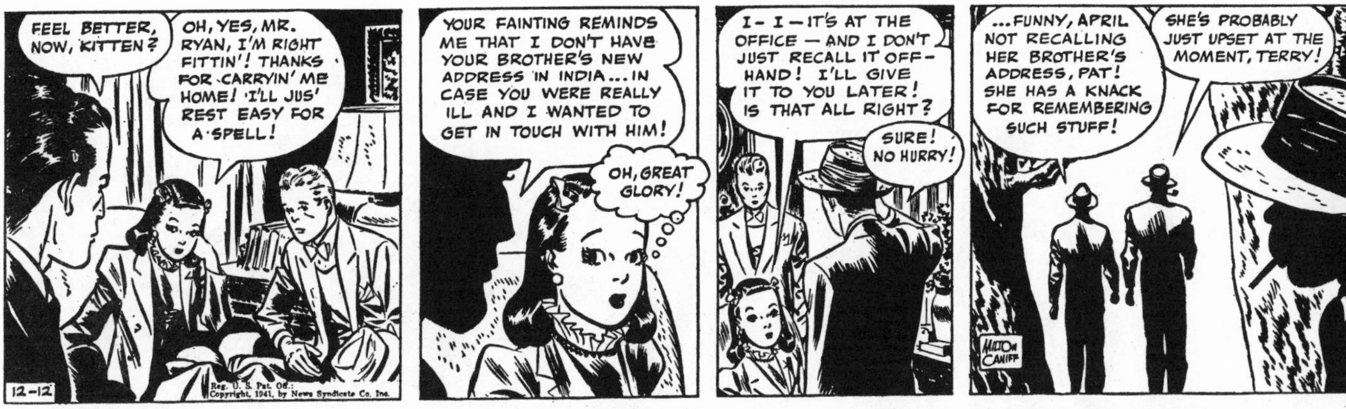
FEEL BETTER, NOW, KITTEN?
OH, YES, MR. RYAN, I'M RIGHT FITTIN'! THANKS FOR CARRYIN' ME HOME! I'LL JUS' REST EASY FOR A SPELL!
YOUR FAINTING REMINDS ME THAT I DON'T HAVE YOUR BROTHER'S NEW ADDRESS IN INDIA... IN CASE YOU WERE REALLY ILL AND I WANTED TO GET IN TOUCH WITH HIM!
OH, GREAT GLORY!
I- I- IT'S AT THE OFFICE — AND I DON'T JUST RECALL IT OFF-HAND! I'LL GIVE IT TO YOU LATER! IS THAT ALL RIGHT?
SURE! NO HURRY!
...FUNNY, APRIL NOT RECALLING HER BROTHER'S ADDRESS, PAT! SHE HAS A KNACK FOR REMEMBERING SUCH STUFF!
SHE'S PROBABLY JUST UPSET AT THE MOMENT, TERRY!
MILTON CANIFF
12-12
Reg. U. S. Pat. Off.: Copyright, 1941, by News Syndicate Co. Inc.

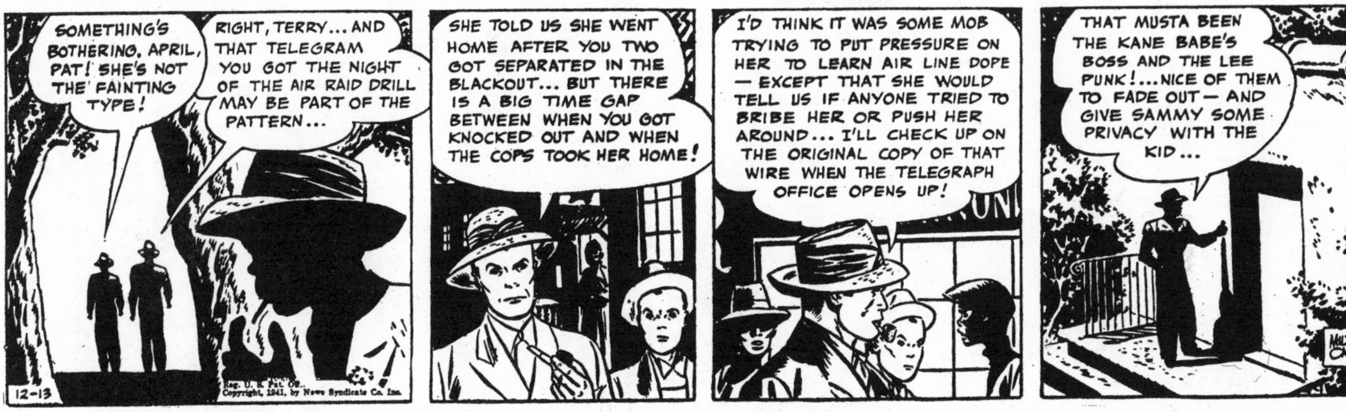
SOMETHING'S BOTHERING APRIL, PAT! SHE'S NOT THE FAINTING TYPE!
RIGHT, TERRY... AND THAT TELEGRAM YOU GOT THE NIGHT OF THE AIR RAID DRILL MAY BE PART OF THE PATTERN...
SHE TOLD US SHE WENT HOME AFTER YOU TWO GOT SEPARATED IN THE BLACKOUT... BUT THERE IS A BIG TIME GAP BETWEEN WHEN YOU GOT KNOCKED OUT AND WHEN THE COPS TOOK HER HOME!
I'D THINK IT WAS SOME MOB TRYING TO PUT PRESSURE ON HER TO LEARN AIR LINE DOPE — EXCEPT THAT SHE WOULD TELL US IF ANYONE TRIED TO BRIBE HER OR PUSH HER AROUND... I'LL CHECK UP ON THE ORIGINAL COPY OF THAT WIRE WHEN THE TELEGRAPH OFFICE OPENS UP!
THAT MUSTA BEEN THE KANE BABE'S BOSS AND THE LEE PUNK!... NICE OF THEM TO FADE OUT — AND GIVE SAMMY SOME PRIVACY WITH THE KID...
MILTON CANIFF
12-13
Reg. U. S. Pat. Off.: Copyright, 1941, by News Syndicate Co. Inc.

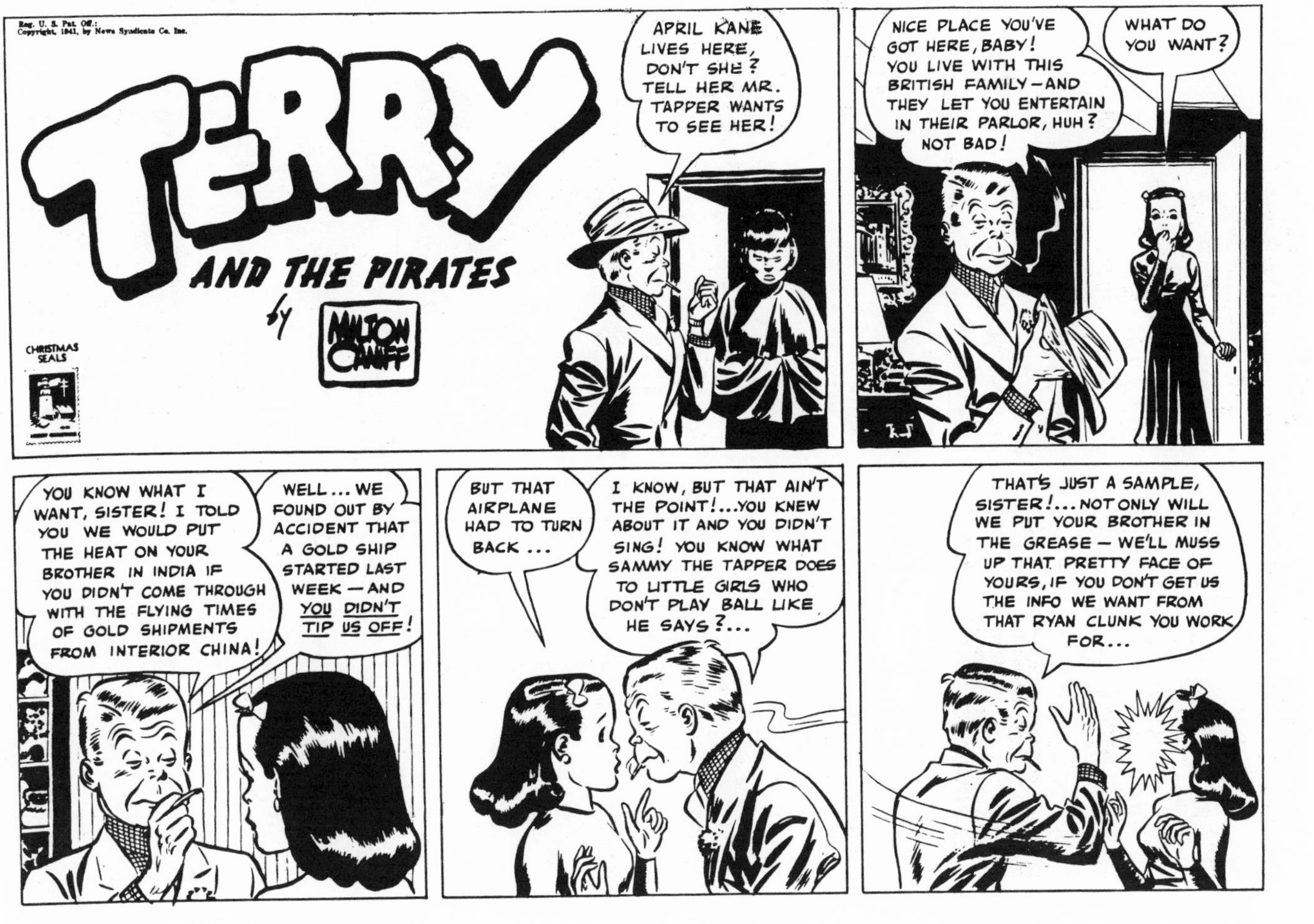
Reg. U. S. Pat. Off.: Copyright, 1941, by News Syndicate Co. Inc.
TERRY
AND THE PIRATES
by MILTON CANIFF
CHRISTMAS SEALS
APRIL KANE LIVES HERE, DON'T SHE? TELL HER MR. TAPPER WANTS TO SEE HER!
NICE PLACE YOU'VE GOT HERE, BABY! YOU LIVE WITH THIS BRITISH FAMILY — AND THEY LET YOU ENTERTAIN IN THEIR PARLOR, HUH? NOT BAD!
WHAT DO YOU WANT?
YOU KNOW WHAT I WANT, SISTER! I TOLD YOU WE WOULD PUT THE HEAT ON YOUR BROTHER IN INDIA IF YOU DIDN'T COME THROUGH WITH THE FLYING TIMES OF GOLD SHIPMENTS FROM INTERIOR CHINA!
WELL... WE FOUND OUT BY ACCIDENT THAT A GOLD SHIP STARTED LAST WEEK — AND YOU DIDN'T TIP US OFF!
BUT THAT AIRPLANE HAD TO TURN BACK...
I KNOW, BUT THAT AIN'T THE POINT!... YOU KNEW ABOUT IT AND YOU DIDN'T SING! YOU KNOW WHAT SAMMY THE TAPPER DOES TO LITTLE GIRLS WHO DON'T PLAY BALL LIKE HE SAYS?...
THAT'S JUST A SAMPLE, SISTER!... NOT ONLY WILL WE PUT YOUR BROTHER IN THE GREASE — WE'LL MUSS UP THAT PRETTY FACE OF YOURS, IF YOU DON'T GET US THE INFO WE WANT FROM THAT RYAN CLUNK YOU WORK FOR...

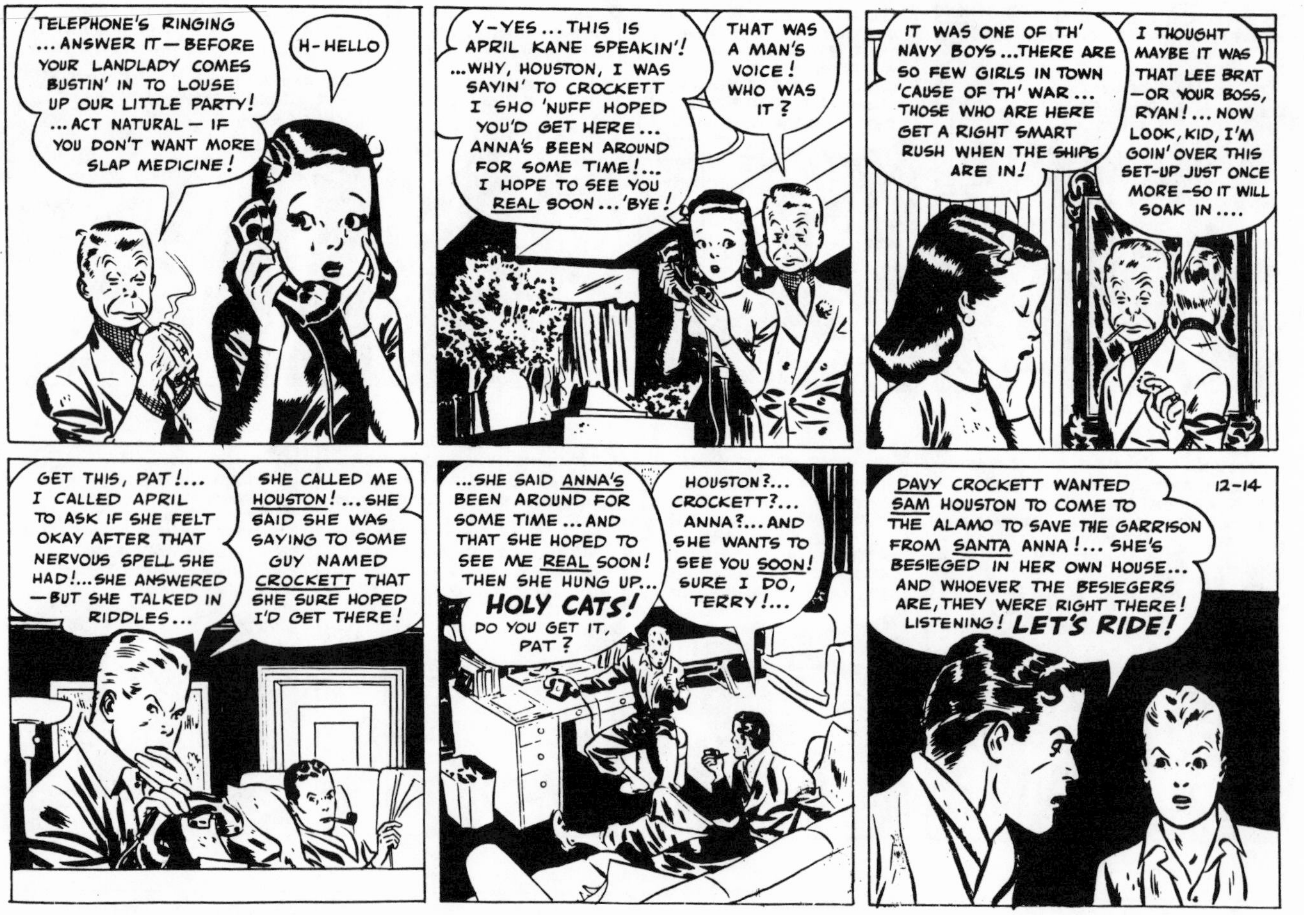
TELEPHONE'S RINGING ... ANSWER IT — BEFORE YOUR LANDLADY COMES BUSTIN' IN TO LOUSE UP OUR LITTLE PARTY! ... ACT NATURAL — IF YOU DON'T WANT MORE SLAP MEDICINE!
H-HELLO
Y-YES ... THIS IS APRIL KANE SPEAKIN'! ...WHY, HOUSTON, I WAS SAYIN' TO CROCKETT I SHO 'NUFF HOPED YOU'D GET HERE ... ANNA'S BEEN AROUND FOR SOME TIME! ... I HOPE TO SEE YOU REAL SOON ... 'BYE!
THAT WAS A MAN'S VOICE! WHO WAS IT?
IT WAS ONE OF TH' NAVY BOYS ... THERE ARE SO FEW GIRLS IN TOWN 'CAUSE OF TH' WAR ... THOSE WHO ARE HERE GET A RIGHT SMART RUSH WHEN THE SHIPS ARE IN!
I THOUGHT MAYBE IT WAS THAT LEE BRAT — OR YOUR BOSS, RYAN! ... NOW LOOK, KID, I'M GOIN' OVER THIS SET-UP JUST ONCE MORE — SO IT WILL SOAK IN ....
GET THIS, PAT! ... I CALLED APRIL TO ASK IF SHE FELT OKAY AFTER THAT NERVOUS SPELL SHE HAD! ... SHE ANSWERED — BUT SHE TALKED IN RIDDLES ...
SHE CALLED ME HOUSTON! ... SHE SAID SHE WAS SAYING TO SOME GUY NAMED CROCKETT THAT SHE SURE HOPED I'D GET THERE!
...SHE SAID ANNA'S BEEN AROUND FOR SOME TIME ... AND THAT SHE HOPED TO SEE ME REAL SOON! THEN SHE HUNG UP ... HOLY CATS! DO YOU GET IT, PAT?
HOUSTON? ... CROCKETT? ... ANNA? ... AND SHE WANTS TO SEE YOU SOON! SURE I DO, TERRY! ...
12-14
DAVY CROCKETT WANTED SAM HOUSTON TO COME TO THE ALAMO TO SAVE THE GARRISON FROM SANTA ANNA! ... SHE'S BESIEGED IN HER OWN HOUSE ... AND WHOEVER THE BESIEGERS ARE, THEY WERE RIGHT THERE! LISTENING! LET'S RIDE!

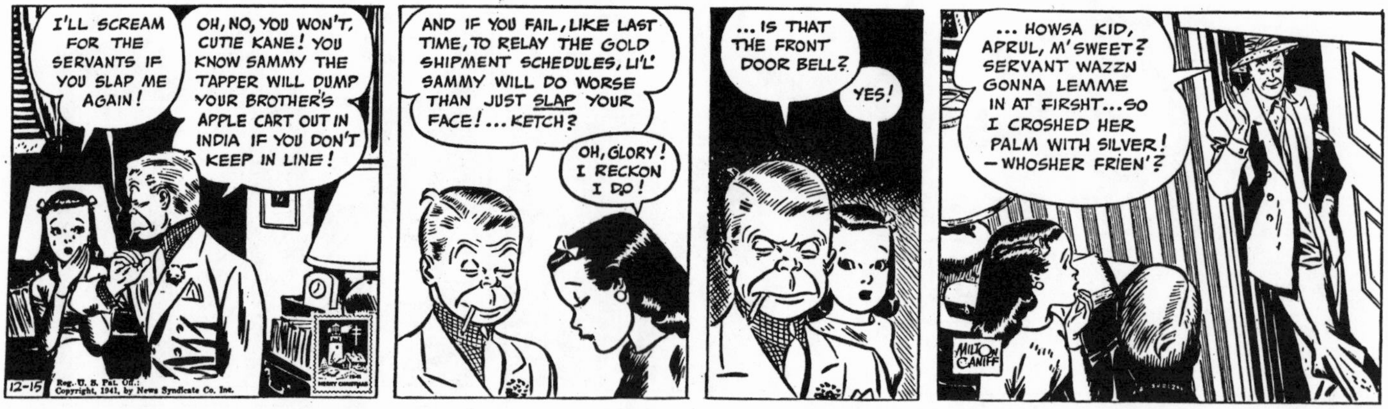
I'LL SCREAM FOR THE SERVANTS IF YOU SLAP ME AGAIN!
OH, NO, YOU WON'T, CUTIE KANE! YOU KNOW SAMMY THE TAPPER WILL DUMP YOUR BROTHER'S APPLE CART OUT IN INDIA IF YOU DON'T KEEP IN LINE!
12-15
Reg. U. S. Pat. Off.: Copyright, 1941, by News Syndicate Co. Inc.
AND IF YOU FAIL, LIKE LAST TIME, TO RELAY THE GOLD SHIPMENT SCHEDULES, LI'L SAMMY WILL DO WORSE THAN JUST SLAP YOUR FACE! ... KETCH?
OH, GLORY! I RECKON I DO!
... IS THAT THE FRONT DOOR BELL?
YES!
... HOWSA KID, APRUL, M'SWEET? SERVANT WAZZN GONNA LEMME IN AT FIRSHT ... SO I CROSHED HER PALM WITH SILVER! — WHOSHER FRIEN'?
MILTON CANIFF

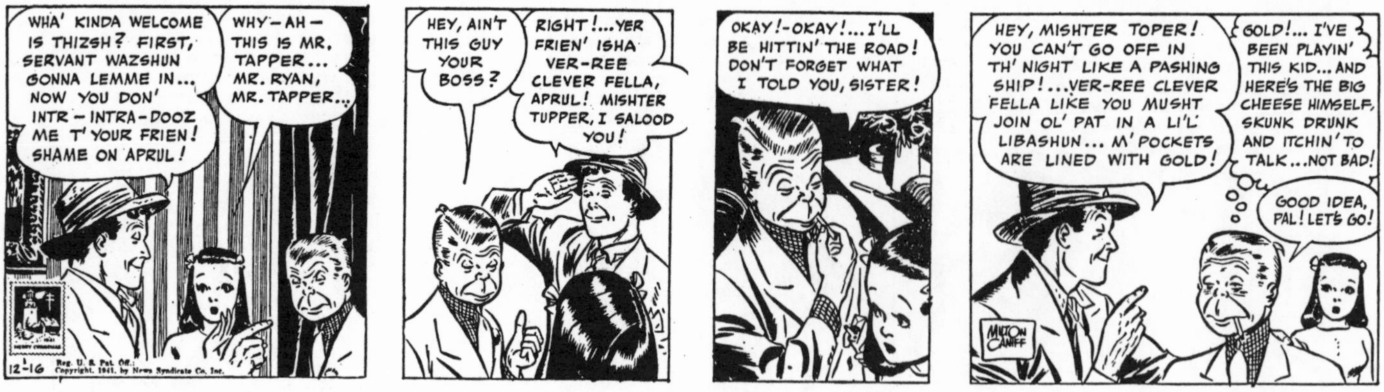
WHA' KINDA WELCOME IS THIZSH? FIRST, SERVANT WAZSHUN GONNA LEMME IN ... NOW YOU DON' INTR — INTRA-DOOZ ME T' YOUR FRIEN! SHAME ON APRUL!
WHY — AH — THIS IS MR. TAPPER ... MR. RYAN, MR. TAPPER ...
12-16
Reg. U. S. Pat. Off. Copyright, 1941, by News Syndicate Co. Inc.
HEY, AIN'T THIS GUY YOUR BOSS?
RIGHT! ... YER FRIEN' ISHA VER-REE CLEVER FELLA, APRUL! MISHTER TUPPER, I SALOOD YOU!
OKAY! — OKAY! ... I'LL BE HITTIN' THE ROAD! DON'T FORGET WHAT I TOLD YOU, SISTER!
HEY, MISHTER TOPER! YOU CAN'T GO OFF IN TH' NIGHT LIKE A PASHING SHIP! ... VER-REE CLEVER FELLA LIKE YOU MUSHT JOIN OL' PAT IN A LI'L' LIBASHUN ... M' POCKETS ARE LINED WITH GOLD!
GOLD! ... I'VE BEEN PLAYIN' THIS KID ... AND HERE'S THE BIG CHEESE HIMSELF, SKUNK DRUNK AND ITCHIN' TO TALK ... NOT BAD!
GOOD IDEA, PAL! LET'S GO!
MILTON CANIFF

# OTHER CANIFF BOOKS FROM NBM:

### TERRY & THE PIRATES COLLECTOR'S EDITION SPECIAL SALE!

Beautiful hardbound volumes, gold stamped, 320 pp. each, jacketed. Normally $36.50 each; NOW ONLY $19.95!

Volumes remaining: 7 (1940-'41), 8 ('41-'42), 11 ('44-'45), 12 ('45-'46).

### "MILTON CANIFF, REMBRANDT OF THE COMIC STRIP"

Biography of Caniff with an introduction by comics historian Rick Marschall, editor of Nemo. Many rare illustrations and stunning blow-ups of Caniff's art.

Paperback, 64 pp., 8½x11: $6.95

KLANG THE WARLORD
TERRY
AND THE PIRATES
NO. 6
1938

## GET 'EM HOT OFF THE PRESS! *SUBSCRIBE!*

This Terry & the Pirates reprint is quarterly like clockwork. Make sure to get each new volume hot off the press, sent in a sturdy carton mailer. You can start with any volume, past or future!

**$25 for 4 volumes**

### MISSING ANY PAST VOLUMES?

Vol. 1 Welcome to China (1934) $6.95
Vol. 2 Marooned with Burma (1935) $5.95
Vol. 3 Dragon Lady's Revenge (1936) $5.95
Vol. 4 Getting Snared (1936-37) $5.95
Vol. 5 Shanghaied (1937) $5.95
Vol. 6 The Warlord Klang (1937-38) $6.95
Vol. 7 The Hunter (1938) $6.95
Vol. 8 The Baron (1938-39) $6.95
Vol. 9 Feminine Venom (1939) $6.95
Vol. 10 Network of Intrigue (1939-40) $6.95
Vol. 11 Gal Got Our Pal (1940) $6.95
Vol. 12 Flying Ace Dude (1940-41) $6.95
Vol. 13 "Into the Frying Pan..." (1941) $6.95
Vol. 14 Raven... (1941) $6.95

THE HUNTER
TERRY
AND THE PIRATES
NO. 7
1938

### HANDSOME SLIPCASED SETS

4 volumes in each for a total of 256 pages of intense reading, slipcased in a leathery cloth, gold-stamped with the Terry logo.

Vols. 1-4: $29.50
Vols. 5-8: $29.50
Vols. 9-12: $29.50
SLIPCASE ALONE: $7.50

THE BARON
TERRY
AND THE PIRATES
NO. 8
1938-1939

P&H: Add $2 first item, $1 each addt'l.
No P&H on subscriptions!

NBM
35-53 70th St.
Jackson Heights, NY 11372

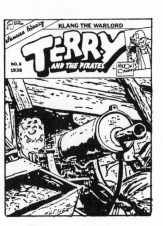

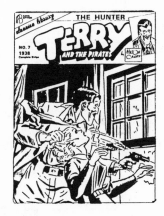

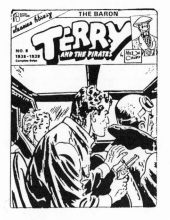